The Boundless Present

UNC | COLLEGE OF ARTS AND SCIENCES
Germanic and Slavic Languages and Literatures

From 1949 to 2004, UNC Press and the UNC Department of Germanic & Slavic Languages and Literatures published the UNC Studies in the Germanic Languages and Literatures series. Monographs, anthologies, and critical editions in the series covered an array of topics including medieval and modern literature, theater, linguistics, philology, onomastics, and the history of ideas. Through the generous support of the National Endowment for the Humanities and the Andrew W. Mellon Foundation, books in the series have been reissued in new paperback and open access digital editions. For a complete list of books visit www.uncpress.org.

The Boundless Present

Space and Time in the Literary Fairy Tales of Novalis and Tieck

GORDON BIRRELL

UNC Studies in the Germanic Languages and Literatures
Number 95

Copyright © 1979

This work is licensed under a Creative Commons CC BY-NC-ND license. To view a copy of the license, visit http://creativecommons.org/licenses.

Suggested citation: Birrell, Gordon. *The Boundless Present: Space and Time in the Literary Fairy Tales of Novalis and Tieck.* Chapel Hill: University of North Carolina Press, 1979. DOI: https://doi.org/10.5149/9781469657127_Birrell

Library of Congress Cataloging-in-Publication Data
Names: Birrell, Gordon.
Title: The boundless present : Space and time in the literary fairy tales of Novalis and Tieck / by Gordon Birrell.
Other titles: University of North Carolina Studies in the Germanic Languages and Literatures ; no. 95.
Description: Chapel Hill : University of North Carolina Press, [1979] Series: University of North Carolina Studies in the Germanic Languages and Literatures. | Includes bibliographical references.
Identifiers: LCCN 78-31202 | ISBN 978-1-4696-5711-0 (pbk: alk. paper) | ISBN 978-1-4696-5712-7 (ebook)
Subjects: German fiction — 18th century — History and criticism. | Hardenberg, Friedrich, Freiherr von, 1772-1801 — Criticism and interpretation. | Tieck, Johann Ludwig, 1773-1853 — Criticism and interpretation. | Space and time in literature.
Classification: LCC PT759 .B5 | DDC 833/.609

Contents

	Acknowledgments	ix
	Introduction	3
I.	Self-Appropriation and the Long Journey Home: Space in the *Märchen* of Novalis	8
	1. "Hyazinth und Rosenblüte"	9
	2. "Arion" and "Atlantis"	20
	3. "Eros und Fabel"	25
II.	Split Terrain: Space in the *Märchen* of Tieck	39
	1. "Der blonde Eckbert"	39
	2. "Der Runenberg"	52
III.	Waiting for Fabel: Time in the *Märchen* of Novalis	63
	1. "Hyazinth und Rosenblüte"	63
	2. "Arion" and "Atlantis"	70
	3. "Eros und Fabel"	78
IV.	Between "Waldeinsamkeit" and Community: Time in the *Märchen* of Tieck	90
	1. "Der blonde Eckbert"	90
	2. "Der Runenberg"	103
V.	Space, Time, and the Romantic Fairy Tale	116
	Notes	141
	Bibliography of Works Cited	157

Acknowledgments

It is a pleasure to record my gratitude to the colleagues and friends who have assisted me in the course of this project. I am indebted above all to Professor Walter H. Sokel, who gave me the initial idea for the book and supported its progress at every stage with astute advice and unfailing loyalty. Professors Flora Kimmich and André Winandy encouraged and counseled me in placing the manuscript with a publisher. Princeton University and Southern Methodist University granted me two leaves of absence during which the bulk of the work on the manuscript was accomplished. I also wish to extend particular thanks to Evan Higgon for his faithful and untiring assistance in the preparation of the manuscript.

The Boundless Present

". . . in jedem Hügel regt sich neu erglimmende Asche, überall lodern Flammen des Lebens empor, alte Wohnstätten werden neu erbaut, alte Zeiten erneuert, und die Geschichte wird zum Traum einer unendlichen, unabsehlichen Gegenwart."
—Novalis, *Die Lehrlinge zu Sais*

Introduction

For many people, the idea of interpreting fairy tales evokes uncomfortable memories of Freudian analysts going to work on "Little Red Riding Hood" and *Alice in Wonderland*, finding meanings which no one had guessed, or wanted to guess, and singling out only those elements of the tales which seemed to substantiate their own theses. Although the psychological approach is an extreme example of what can be done in the name of interpretation, one often enough encounters the conviction that fairy tales should be spared any sort of critical examination at all, that no one needs to be told what the tales "mean," for their ingenuous charm lies precisely in the fact that they are immediately accessible to everyone.

Quite apart from the fact that it *is* possible to interpret the folk fairy tale with delicacy and understanding, as the Swiss folklorist Max Lüthi has demonstrated, the tales under discussion in this study are of a different order than the folk variety. They not only yield to interpretation but demand it. Neither Novalis nor Tieck had any intention of accommodating a reading audience of children. Their tales were directed to intelligent, informed adults who were willing to think about what they read and to grapple with complexities of theme and allusion which would have been unthinkable in the folk tale. There are still those, of course, who feel that even the *Kunstmärchen* is too fragile to touch with the tools of literary criticism. Friedrich Schlegel's answer to such sentiments is as good as any: "Wenn manche mystische Kunstliebhaber, welche jede Kritik für Zergliederung, und jede Zergliederung für Zerstörung des Genusses halten, konsequent dächten: so wäre potztausend das beste Kunsturteil über das würdigste Werk. Auch gibts Kritiken, die nichts mehr sagen, nur viel weitläufiger."[1]

My aim in writing this book has been to illuminate one of the central aspects of the German Romantic fairy tale: its treatment of space and time. By treatment I mean primarily the way in which space and time function as structural elements, the way, in other words, in which they help to constitute and shape the imaginative world of the *Märchen*. Only rarely do the tales deal with space and time explicitly on a thematic level. Nevertheless, there is scarcely a major thematic problem in these narratives that is not either directly related to their spatial and temporal structure or revealed through it. The estrangement of mind from nature, the synthesizing activity of poetry, the distinction between true and false death, the nature of narcissism and insanity: all of these topics are expressed in the organization of space and time, and usually in a way which substantially deepens our understanding of the thematic problems. It has frequently been observed, for instance, that the old woman in Tieck's "Der blonde Eckbert" represents the mysterious forces of Nature; but what Nature itself is supposed to signify has eluded most commentators. Through a structural analysis, on the other hand, it can be shown that the old woman's domain represents an ideal fusion of time and timelessness, form and formlessness, an integration of internal and external space which Eckbert and Bertha, the adult protagonists of the tale, are expected to imitate on a higher, more complex level. An understanding of the Romantic *Märchen* is scarcely possible without reference to formal devices such as imagery and structure. This is certainly not the least of the reasons why the tales are as difficult and perplexing today as they were nearly two hundred years ago.

The tales under discussion here are Novalis's "Hyazinth und Rosenblüte" (from *Die Lehrlinge zu Sais*), "Atlantis," "Arion," and the Klingsohr tale (all from *Heinrich von Ofterdingen*); and Ludwig Tieck's "Der blonde Eckbert" and "Der Runenberg."[2] This is, of course, a very limited selection, for the entire corpus of Romantic *Märchen* encompasses several dozen works; almost every important writer of the period felt challenged enough by the genre to turn out at least one tale. Those who are interested in a broader account of the Romantic fairy tale may consult Marianne Thalmann's *Das Märchen und die Moderne* (Stuttgart: Kohlhammer, 1961), Richard Benz's *Märchen-Dichtung der Romantiker* (Gotha: Perthes, 1908), and Rudolf Buchmann's *Helden und Mächte des romantischen Kunstmärchens* (Leipzig: Haessel, 1910). If nothing else, these works illustrate the shortcomings of a survey approach. With the exception of lyric poetry, no Romantic genre so stubbornly resists classification as the fairy tale. Thalmann's book, while easily the most worthy of the three, lumps the tales of a given writer together as if they were all variations on a single model ("Das Novalis-Märchen," "Das Brentano-Märchen," etc.), a procedure that not only does violence to the complexity of the individual works but occasionally leads to some very serious misreadings. If we are to acknowledge the intelligence and inventiveness of Romantic writers, we must ultimately take the time to interpret their works carefully and to honor all those triumphs of originality that have been ignored because they fail to support preconceived notions or generalized schemes of interpretation.

I have attempted throughout the book, however, to relate the tales to Romanticism in general, particularly where it could be demonstrated that prevailing opinion is in need of correction or modification. It will be seen, for example, that Tieck, despite his close relationship with the Jena group, anticipates in many respects the mood and concerns of Late Romanticism; and that Novalis's later tales, especially "Eros und Fabel," betray the imminent collapse of the Early Romantic belief in progressivity. In addition, it seemed useful to balance the detailed textual analyses with a more general investigation of space and time in the Romantic fairy tale at large. In the concluding chapter, I have shown that the *Märchen* of Novalis and Tieck exemplify two major groups of Romantic tales, and that these groups in turn point to two quite divergent directions within the Romantic tradition.

Above, I indicated that my interpretations are based on structural analysis. It must be emphasized from the outset that this approach has little in common with the highly formalized techniques of French structuralism. Instead, I have preferred to use an eclectic approach, which is, I think, the only adequate way of dealing flexibly with texts as various and innovative as the Romantic fairy tales.

Since eclectic approaches are generally open to the charge of methodological untidiness, a brief discussion of theory is in order here. Speaking quite broadly, spatial and temporal structure in a literary work may be defined as the total set of data which inform the reader's experience of space and time. Since any work of art represents a selective ordering of reality, fictive space and time are necessarily schematic. Unlike the space and time of real experience, they are not, and cannot be, completely determined in every respect. As a preliminary operation, the critical reader must establish the general spatial and temporal outlines of a work: he must take note of those passages in which space and/or time are articulated with a high degree of specificity, as well as those gaps in which space and time must be presumed to exist but remain indeterminate.[3] Certain fundamental questions arise from such a procedure: what purpose, for instance, is served by the precise delineation of a certain segment in the temporal flow, or by the detailed description of a certain spatial area? Conversely, does the lack of spatial and temporal data in other passages simply imply that such data are irrelevant in the general context of the work? Or, as in the case of the Romantic fairy tale, is the lack of determination itself thematically significant?

In a traditional and somewhat less precise sense, structure has also referred to the architecture of a work: the number of discrete parts, or phases, that the work contains, the ways in which transitions between the phases are handled, the temporal relationship of the various parts, the significance of the arrangement in which the phases appear.[4] In terms of space and time, significant arrangement applies above all to those patterns and configurations which symbolically underscore the principal themes of a text. Spatially, such patterns include horizontal and vertical polarities, the opposition of interior and exterior space, circular or linear configurations, and the duplication of spatial arrangements at different points in the narrative. By the same token, time as articulated by specific events may assume a variety of meaningful forms: acceleration, progression, stasis or regression, repetition of individual events or phases, temporal spirals (return to an original state on a higher level), linking of past and present through associative flashbacks, simultaneity of two or more temporal levels (e.g., everyday reality and myth).

This does not mean, however, that the spatial/temporal organization of a work necessarily carries thematic or symbolic freight. In naturalistic narratives, for instance, spatial pointers may serve merely to establish a specific locale (Paris, a back street, the interior of a jute mill).[5] At the other end of the spectrum are allegorical works such as Novalis's *Klingsohrmärchen* or Goethe's *Märchen*, in which spatial structure operates almost totally in the service of ideas and specific concepts. With Romantic narrative in general, it is legitimate to expect that spatial data will fall into suggestive patterns. The Romantic belief in a hidden correspondence between nature and mind implies that external space represents a symbolic image of the consciousness which perceives it. It is scarcely overstating the case, in fact, to maintain that the analysis of spatial structure is an all but indispensable critical tool in dealing with Romantic narrative. Similarly, the Romantic preoccupation with time and temporal process—the dynamics of personal and historical transformation—suggests that the temporal structures of Romantic narratives are likely to be as rich and as significant as their spatial counterparts.

Beyond this, from a philosophical standpoint one may argue that space and time are in fact inseparable phenomena, that a complex spatial structure automatically implies a comparably complex temporal structure. Philosophical "rightness" and literary technique do not always go hand in hand, of course; and it is easy enough to cite texts in which one of the variables is left at a rudimentary level while the other is extravagantly developed. The temporal scheme of Thomas Mann's *Doktor Faustus*, for example, is elaborate beyond any comparison with its spatial structure. Nevertheless, the interrelatedness of space and time leads to an additional methodological problem: the difficulty of dealing with, and doing justice to, two quite distinct literary techniques (spatial and temporal structure) while forever keeping a vigilant eye on the ways each complements the other. In this work, the problem is further compounded by the demands of a comparative approach. In order to relate five or six different narratives to each other in a clear and disciplined manner, it was necessary to impose some limitation on the points of comparison. For this reason I have decided to deal with space and time sequentially. The first two chapters discuss and relate the spatial structures of Novalis's and Tieck's *Märchen*, while the next two chapters take up their temporal structures. To compensate for the inevitable shortcomings of this approach, however, I have attempted, particularly in the third and fourth chapters, to illuminate the extent to which space and time in fact interpenetrate each other and how the seemingly separate techniques of spatial and temporal organization emerge in the end as interlocking facets of a single formal principle.

I

Self-Appropriation and the Long Journey Home
Space in the *Märchen* of Novalis

In October 1798, while he was at work on the voluminous collection of notes for his projected encyclopedia, the *Allgemeine Brouillon*, Novalis jotted down the following thought: "Entsteh[ung] der Zeiten—aus relativer, und daher sich allmählich vermindernder Elasticität unsrer GedankenAction. Räume und Zeiten sind Symptome von Schwäche."[1] That space and time should be merely symptoms of mental weakness or insufficient elasticity of thought is an astonishing and disturbing idea, but it was a notion that appeared altogether feasible to the Romantic mind. No less an authority than Kant had maintained that space, time, and causality are essentially nothing more than mental tools for correlating and ordering experience, modes of perception rather than perceptions themselves. Thus it cannot be said that space and time exist independently of our minds. Objects only *appear* to exist in space and time because the intellect cannot conceive them in any other way. Romantics, however, went one decisive step beyond Kant. Rather than viewing the a priori categories of perception as inevitable limits on human understanding, they contended that it was possible for the mind to transcend these fundamental operations of ordering experience. Johann Gottlieb Fichte, whose ideas formed one of the bases of Romantic philosophy, conceived the intellect as an active, dynamic force incessantly at work reflecting on its own activities. Through each successive act of self-analysis, the mind rose above itself and recreated itself on a higher level. Thus it seemed possible that space and time, as rudimentary and limited forms of perception, could be overcome by means of repeated acts of self-reflection. The inability to liberate oneself from the coordinates of time and space was, in effect, a sign of mental lassitude.

The supreme task of the fairy tale was to give literary expression to this process of self-transcendence, and no other genre could have suited the purpose so well. The novel might express universality, but it was too much bound to empirical reality. Lyric poetry might represent an individual ego rising above itself, but it could not depict the *process* of ascent. The fairy tale, unlike the novel, was not expected to deal with the everyday world, but presented a heightened reality in which marvelous figures and situations could readily function as symbols for mental events or for higher forces acting on or in the mind. Moreover, as a narrative with a plot, the fairy tale could describe the dynamic development of the mind from one level to the next; and with the aid of various figurative devices it might even suggest the final state of perfection in which space and time were transcended altogether. In the following studies, we shall be concerned primarily with two aspects of the fairy tales: first of all, the way in which the development of the mind is reflected in the spatial and temporal structure of the tales; secondly—and this is perhaps the more intriguing aspect—the way in which Novalis and Tieck envisioned the final state beyond space and time, and the poetic means which they utilized to depict this state.

"Hyazinth und Rosenblüte"

It is no easy matter to establish the chronological order of the composition of Novalis's *Märchen*. The last two years of his life were marked by a fury of creative activity which produced almost simultaneously the *Hymnen an die Nacht*, *Heinrich von Ofterdingen*, the essay *Die Christenheit oder Europa*, and thousands of fragments. The Klingsohr tale, in many respects the most advanced of his works, may very well have been conceived as early as March of 1797, shortly after the death of his fiancée Sophie von Kühn.[2] There seems to be little doubt, however, that the earliest completed *Märchen* is the tale of Hyazinth and Rosenblüte in the second chapter of *Die Lehrlinge zu Sais*, which dates approximately from January of 1799. With the exception of the Klingsohr tale in *Ofterdingen*, this earliest *Märchen* is also the most complex, though its intricacies are less immediately apparent than those of the larger tales that were to follow.

"Hyazinth und Rosenblüte," like all of Novalis's other *Märchen*, is a tale within a tale. The narrating voice is that of a "cheerful fellow" who laughingly chides the young apprentice at the temple of Sais for sitting forlornly apart in meditation. "Wie kannst du nur in der Einsamkeit sitzen?" he cries (I, 91). To illustrate his point he relates the story of Hyazinth, a very good but exceedingly strange boy in love with a beautiful girl named Rosenblüte. The tale opens in Hyazinth's homeland, which is described as "weit gegen Abend"—that is, far to the west of the temple at Sais, where the narrator and his listener are situated. The uncommon collection of animals and plants that surrounds the Hyazinth in his homeland—a squirrel, a monkey, a parrot, a bullfinch, a rose, a strawberry, and so forth—obstructs any attempt to pinpoint the geographical location of this land. The harmonious coexistence of such diverse fauna and flora, however, suggests a parallel to the biblical garden of Eden. At the same time, however, such diversity invokes quite a different garden, the fabulous Garden of the Hesperides, or the Islands of the Blessed, which ancient accounts located "far to the West," beyond all known land.[3] It was here that the departed souls of heroic and good men went to a reward of timeless contentment. Through this double allusion, to Eden and the Hesperides, Hyazinth's homeland ascends to the level of myth. Moreover, it is indirectly associated with *two* earthly paradises: one before the beginning of time, the other after the ending of time. As we shall see, this reading is altogether in keeping with a general interpretation of the tale.

Chronologically, the first phase of "Hyazinth und Rosenblüte" begins with " . . . er war auch bis vor wenig Jahren fröhlich und lustig gewesen, wie keiner" (I, 92). What is striking about this first phase is the vague and disorganized quality of spatial data. While numerous plants and animals are mentioned, they fail to fall into any distinct spatial arrangement. From the rapid transmission of gossip throughout the garden and forest, however, one may gather that the plants and animals live together in close proximity and rather jocose solidarity: "Das Veilchen hatte es der Erdbeere im Vertrauen gesagt, die sagte es ihrer Freundin der Stachelbeere, die ließ nun das Sticheln nicht, wenn Hyazinth gegangen kam; so erfuhrs denn bald der ganze Garten und der Wald, und wenn Hyazinth ausging, so riefs von allen Seiten: 'Rosenblütchen ist mein Schätzchen!' " (I, 92).

In contrast to the spatially indefinite but naively unified and harmonious world of nature, Hyazinth and Rosenblüte appear in a spatial configuration that immediately suggests a certain disunity: "Wenn nun Hyazinth die Nacht an seinem Fenster stand und Rosenblüte an ihrem, und die Kätzchen auf dem Mäusefang da vorbeiliefen, da sahen sie die Beiden stehn, und lachten und kicherten oft so laut, daß sie es hörten und böse wurden" (I, 92). This first clear spatial image in the tale was to become standard equipment in all three of Novalis's major fairy tales: an initial separation of the main characters into two enclosed spaces, a state of both confinement and remoteness. The image of the stationary figures at their separate windows reflects more, however, than the partial (and at first enigmatic) estrangement of the two lovers. As becomes evident in the course of the tale, the spatial distance between Hyazinth and Rosenblüte is an expression of the simultaneous alienation between Hyazinth and the world of nature. Thus even in this first phase there are signs of tension between Hyazinth and the various plants and animals. The gooseberry teasingly pricks Hyazinth, the two lovers become angry at the giggling of the housecats who see them standing alone, and Hyazinth is temporarily annoyed at the song of the lizard. As we shall see, two sets of spatial relationships operate simultaneously throughout the tale as manifestations of the same process: the relationship between Hyazinth and Rosenblüte and the relationship between Hyazinth and nature.

The detail of the windows here is also worth noting. While windows appear only infrequently in Novalis's writings, their importance for Romanticism in general can scarcely be underestimated.[4] One could, in fact, view the solitary figure at the open window as the single most characteristic image of Romanticism. The early eighteenth century, with its love of visual clarity and its commitment to enlightened pedagogy, had been drawn to pictorial forms of representation that offered a significant and easily comprehensible slice of reality in the confines of a neat frame.[5] The extraordinary popularity of copper engravings, *Guckkasten* pictures, and novels organized around isolated scenes or tableaus bears testimony to the eighteenth-century delight in contained and carefully composed images. Romantic aesthetics, on the other hand, took a dim view of such tidy reductions of reality. Provocative vagueness was glorified over lucidity, totality over limited selection, interesting arrangement of materials over painstaking composition. The frame, however, remained. In the form of a window opening out onto a magnificent panorama or a nocturnal landscape, it answered one of the fundamental needs of the Early Romantic sensibility: that is, to put it succinctly, the need to juxtapose infinity and limitation. For Romantic and rationalist alike, the frame served as a reminder of the presence of an interpreting consciousness, a standpoint or perspective from which the subject matter was viewed. But while the Enlightenment was interested in the frame as a means of establishing and displaying the clearest, most explicit relationship between viewer and subject matter (hence the preoccupation with finding the proper standpoint),[6] Romantics exploited the view through the windowframe as an image of limited consciousness in confrontation with the infinite. The window is thus closely connected with, and is certainly the most striking spatial expression of, the concept of Romantic irony.[7] Friedrich Schlegel, who was responsible for enunciating the concept and exploring its intricacies, himself provided one of the most revealing passages involving a window in the opening pages of *Lucinde*:

Das Wahre an der Sache ist, daß ich vorhin am Fenster stand; wie lange, das weiß ich nicht recht; denn mit den andern Regeln der Vernunft und der Sittlichkeit ist auch die Zeitrechnung dabei ganz von mir vergessen worden. Also ich stand am Fenster und sah ins Freie. . . . Und wie sich die weite Ebne bald hebt bald senket, so windet sich der ruhige, breite silberhelle Strom in großen Schwüngen und Bogen, bis er und die Fantasie des Liebenden, die sich gleich dem Schwane auf ihm wiegte, in die Ferne hinziehen und sich in das Unermeßliche langsam verlieren.[8]

Eichendorff's works are so full of windows that the effect is almost humorous. The window hurled open at break of dawn inevitably reveals a spectacular landscape tremulous with birdsong and sunlight, while the night window opens to a poetically atmospheric world of moonlit vistas, nightingale tones, and the remote sound of a post horn.[9] By the mid-nineteenth century, the Romantic window had been worked to the point of exhaustion. Its usefulness in serious literature was confined to parody. Heinrich Heine, in his mischievously witty *Die romantische Schule* (1836), was able to characterize Novalis, not altogether unsympathetically, through the portrait of a frail, sickly young girl who sits forever at her window, leafing through *Heinrich von Ofterdingen* and gazing longingly at the graveyard outside.[10]

The second phase of "Hyazinth und Rosenblüte" is ushered in by the arrival of a strange old man who captivates Hyazinth with tales of strange lands, descends with the boy into deep pits, and gives him a book "das kein Mensch lesen konnte" (I, 93). Following the departure of the old man, Hyazinth spends all of his time alone in the woods and caves, speaking "lauter närrisches Zeug" (I, 91) to the animals, birds, trees, and rocks. The old man and his book have awakened in Hyazinth an awareness of his own mental limitations, but leave him stranded in a state of inadequacy. He can neither read the book of wisdom nor, any longer, speak with the various natural beings around him. What he wishes to gain from the plants, animals, and rocks is knowledge into the essence of nature, but they are unable to understand him or give any sort of intelligible response. The most they can do to set him on the right path is to tell him fairy tales or sing ballads to him, but Hyazinth, like many somber eighteenth-century intellectuals, has no use for these naive forms of expression. In comparison with the first phase of the tale, space here is more extensive (forests and caves instead of garden and wood) and populated by much more diverse forms of wild life: a squirrel, a monkey, a parrot, a rose, an ivy plant. Once again, however, there is no indication of spatial arrangement. The external world corresponds here to the new state of Hyazinth's mind, which has expanded to an awareness of the diversity of nature but is unable to impose any sort of order on its perceptions. If the landscape of the first phase represented a relatively harmonious chaos, in the second phase the chaos is experienced as disturbing; instead of reacting to the natural world with momentary annoyance, Hyazinth is now invariably sullen and morose. At the same time, the spatial distance between Hyazinth and Rosenblüte increases. Formerly they were no further apart than their two houses; now Hyazinth wanders alone in the forests while Rosenblüte remains in the village.

It is here that Novalis's break with Fichte becomes apparent. While the influence of the old man leads to a certain enlargement of Hyazinth's mind, the boy is unable to continue the process of mental expansion on his own. The mind cannot deduce higher and higher levels of reality through itself alone, as Fichte had maintained, but must rely on the influx of external reality or nature. Novalis had already reached this conclusion by the summer of 1796, as a passage from the *Fichte-Studien* indicates:

Hieraus sehn wir beyläufig, daß Ich im Grunde nichts ist—Es muß ihm alles *Gegeben* werden—Aber es kann nur ihm etwas gegeben werden und das Gegebene wird nur durch Ich etwas. Ich ist keine Encyclopaedie, sondern ein universales Princip. Dis hellt auch die Materie von Deductionen a priori auf. Was dem Ich nicht gegeben ist, das kann es nicht aus sich deduciren—aber mit dem Gegebenseyn tritt auch seine Befugniß und Macht ein, dasselbe zu deduciren. Was ihm gegeben ist, ist auf Ewigkeit sein—denn Ich ist nichts als das Princip der Vereigenthümlichung. (II, 273–274)

What is given to Hyazinth at this stage is a fragmented reality, a varied assortment of single impressions (the rose, the brook, the bullfinch) which fail to coalesce into an ordered whole. The discrepancy between this limited awareness and the more complete knowledge represented by the seemingly incomprehensible book results in a persistent feeling of frustration and depression in Hyazinth. Thus an old woman in the woods who perceives what is wrong with him hurls the book into the fire and bids him to set out on a journey to the "Mother of All Things," a journey which is to lead to his mental appropriation (in the sense of the above quotation) of the whole of nature.

After a short farewell speech to his parents and an offhand "Grüßt Rosenblütchen," Hyazinth feverishly sets out on the long journey to the "fremde Lande." Rosenblüte retires in tears to her chamber. Here the spatial relationship between the two figures shifts once again, this time to a juxtaposition of the stationary Rosenblüte and the mobile Hyazinth. This juxtaposition reinforces the symbolic interpretation of the two characters as Nature (passive, immobile) and Mind (active, questing), an interpretation that is further underscored at the conclusion by the revelation that Rosenblüte herself is the "Mother of All

Things." An identical assignment of symbolic roles to mobility and immobility also obtains, as we shall see, in "Atlantis" and the Klingsohr tale.[11]

Hyazinth's travels take him through valleys and wildernesses and over mountains and rivers. Here again one may note a lack of distinct spatial organization. The repeated plurals indicate diversity without any clear succession. It is impossible to determine the direction of Hyazinth's journey, or even if he is traveling in a straight line. The whole geography of the earth sweeps by with Hyazinth's dizzying progress, but no single region or landscape is specifically articulated until he reaches the spring and the flowers late in his journey. On the other hand, the generalized landscape he traverses undergoes a significant development: "Im Anfange kam er durch rauhes, wildes Land, Nebel und Wolken warfen sich ihm in den Weg, es stürmte immerfort; dann fand er unabsehliche Sandwüsten, glühenden Staub, und wie er wandelte, so veränderte sich auch sein Gemüt" (I, 94). There are four distinct shifts in landscape up to this point, accompanied in each instance by a different spatial relationship with Rosenblüte:

1. the harmonious chaos of Hyazinth's immediate surroundings in his homeland; some diversity of detail; slight tension between Hyazinth and the natural world (slight distance between Hyazinth and Rosenblüte)

2. expanded space; much greater diversity of detail; considerable tension between Hyazinth and the natural world (greater distance from Rosenblüte)

3. continually expanding space; less detail; outright hostility between Hyazinth and nature: "Nebel und Wolken warfen sich ihm in den Weg, es stürmte immerfort" (increasing separation from Rosenblüte)

4. the vast deserts, totally devoid of detail, except for the "glowing sand" (greatest distance from Rosenblüte)

As we have seen, the organization, or more precisely lack of organization, of the external world in the first two phases corresponded to Hyazinth's internal condition. This correspondence persists into the next two phases. His impulsive, aggressive attempt to embrace all of nature in the first part of his journey is mirrored by the wildernesses and storms of the external world, and all communication between Hyazinth and the natural beings breaks down. Instead of telling him ballads and fairy tales, the trees, animals, and rocks remain silent or ridicule him. As he reaches the deserts, however, a crucial change takes place, both inside and outside of him: " . . . wie er wandelte, so veränderte sich auch sein Gemüt, die Zeit wurde ihm lang und die innere Unruhe legte sich, er wurde sanfter und das gewaltige Treiben in ihm allgemach zu einem leisen, aber starken Zug, in den sein ganzes Gemüt sich auflöste" (I, 94). In the infinite void of the deserts,

Hyazinth is no longer able to grasp at isolated phenomena, but is forced to readjust his thinking to cosmic proportions; his mind "dissolves" in the sense that he becomes receptive to the totality of an experience rather than to mere disconnected fragments of it. Limited cognition yields to infinite receptivity, and at this point Hyazinth is ready to reenter the phenomenal world. He has regained the capacity ascribed to the Ancients in an earlier passage of *Die Lehrlinge zu Sais*: "Wir finden, daß gerade die erhabensten Fragen zuerst ihre Aufmerksamkeit beschäftigten, und daß sie den Schlüssel dieses wundervollen Gebäudes bald in einer Hauptmasse der wirklichen Dinge, bald in dem erdichteten Gegenstande eines unbekannten Seins aufsuchten. Bemerklich ist hier die gemeinschaftliche Ahndung desselben im Flüssigen, im Dünnen, Gestaltlosen" (I, 83).

The infinite openness of the deserts corresponds, then, to the openness of a mind which has gone beyond the scraps and fragments of limited awareness. It is in this consistent correspondence between the external world of nature and the internal world of Hyazinth's mind that the miracle of Novalis's tale lies, long before the marvelous reunion with Rosenblüte. Hyazinth's interminable journey through physical space is simultaneously a journey through the vastness of his own soul. To say that one symbolizes the other is to miss the point, for Novalis presents the two journeys as parallel manifestations of the same process. As he observes in one of his most penetrating fragments: "Jetzt sehn wir . . . , daß es auch eine Außenwelt in uns giebt, die mit unserm Innern in einer analogen Verbindung, wie die Außenwelt außer uns mit unserm Äußern und jene und diese so verbunden sind, wie unser Innres und Äußres. Daß wir also nur durch Gedanken das Innre und d[ie] Seele der Natur vernehmen können, wie nur d[urch] Sensationen das Äußre und d[en] Körper der Natur" (III, 429). The notion of an internalized external world is a heady one, but it is crucial to an understanding of Novalis's thought. Human existence is conceived as being in a mediating position, confronted on the outside by the awesome body of nature and on the inside by the equally awesome soul of nature; and it is man's own division into body and spirit which makes it possible for him to comprehend the totality of nature in its double aspect. Comprehension is, moreover, only the beginning. The higher task faced by humanity is to reconcile and unify the corporeal and spiritual sides of nature. It follows from man's medial position that this operation must entail self-extension in both directions, physical as well as intellectual. The appropriation of nature is simultaneously self-appropriation. Through a ceaseless process of cross reference, the latent external world within us acquires shape and substance in the same measure that our perceptions of physical nature become increasingly inclusive and refined.

One should not, however, overlook the implicit danger of self-alienation in this "äußere Welt in unserm Innern." Barely disguised beneath the optimism of Novalis's writings is a considerable degree of personal risk; the philosophical system that he established with the headstrong confidence of youth imposes severe and unabating demands on human consciousness. His endless attempts, in the last two years of his life, to synthesize the most divergent forms of physical and spiritual reality may well have brought him to the very threshold of madness. It was surely this self-imposed and uncompromising sense of personal imperative which caused Goethe to react with such discomfort to the Romantics, despite the remarkable affinity between their philosophy and his own.

The landscapes of "Hyazinth und Rosenblüte" are thus external manifestations of the internal states of Hyazinth's mind, and vice versa. Having achieved a kind of *tabula rasa*, an infinite openness devoid of content, in the spacelessness of the desert, he is ready to reenter a fuller, more diversified world: "Nun wurde die Gegend auch wieder reicher und mannigfaltiger, die Luft lau und blau, der Weg ebener, grüne Büsche lockten ihn mit anmutigem Schatten, aber er verstand ihre Sprache nicht, sie schienen auch nicht zu sprechen, und doch erfüllten sie auch sein Herz mit grünen Farben und kühlem, stillem Wesen" (I, 94). Notable here, but predictable, is the lack of specific landscape detail. Nouns such as "die Gegend," "die Luft," and "der Weg" are too general to evoke anything more than the most abstract countryside, and the adjectives "reicher und mannigfaltiger," "lau und blau," and "ebener" only indicate that the climate and the terrain are improving as the landscape fills up again with unspecified details. To to be sure, the balmy skies and the increasingly level path signify that Hyazinth is descending again from the mountains, thereby reversing the sequence of landscapes up to the desert.[12] In contrast to the earlier episode, however, there is no further talk of a chaotic diversity of valleys and wildernesses, mountains and streams, rocks and trees. The only relatively concrete detail here is the reference to green bushes, and this, too, is immediately generalized in the striking and rather lovely image: "sie schienen auch nicht zu sprechen, und doch erfüllten sie auch sein Herz mit grünen Farben." What Hyazinth perceives is no longer isolated green bushes. He has achieved the ability to internalize reality on an abstract level. He registers the quality of greenness rather than the myriad of specific details such as stems, leaves, branches, and so forth. Moreover, we see that he has become capable of transforming perceptions into emotions. The plants fill his *heart*, rather than his mind, with green colors.

If the disorganized conglomeration of spatial detail in Hyazinth's homeland suggested his inability to coordinate his perceptions of reality, the selectively determined and generalized quality of space during the latter phase of his journey reflects his new-found capacity to absorb nature in its unity and totality. This flow of indefinite space is interrupted briefly, however, when he meets the flowers and the spring: "Eines Tages begegnete er einem kristallnen Quell und einer Menge Blumen, die kamen in ein Tal herunter zwischen schwarzen himmelhohen Säulen. Sie grüßten ihn freundlich mit bekannten Worten" (I, 94). The abrupt reappearance of specific spatial detail here is at first baffling and apparently inconsistent. There is, however, a fundamental difference between the woods, caves, and rocks of Hyazinth's home and these black, sky-high columns and valley. The latter do not function as disconnected, isolated objects, but fuse together to form a single image, and this image is quite clearly that of a natural temple. In keeping with the traditional conception of the temple as a site at which the earthly and the divine meet, it is here that Hyazinth at last regains the capacity to speak with the representatives of nature (the spring and the flowers) rather than responding to nature only on an emotional level. The spoken—and understood—word implies an immediate bridging of internal and external reality, an externalization of Hyazinth's mental processes as well as his own ability to internalize the thoughts of nature. The encounter has yet another meaning. While the flowers and spring are preparing the way for the descent of a family of spirits from the ideal realm (the abode of the "Mother of All Things") to the natural world, Hyazinth himself represents a spirit who is preparing the way for the ascent of nature to the ideal, as we shall see.[13]

The sudden emergence of a specific landscape makes sense not only in symbolic terms. From a quite different angle, it is further justified as the first appearance of a recognizable *geographical* location, for the black, sky-high columns are in all probability an allusion to the Columns of Hermes in Upper Egypt.[14] As Hyazinth begins his final ascent into the realm of the ideal, the narrative itself descends for the first time to a realistic plane. It is significant, and very much in keeping with what was said above, that these converging directions should meet at the site of the temple.

At the dwelling of Isis, Hyazinth falls asleep, "weil ihn nur der Traum in das Allerheiligste führen durfte." The implied equation of internal and external space that underlies the entire tale of Hyazinth and Rosenblüte makes the continuation of Hyazinth's journey into a dream possible. Ultimately it explains his miraculous return to Rosenblüte and his homeland via the dream. Even as the external journey through mountains and valleys, wildernesses and deserts represented his simultaneous internal journey, the endless chambers that he traverses in the internal world of the dream may be taken to represent his continuing progress through external space to Rosenblüte. Nevertheless, the explicit correspondence between Hyazinth's mind and the world of nature is abandoned here. The implication of the dream would appear to be that the ultimate ascent to totality and perfection can only be achieved through acts of autonomous creativity on the part of the mind. By the time he reaches the temple at Sais, Hyazinth has assimilated everything that the external world has to offer; the final consolidation must be accomplished internally. It seems likely that the strange objects that Hyazinth encounters in the endless chambers of his dream are intended to represent purely mental images, possibilities of the free imagination, which must also be incorporated into the final unity.

What is particularly significant about the dream is its intriguing mixture of definiteness and indefiniteness: "Wunderlich führte ihn der Traum durch unendliche Gemächer voll seltsamer Sachen auf lauter reizenden Klängen und in abwechselnden Akkorden" (I, 95). Hyazinth wanders through enclosed chambers, but these chambers extend into infinity. He sees nothing but strange objects, but these objects are not described specifically; and he appears to be walking on music, itself a combination of form and fluidity.

If the separation from Rosenblüte consistently functioned as a reflection of Hyazinth's estrangement from nature, the embrace of the two lovers signifies the end of all former disunity. While Hyazinth's external sense has comprehended the body of nature, his internal sense has encompassed the soul of nature within him. The union with Rosenblüte represents not only a union with the objective world but a total realization of his inner self.[15] Equally miraculous, however, is a less obvious point. Because the natural world has proceeded step by step along with Hyazinth through his transformations toward perfection, one must assume that it too shares in the final apotheosis. Through his long journey, Hyazinth has not only fulfilled himself, but in the process redeemed his homeland from the original state of chaos. The redemption of nature through mind is a major theme of the Klingsohr tale and, to a certain degree, of "Atlantis." Here, in Novalis's most subtle and understated *Märchen*, the point is much less dramatically demonstrated.[16] Following the mystical embrace of the two lovers, the narrative concludes briskly without a single further reference to landscape: "Hyazinth lebte nachher noch lange mit Rosenblütchen unter seinen frohen Eltern und Gespielen, und unzählige Enkel dankten der alten wunderlichen Frau für ihren Rat und ihr

Self-Appropriation 19

Feuer; denn damals bekamen die Menschen so viel Kinder, als sie wollten" (I, 95). It is evident, however, from the presence of Hyazinth's parents and playmates, as well as the old woman, that he has returned to his homeland. The reunion with Rosenblütchen establishes the climactic moment of transition to the familiar but wondrously transformed space of childhood. The exalted temple of Isis fuses with Rosenblütchen's chamber, which Hyazinth has entered not from without but, in the deepest sense of the word, from within. Through his limitless appropriation of the external world, Hyazinth's soul itself has become the temple—and the simple chamber—that contains Rosenblütchen.

While Novalis does not describe the landscape of the final phase, one must assume that it is precisely as chaotic as in the beginning, but with one crucial difference. The chaos is now unified through Hyazinth's perfect knowledge. It would be quite wrong, and an injustice to the complexity of Novalis's thought, to picture the landscape here as dissolving into serene spacelessness as a result of Hyazinth's journey. To be sure, Hyazinth has overcome his initial experience of space, but this must not be taken to mean that he no longer experiences space at all. Rather the final condition is to be thought of as a wonderful synthesis of space and spacelessness, in which space represents not separation and disunity, as in the beginning, but the possibility of infinite variation and abundance, a unified chaos in which all things are immediately present.[17] Thus Novalis writes earlier in the *Lehrlinge* of the second Golden Age as "the dream of an infinite, boundless presence": "Dann finden sich die alten verwaisten Familien, und jeder Tag sieht neue Begrüßungen, neue Umarmungen; dann kommen die ehemaligen Bewohner der Erde zu ihr zurück, in jedem Hügel regt sich neu erglimmende Asche, überall lodern Flammen des Lebens empor, alte Wohnstätten werden neu erbaut, alte Zeiten erneuert, und die Geschichte wird zum Traum einer unendlichen, unabsehlichen Gegenwart"[18] (I, 86–87). In "Hyazinth und Rosenblüte" the concluding fusion of space and spacelessness is not directly expressed but can be deduced from the preceding development of the tale. In the later tales, Novalis was to invent spatial images that could depict this synthesis explicitly.

To recapitulate: throughout the tale, the structure of external space parallels and corresponds to the internal situation in Hyazinth's mind. The disjointed quality of space in the opening passages, for instance, reflected an underdeveloped intellect which could perceive isolated phenomena but not coordinate them. The less determined but equally chaotic space of the first phase of Hyazinth's journey corresponded to his frantic, and futile, attempt to assimilate the external world all at once. In the immense void of the deserts, his mind becomes calm and clear, and he achieves for the first time an all-embracing emotional and intellectual receptivity toward nature. From this second starting point, he reenters the phenomenal world, which he experiences both as space (in the sense of increasing diversity of perception) and spacelessness (in the sense of unified perception). On a structural level, this new relationship with nature is expressed in the quasi definiteness of spatial data. Later it is suggested by the combination of form and formlessness in the music of Hyazinth's dream. The two spatial poles of the tale are, in effect, the desert and Hyazinth's homeland. While the former represents unity devoid of content, the latter (initially) represents diversity devoid of unity. Through his journey back to Rosenblüte, Hyazinth gradually fuses the two poles. The final state is one of greatest unity combined with greatest abundance.

"Arion" and "Atlantis"

The tales of "Arion" and "Atlantis" in the second and third chapters of *Heinrich von Ofterdingen* are generally considered *Märchen* by virtue of their formal compactness and miraculous events. Nevertheless, the merchants who relate these tales refer to them merely as stories (*Geschichten*), and their spatial structure only infrequently transcends the laws of natural science.

In "Arion," a poet living in ancient times travels across the sea to a foreign land, taking with him precious jewels and treasures that he has received in gratitude for the beauty of his song. En route the boatmen take him captive and announce their intention of throwing him overboard and confiscating his treasures. The poet begs them to permit him to sing one last song before his death. The evil boatmen, aware of the power of his poetry, stuff their ears in order to remain unmoved; but all of nature responds to the wonderful song. The poet then leaps into the sea. Before he sinks beneath the waves, a thankful sea monster rises from under him and carries him safely to his destination. Some time later, as the poet walks on the shore lamenting the loss of his treasures, the sea monster appears again and drops the stolen jewels from his jaws. In the meantime the boatmen had quarreled over the booty, fallen into a violent battle, and lost control of the ship, which shattered against the shore and sank with the treasure. The few survivors of the murderous quarrel straggle onto land tattered and penniless.

The journey over the sea thus represents a potential threat to the poet's life and happiness, a threat he is able to counter with the power of his song, which enchants all of nature into harmonious resonance. In his departure from the safe land and his ensuing isolation on the high seas he is subject to the spatial danger of separation which recurs in all of Novalis's works. Dislocation from the mainland brings with it the threat of separation from treasures, happiness, and ultimately from life itself. The conflict which ensues may be seen as the struggle between the forces of isolation (the evil boatmen) and the forces of unity and organization (the poet and his song).[19] In its spiritual manifestation as greed, isolation finally turns the boatmen against each other. In the resultant turmoil, the ship is destroyed. The jewels sink to the bottom of the ocean, where they are collected by the sea monster and eventually returned to the hands of their rightful owner. The fortunes and misfortunes of the jewels may not seem particularly remarkable in themselves, but the sequence of dispersal, descent and loss, and final resurrection prefigures important spatial movements in both the Klingsohr tale and "Atlantis."

A shore, a ship on an ocean, a shore: with almost mathematical spareness, Novalis sketches the landscape of the linear journey. Again all local geographical detail is avoided, including the name Arion, which would set the tale in ancient Greece.[20] Sea and shore take on an abstract quality which intensifies the effect of the figural groupings: poet and boatmen, poet alone on the shore, poet and sea monster. This isolation of characters against an absolute minimum of scenery gives "Arion," more than any of the other tales of Novalis, the spatial feeling of the folk fairy tale.[21] Only in the description of the response of nature to the poet's song does the landscape suddenly spring to life. From the ship to the waves, up to the skies and back down to the sea, the narrative follows the reverberation of the cosmos to the song: "Das ganze Schiff tönte mit, die Wellen klangen, die Sonne und die Gestirne erschienen zugleich am Himmel, und aus den grünen Fluten tauchten tanzende Scharen von Fischen und Meerungeheuern hervor" (I, 212). The poet's song momentarily reunites all of the diverse aspects of nature: the sun and the stars appear simultaneously, fish and sea monsters emerge from the depths, and even the wood of the boat sings along. As in "Hyazinth und Rosenblüte," Novalis is careful to include representatives from all three natural kingdoms (plant, animal, and mineral) in the image of unified existence. Here again we may note the redemption of nature from a condition of disarray through the synthesizing activity of the mind; thus the sea monster is twice described as grateful to the poet. Like Hyazinth at the conclusion of his journey, the poet does not experience space as separation, or rather he only briefly experiences it as separation, as he walks alone on the shore singing mournfully of his lost jewels. In the end, his situation on the second shore is precisely the same as his situation on the first shore; the jewels he had once received as "tokens of love and gratitude" are regained, again through thankfulness and love. What is significant here—and indicative of the development from intellectual Romanticism to aesthetic Romanticism—is the fact that the synthesizing agent is no longer the mind per se, as in "Hyazinth und Rosenblüte," but the artistic mind.

The second story of the merchants is, like "Hyazinth und Rosenblüte," the tale of a boy and a girl. As in the folk fairy tale, with its preference for extreme social types,[22] the girl in "Atlantis" is a beautiful princess, the boy the only son of an old man living in a small house in the forest adjoining the royal palace. In the opening pages of the tale, a clear spatial configuration is established. Court and country house, both enclosed spaces, represent the two pivotal points of the narrative. Between them, and surrounding the house, stretches the forest, a nondetermined mass. More than a boy and a girl are separated by this forest. While it took some philosophical consideration to see the two houses in "Hyazinth und Rosenblüte" as representing anything more than two houses, here the spatial configuration assumes specific, and unmistakable, thematic content.

The court represents the world of poetry and song; the old king has surrounded himself with singers and bards who continually celebrate the muses in magnificent ceremonies. The princess herself is the reigning glory of this aesthetic world. For all who behold her, she represents the "visible soul of poetry." The old man and the youth, on the other hand, have devoted themselves to the study of nature and have avoided the glittering life of the court. Strange and wonderful specimens of nature fill their simple dwelling. Thus, whereas Hyazinth could still be regarded as a complete though psychologically nondetermined human being, the characters of "Atlantis" are on their way to becoming the abstracts that people the Klingsohr tale. For all their one-dimensionality, however, the princess and the youth are not yet Poetry and Natural Science incarnate, and the space that separates them still exists on its own terms as physical reality.

One day the princess rides into the forest and stumbles on the old man's house. In the days that follow, she returns often, and she and the boy fall in love. With the motion of the princess back and forth between the court and the house, a pendulumlike movement that anticipates the repeated visits of Fabel to Arcturus's kingdom in "Eros und Fabel," the initial static polarity between the two points begins to dissolve. Again we may note, in contrast to "Hyazinth und Rosenblüte," that it is no longer the entire mind which is mobile, but only the poetic faculty (that is, the princess), which passes with ease from court to house and back again. Prior to the princess's first visit, the youth, predictably enough, was all but stationary. Even his occasional sorties into the forest were circumspect and infrequent: "Es war dem Jüngling nie eine Lust angekommen, den Festen des Hofes beizuwohnen, besonders da er seinen Vater höchstens auf eine Stunde zu verlassen pflegte, um zuweilen im Walde nach Schmetterlingen, Käfern und Pflanzen umherzugehen" (I, 217). After the princess's arrival, however, he becomes remarkably mobile. He secretly follows her back to the very gates of the palace garden, and during her subsequent visits he gradually falls into a routine of picking her up at the garden and accompanying her to the house and back. In other respects, too, the former one-dimensionality of the two figures begins to break down: the youth gains facility in the art of the lute, and the princess verses herself in nature lore. Their final union is represented first in an intricate piece of symbolism, as the youth incorporates the princess's lost carbuncle, an artifact of the natural world, into his first poem. Later they consummate their love in sexual union, which appropriately takes place in a cave in the spatially nondetermined intermediary zone of the forest. In both "Atlantis" and the Klingsohr tale, Novalis repeatedly combines enclosure with openness to suggest the synthesis of space and spacelessness.

After the union in the cave, the princess settles in subterranean rooms adjoining the old man's house. Her descent into the ground and subsequent resurrection to a higher unity recall the fate of Arion's jewels, as well as the spatial movement of the *Hymnen an die Nacht*, in which the grave is conceived as an intermediary step before the ascent to a final resolution.[23]

Following the symbolic interment of the princess, the spatial organization of "Atlantis" shifts functions. In the place of the previous polarity between poetry and nature, a new tension arises. The king and his court represent a society threatened more than ever by sterility and ultimate chaos in the event of the king's death without an heir, while the house of the old man shelters the forces capable of rejuvenating this society. Whereas, however, both the initial polarity between science and poetry and the process leading to the dissolution of this polarity were represented spatially, the process that brings about the final resolution of the new tension is psychological and not spatial in nature. The perspective switches to the interior of the king's mind, where a monumental struggle rages between his ancestral pride and his new sense of oneness with humanity through suffering and deprivation. It is, of course, the familiar theme of isolation versus unity, but without any kind of spatial representation. As a result of this internal discord and its mellowing effect on his regal pride, the king is able ultimately to forgive his daughter for the indignity she has brought upon him. More significantly for the fate of the kingdom, he accepts as his heir the young scientist-cum-poet, who has forged a totally new and vital literature to replace the ossified traditional creations of the court poets.[24]

The reconciliation scene takes place in the royal gardens, an inspired choice of setting. While the previous scenes of the tale have unfolded either in a series of enclosed spaces (the court, the house, the underground rooms) or in the open, formless mass of the forest, here the two spatial categories are fused. The garden is both external and internal space, both open to the sky and closed on the sides. If the enclosed spaces of the tale generally represented containment, order, and stability, while the open space of the forest represented expansion and movement, here the opposing impulses merge together into a new totality.[25] Moreover, the garden per se reflects a special kind of synthesis, and one which is very much in accordance with the symbolic framework of "Atlantis." In eighteenth-century aesthetics, the garden was widely regarded as a wedding of nature and art, as nature organized into pleasing form.

Following the reconciliation scene in the garden, Novalis provides yet another, and considerably bolder, spatial image: the entire land sinks into the sea. This does not mean that the kingdom dissolves into the all-encompassing spatial unity of an aqueous solution, as one might first surmise. Such a reading would only perpetuate the widespread misconception that views the goal of Romanticism as a formless and substanceless blue infinity. By having Atlantis descend into the sea, Novalis places the articulated space of the kingdom in a unified spatial medium (the sea), thereby suggesting once again a synthesis of space and spacelessness, diversity and unity. At the same time, this final image, which is added as a speculative afterthought by the merchant narrators—"Nur in Sagen heißt es, daß Atlantis von mächtigen Fluten den Augen entzogen worden sei" (I, 229)—goes beyond the empirical reality of the rest of the tale. Through the coalition of science and poetry the kingdom is not only regenerated, but elevated to a plane of reality that is inaccessible to the view of mere mortals.[26]

While "Atlantis" displays nothing so intricate as the two simultaneous sets of spatial relationships in "Hyazinth und Rosenblüte," it does in one respect represent a significant advance over the earlier tale. Here for the first time Novalis attempts to express the final transcendent state through spatial images such as the garden and the submerged kingdom, which suggest a blending of enclosure and openness as well as space and spacelessness. In Novalis's last tale, we will observe a similar but much more complex employment of visual symbols to signify the overcoming of empirical space.

"Eros und Fabel"

The tale that the poet Klingsohr relates in the ninth chapter of *Heinrich von Ofterdingen* is a creation of such staggering complexity that critics were long content to follow Ricarda Huch's example in labelling it "incomprehensible."[27] Interpreters who dealt with the tale in any detail tended to resort to florid, lyrical descriptions that obscured rather than illuminated the text; even such an authority as H. A. Korff could write, for instance; "Dieses Märchen ist mit Champagner geschrieben und schäumt in flüchtig schimmernden Bildern aus dem Kelche der Phantasie."[28] The last few decades, however, have witnessed a growing respect for what Novalis was trying to do in the Klingsohr tale. Studies such as Marianne Thalmann's *Das Märchen und die Moderne*, Luitgard Albrecht's *Der magische Idealismus in Novalis' Märchen*, and Max Diez's essay, "Novalis und das allegorische Märchen," have made considerable progress toward clarifying the maddeningly complicated references and relationships in which the work abounds. The best general study in English is provided by Bruce Haywood's *Novalis: The Veil of Imagery*, which manages to convey a sense of the totality of the work while illuminating numerous details.

The problems of spatial and temporal organization in "Eros und Fabel," on the other hand, have never been adequately analyzed; an unfortunate circumstance, considering that Novalis's willful experiments with space and time are equally as aggravating as the tangled allegorical connections. His use of space in particular is anything but consistent. In this whimsically abstract tale, spatial systems, once established, refuse to stay put. The reader is continually made to readjust his conceptualization not only of space, but of the allegorical relationships which are expressed by means of spatial configurations.

For this reason, any attempt to explain the incessant motion of Fabel from one realm to another and the simultaneous travels of Eros and Ginnistan in terms of a neat spatial alignment like the juxtaposition of court and house in "Atlantis" is bound to result in an oversimplification not only of the structural complexities of the tale but also of its thematic implications. We may, however, establish at the outset certain general parallels which exist between "Eros und Fabel" and "Atlantis." Here again, spatial separation represents the dissociation of immanently nonspatial concepts. Arcturus's kingdom, located at the North Pole, encompasses the world of terrestrial and celestial nature. Surrounding Arcturus's kingdom at a distance is a circular mountain belt, and somewhere in or beyond this mountain belt is situated a house in which the manifestations of the spirit (Love, Poetry, Heart, Sense, Fantasy, and so forth) dwell. Between the two foci stretches the nondetermined expanse of a frozen sea, which corresponds structurally to the forest of "Atlantis." In addition to this now familiar constellation representing the division of nature and spirit,[29] two new realms appear: the black subterranean world of the Fates, and the mobile dream world of the Moon. With the exception of the last, these realms appear at the beginning of the tale in a static configuration, recalling once again the initial situation in "Atlantis."

Now we must attempt to determine a general scheme for the spatial development of the Klingsohr tale. Such a scheme does exist, and it appears in miniature no less than three times during the course of the narrative. Novalis was not afraid to furnish repeated clues toward the understanding of his incomprehensible tale. The three key passages are, in the order of their appearance, the movement of the figures in the high windows of Arcturus's castle at the outset of the tale, the motion of the stars in Arcturus's throne room during the mysterious card game, and the drama that Eros and Ginnistan view in Father Moon's treasure chamber. Although all three of these scenes reiterate the basic structure of the tale as a whole, each emphasizes a slightly different aspect of the larger process. Our understanding of the intermediate development represented in the travels of Fabel, Eros, and Ginnistan is best served by the second passage, the dance of the stars in Arcturus's throne room. While Arcturus and his daughter Freya engage themselves in an occult card game which forecasts the destiny of the world, innumerable stars that have entered the hall in graceful groups begin to move in mysterious patterns, accompanied by soft music:

Die Sterne schwangen sich, bald langsam, bald schnell, in beständig veränderten Linien umher, und bildeten, nach dem Gange der Musik, die Figuren der Blätter auf das kunstreichste nach. . . . Mit einer unglaublichen Leichtigkeit flogen die Sterne den Bildern nach. Sie waren bald in *einer* großen Verschlingung, bald wieder in einzelne Haufen schön geordnet, bald zerstäubte der lange Zug, wie ein Strahl, in unzählige Funken, bald kam durch immer wachsende kleinere Kreise und Muster wieder *eine* große, überraschende Figur zum Vorschein. (I, 293)

The movement of the stars thus represents a visual magnification of the process which the images on the cards are undergoing. Simultaneously, however, this ever-changing stellar configuration, with its alternation between movement and temporary alignment, anticipates the spatial interaction of the figures of the mind.[30] One's first impression of them is that of a tableau. Eros lies asleep in the cradle, which Ginnistan rocks while holding Fabel at her breast; nearby the Scribe writes busily at his desk, and Sophie stands at the altar. When the Father arrives with a metal splinter from Arcturus's realm, this tranquil if not entirely harmonious group begins to scatter and regroup. Eros, having suddenly grown to manhood at the touch of the metal splinter, embraces his mother. The Scribe and Sophie leave the room, and Ginnistan and the Father withdraw together into a chamber. After some time, the whole group draws together again without any indication of spatial configuration, suggesting the "Verschlingung" of the stars, and then diverges again, the Father to the courtyard, Eros and the Mother to other parts of the House in preparation for the journey.[31] All except the Father converge in the room again, as Eros and Ginnistan kneel to receive a sacramental blessing from Sophie (second tableau). After the departure of Eros and Ginnistan, the Scribe kindles a revolt among the servants and lays the Mother and Father in chains. Sophie and Fabel escape. After lengthy individual journeys ("bald zerstäubte der lange Zug . . . in unzählige Funken"), Eros, Ginnistan, and Fabel meet again on the shore. Fabel sings Eros to sleep and leaves him in Ginnistan's arms, his wings spread over her (third tableau). Fabel continues her journey, destroying the Fates and rejuvenating Atlas; finally she returns to the House. Sophie is once again at the altar, with Eros in full armor at her feet. Ginnistan leans over a bed in which the Father lies (fourth tableau). After the galvanic reawakening of the Father, the group scatters again, to converge finally at Arcturus's palace for a magnificent closing tableau, in which all the figures of the tale except the Scribe are present in one form or another.

What, then, is the function of this alternating spatial dissociation and convergence? Once again Novalis provides a key to interpretation in a seemingly subsidiary passage. The tale begins with a lengthy description of the mysterious light that begins to emanate from Arcturus's palace following three blows which the Old Hero sounds on his shield:

Da fingen die hohen bunten Fenster des Palastes an von innen heraus helle zu werden, und ihre Figuren bewegten sich. Sie bewegten sich lebhafter, je stärker das rötliche Licht ward, das die Gassen zu erleuchten begann. Auch sah man allmählich die gewaltigen Säulen und Mauern selbst sich erhellen; endlich standen sie im reinsten, milchblauen Schimmer, und spielten mit den sanftesten Farben. Die ganze Gegend ward nun sichtbar, und der Widerschein der Figuren, das Getümmel der Spieße, der Schwerter, der Schilder, und der Helme, die sich nach hier und da erscheinenden Kronen von allen

Seiten neigten, und endlich wie diese verschwanden, und einem schlichten, grünen Kranze Platz machten, um diesen her einen weiten Kreis schlossen: alles dies spiegelte sich in dem starren Meere, das den Berg umgab, auf dem die Stadt lag, und auch der ferne hohe Berggürtel, der sich rund um das Meer herzog, ward bis in die Mitte mit einem milden Abglanz überzogen. Man konnte nichts deutlich unterscheiden; doch hörte man ein wunderliches Getöse herüber, wie aus einer fernen ungeheuren Werkstatt. Die Stadt erschien dagegen hell und klar. (I, 290-91)

Here we find the first passage mentioned above, encased in some of the most complex syntax that Novalis ever wrote. Its depiction of the development from spatial chaos (the tumult of spears, swords, shields, and helmets) to a simple circular tableau representing spatial unity anticipates in an abbreviated way the following development of the tale. More important for our purposes here, however, is the process of *reflection* which the light emanating from the palace undergoes. From one sentence to another, our eye follows the progress of this light. First the palace windows appear, then the streets of the city. The palace itself begins to glow, and we see the reflection of the windows in the frozen sea. Our eyes return to the mountain on which the city is built, then spring back to the far mountain belt beyond the sea, and finally back to the city. Through this verbal imitation of reflection, which recalls the depiction of Arion's song echoing between heaven and earth, we follow the light as it illuminates and reilluminates ever greater expanses of space. This process of widening reflection exactly parallels the movement of Fabel, who, as the spirit of song, literally reverberates from one place to another in effortless motion.[32] Her path gradually lengthens, until she finally bounds around the entire earth to Atlas and back. And just as the light gains in intensity and range each time it is reflected back into the source in the palace, Fabel's power and distance grow with each successive visit to Arcturus's throne room. After her first visit, she returns to the World (that is, the mountain belt) to subdue the wild Eros, after her second she descends to destroy the Fates, and after her third she springs around the earth to awaken Atlas and to bring the Mother's ashes back to the House.

Our picture of alternating dissociation and convergence, movement and tableau, must now be modified to include the specific contribution of Fabel. While all the other figures move within the realms of the World or the Underworld respectively, Fabel alone oscillates back and forth between these realms and the kingdom of Arcturus. Energized, so to speak, by her repeated contact with the latter, she brings one field of forces into harmony (Eros and Ginnistan) and reactivates another (the group around the altar in the House). Thus the spatial movement in "Eros und Fabel" consists of an involved interplay between the process of reflection and the process of alignment and realignment of the conceptual forces represented by the various figures. Each successive convergence causes these forces to be modified and developed through mutual interaction. As we have seen, the movements of the princess between the court and the house in "Atlantis" suggested the same thing, on a much simpler level.

From an abstract viewpoint, it is possible to interpret the opposing movements toward dispersal and convergence as manifestations of centrifugal and centripetal force. In a fragment from 1798, Novalis draws an analogy between the two dynamic forces and synthetic and analytical thinking: "Zentripetalkraft—ist das synthetische Bestreben—Centrifugalkraft—das analytische Bestreben des Geistes—Streben nach Einheit—Streben nach Mannichfaltigkeit—durch wechselseitige Bestimmung beyder durch Einander—wird jene höhere Synthesis der Einheit und Mannichfaltigkeit selbst hervorgebracht—durch die Eins in Allem und Alles in Einem ist" (II, 589). It seems to me that this fragment describes precisely what is going on in "Eros und Fabel": in their development toward that higher synthesis, the various figures, who personify components of the spirit, alternate between movement toward unity and movement toward diversity. The successive contributions of Fabel insure, moreover, that each rearrangement represents a step forward.[33]

This dynamic interplay of convergence and dispersal, which is reminiscent of Goethe's conceptions of systolic and diastolic movement, operates not only among the various characters as a group, but also within the single figure of the Mother, who, though a minor protagonist, undergoes some fairly flashy transformations. At the beginning of the tale, the Mother, who allegorically represents the Heart, is constantly in motion: "Die Mutter des Knaben, die wie die Anmut und Lieblichkeit selbst aussah, kam oft herein. Sie schien beständig beschäftigt, und trug immer irgendein Stück Hausgeräte mit sich hinaus. . . . Die Mutter gab auf einige Augenblicke der kleinen Fabel die Brust; aber bald ward sie wieder abgerufen" (I, 294). This restless, fidgety activity is indicative of a heart incapable of sustained attention to any object. She is continually distracted from one pursuit and drawn to another. A rather nice detail is her magpielike practice of carrying off various household utensils, probably to hide them somewhere. This aimless and unproductive activity is brought to a halt by the Scribe, who locks up both the Mother and the Father.[34] Shortly thereafter the Scribe and his henchmen attempt to destroy the Mother by burning her on a funeral pyre, but their action only succeeds in condensing her hitherto disorganized energy into a magnificent flame. In allegorical terms, the murderous assault of Rationality on the immature Heart only forces it to gather itself together and become transfigured into a new, invincible source of power. At this point, the Mother's essence divides into two aspects. As the pure energy of the flame, she destroys the sun and then proceeds northward to melt the polar ice cap. At the same time, her ashes are scattered over the surface of the earth. Later, Fabel gathers the ashes with the aid of Tourmaline and brings them to Sophie, who dissolves them in her basin of tears. Everyone present partakes of the wondrous fluid, and Sophie pours the remainder into the depths of the earth. This familiar progression (dispersal–convergence–transformation–redispersal) thus culminates in a situation in which the Mother is everywhere present, internalized in each of the characters and in the earth itself. She now represents eternal renewal and the great mystery of regeneration through pain. If at the beginning of the tale she was faced with the spatial dilemma of trying to be everywhere at once, at the conclusion she is, in fact and literally, everywhere at once.[35]

The Mother's metamorphosis into an aqueous solution and a flame is only one of a sizeable group of images which Novalis accumulates to express the final state of spatial unity. Another is the vanishing of geographical disparity. As the ice cap melts, an eternal climate of spring spreads over the face of the earth. Objects which have been vertically isolated (sun and moon in the sky, the realm of the Fates in the core of the earth) rejoin the unified surface of the earth: the sun falls into the sea, Father Moon and his court enter the palace of Arcturus, and the eerie world of the Fates rises up into Arcturus's courtyard. Another former source of polarity, as well as attraction, is Freya's electric charge, which Eros conducts into the sea by way of Iron's sword and a gold chain. Immediately thereafter, all the principal figures gather in a final harmonious tableau in Arcturus's palace, as Eros and Freya join in erotic union. Because the philosophical relationships of the figures are depicted entirely by their spatial alignment, and because conversely the primary function of space is to represent these relationships on a physical level, the final unified tableau represents not only the resolution of all philosophical or conceptual tension, but the annihilation of articulated space itself: "Der Raum verschwindet—als ein banger Traum" ("Studien zu Klingsohrs Märchen," I, 338).

Once again it must be emphasized, however, that the end of the tale by no means suggests a dissolving of the whole universe into cosmic openness. In the place of the former disparate realms there appears the image of concentric circles. Freya's bracelet becomes a luminous band of light that surrounds the earth, while the mountain belt, the sea, and the city enclose Arcturus's palace in ever tighter circles of unified substance. In this way Novalis manages to convey a certain sense of material fullness without sacrificing unity. The separation between the circles no longer expresses artificial separation of things which belong together, but rather the possibility of variation and multiplicity. In the *Allgemeine Brouillon* Novalis contrasts apparent separation with this productive or true separation, which is congruent with, and a reciprocal manifestation of, true unity: "Alles Übel und Böse ist isolirt und isolirend—es ist d[as] *Princip d[er] Trenung*—durch Verbindung wird die Trenung aufgehoben und nicht aufgehoben—aber d[as] Böse und Übel etc. als *Scheinbare* Trenung und Verbindung wird in der That durch wahrhafte Trenung und Vereinigung, die nur *wechselseitig bestehn,* aufgehoben" (III, 390).

As was the case with "Atlantis," Novalis concludes the narrative proper with a tableau but indicates a further spatial movement. As Fabel hovers over the wedding bed of Eros and Freya and the assembled multitudes engage in tender loveplay, Sophie announces: "Die Mutter ist unter uns, ihre Gegenwart wird uns ewig beglücken. Folgt uns in unsere Wohnung, in dem Tempel dort werden wir ewig wohnen, und das Geheimnis der Welt bewahren" (I, 315). Novalis seems to have been uneasy with Arcturus's throne room as the final dwelling place of his figures, and justifiably so. Even in this most abstract of worlds, it is ultimately unsatisfying to envision the whole cast of characters suspended in the same tableau through all eternity. By removing them from sight, he circumvents the irresolvable dilemma of finding visual representation for the state of absolute perfection. The temple functions here much in the same way as the ocean into which Atlantis sinks, but the later image is rather less successful. In both cases, the mystery of the world withdraws into secluded territory; but although the ocean provided a possible medium for the resolution of such dualities as containment and expansion, external and internal space, and mobility and immobility, the temple exhibits little if any symbolic resonance. It is simply an internal space.

Although the spatial structure of the Klingsohr tale parallels that of Novalis's other *Märchen* not only in general organization, but also in many individual features, the ascent of this final tale into the rarified atmosphere of allegory results in a number of new problems concerning spatial determination. The initial configuration of "Eros und Fabel" is unproblematic: a castle in the middle of a frozen sea encircled by a mountain belt. These mountains as a whole, and presumably the global space beyond them, represent the "World," to use the designation of Arcturus himself: "Der alte Held hatte bisher auch sein unsichtbares Geschäft emsig betrieben, als auf einmal der König voll Freuden ausrief: 'Es wird alles gut. Eisen, wirf du dein Schwert *in die*

Welt, daß sie erfahren, wo der Friede ruht.' Der Held riß das Schwert von der Hüfte. . . . Wie ein Komet flog es durch die Luft, und schien an dem Berggürtel mit hellem Klang zu zersplittern" (I, 293; emphasis added). What is meant by "Welt" is by no means apparent at the first glance. The term cannot, for instance, be understood in its usual inclusive sense here, since Arcturus's polar island, the realm of Nature, is quite clearly set off from the mountain belt and everything it represents.[36] If we assume, however, that Arcturus's kingdom embraces only *ideal* natural forms, then the world may be viewed as fallen nature, nature corrupted by the clouded vision of immature Mind. It is the world of time and history, transitoriness and decay; the world, in other words, as it appears at the opening of "Hyazinth und Rosenblüte," distorted by Hyazinth's morose, uncomprehending consciousness. The strange cacophony that resounds from the far mountains is a first, and rather humorous, indication of the state of disorder into which the World has descended: " . . . auch der ferne hohe Berggürtel, der sich rund um das Meer herzog, ward bis in die Mitte mit einem milden Abglanz überzogen. Man konnte nichts deulich unterscheiden; doch hörte man ein wunderliches Getöse herüber, wie aus einer fernen ungeheueren Werkstatt" (I, 291).

In keeping with the Gnostic associations of the tale, the mountain belt is the home of Sophie, the spirit of wisdom fallen away from God and relegated to the precincts of a lower sphere, which in turn encloses and contains all temporal existence (that is, the global space beyond the mountains).[37] The circular mountain belt thus functions as a metaphor for containment, and in this sense Sophie as well as the lesser manifestations of Mind (Sense, Fantasy, Reason, etc.) must be understood as *defining* the circle through their presence everywhere within it.

With the introduction of the House, however, the reader's clear notion of spatial and allegorical relationships begins to crumble. If the mountain-belt landscape presented the world of the Mind as a circle surrounding the kingdom of Nature, the House condenses the territory of the Mind into a single enclosed space (apparently, however, somewhere in the mountains or immediately beyond them). We are confronted, then, with the coexistence of two contradictory spatial configurations with two quite different functions. One represents a mythic cosmorama, according to which Arcturus's mountain island appears as the hub of the universe,[38] the kingdom of ideal Nature at the center of all things, an image which recalls Novalis's notion of the soul of nature at the deepest point within us. The other configuration juxtaposes house and palace as headquarters for two allegorical teams headed by Sophie and Arcturus respectively. It is altogether unlikely that Novalis could have overlooked the contradictory nature of his spatial system here, which in effect equates a point (the house) with a circle (the mountain belt). In all probability, he superimposed the two configurations onto each other in a deliberate attempt to encourage a reading of the tale on at least two levels at once. More important, the very illogic of Novalis's geometry serves to induce a productive feeling of disorientation in the reader; it challenges the seemingly self-evident view of space as an objective medium in which all of us move, and which is fundamentally indifferent to, and unaffected by, human perception. By simultaneously using two conflicting spatial configurations to express different aspects of a single situation (the oppostion of nature and mind), Novalis invites us to reflect on the possibility that objective space is a scientific hoax—that space does not exist independently of consciousness, but is essentially a reflex of one's internal viewpoint.

A similar spatial confusion obtains with regard to the fanciful world of Father Moon. After his departure from the House, Eros is led by the willful Ginnistan to her father's ancient castle in the sky, which soon comes to rest on the mountains beyond the sea. It is possible to interpret these mountains simply as that part of the circular mountain belt which lies opposite the House. Once again, however, the whole topography shifts functions. The spatial reference to mountains beyond the sea has nothing to do with the mythic cosmorama centered around Arcturus's kingdom, nor does it have a place in the allegorical confrontation between palace and house. Its function is entirely poetical. "Beyond the sea" evokes the image of a distant dreamland, a Neverneverland beyond time and place where the moon goes after it has set. Only if we momentarily abandon the allegorical interpretation of the whole mountain belt as the world of the Mind, are we justified in locating this fabulous land on the far side of the mountain belt.

The reader is thus thwarted in every attempt to make this space settle down and behave like physical space or to assign to it a rigid allegorical shape. While Arcturus's island and the mountain belt provide a convenient and flexible spatial framework for the tale as a whole, numerous other landscape details flash into sight and disappear again without any larger purpose than to illuminate a momentary mood or to form a symbolic backdrop for an isolated action. The splendid view, for instance, which one glimpses from the House when Ginnistan opens the window (I, 296), has nothing to do with other spatial arrangements in the tale, but merely reflects her newly awakened concern with the sense of sight. When Fabel journeys around the earth to revitalize the old giant later in the tale, the mythological motif of Atlas holding the world on his shoulders is briefly evoked. Once again, although the content of the scene is closely integrated with the text as a whole, the spatial image is a striking and unexpected departure from the other landscapes of the tale.

Space here is anything but autonomous; it is totally at the service of the ideas it expresses. The realm of the Fates, for example, is described as being "Überall und nirgends" (I, 301), and indeed it is everywhere. It appears directly below such distant points of the compass as the House and Arcturus's palace.[39] But it is also a "nowhere" kingdom, a black counterpart—complete with a black sun—to the external world, which in its own way is also nowhere, a land of unfulfilled existence, a purgatory under the merciless domination of the sun, which ensures an endless continuation of inadequacy and isolation.

At the root of these various manipulations of represented space is the allegorical nature of the tale as a whole. Space here no longer exists on its own terms as physical space, with a semiallegorical structure superimposed on it, as in "Atlantis." The entire ontological function of space is instead exhausted in its representation—on allegorical, mythic, or symbolical levels—of the relationships between personified abstracts. We must not be misled by the apparent location of Arcturus's palace at the North Pole. Details such as the aurora borealis and the position of the northern magnetic pole in Freya's body leave the essentially nonphysical structure of this space unharmed. They are merely superimposed on what amounts to an ideal space, which separates not real objects, but concepts. One might term these details "inverse symbols." If a symbol is said to cause the ideal to shimmer through a real context, details such as these have just the opposite function—to cause the real to shimmer through an ideal context. In a similar sense, Eros and Freya could be said to "symbolize" a boy and a girl. Their conceptual range extends, however, considerably beyond a masculine-feminine opposition, and even this opposition is complicated by an occasional reversal of gender sign. Arcturus speaks of Freya as "der Friede," and Eros is referred to more than once as "die Liebe."[40]

The casual way in which spatial images are established and then abandoned in "Eros und Fabel" is not a sign of incompetent storytelling, nor is it mere capriciousness on Novalis's part. Rather it provides yet another dimension to the theme of the tale. Precisely as the various allegorical figures of the mind are constantly in motion or in flux, the mind of the narrator, too, is felt to be continually on the move, rearranging his narrative materials as he pleases, inserting now a scrap of epic poetry (I, 297–98), now an image from mythology, now a spatial illustration of an allegorical event. The Romantic mistrust of fixed systems extends here to the very spatial structure of the narrative. Rather than permitting himself to be tied down to one self-contained spatial scheme, the narrator continually gives evidence of his own freedom of artistic selection: "Alles *Unwillkührliche* soll in ein *Willkührliches* verwandelt werden" (II, 589). Whether the active mind of the narrator can be said to move toward the synthesis which his allegorical figures achieve, is another question. It must be conceded that Novalis is flirting with disintegration of form in the Klingsohr tale. Despite the final conglomeration of images suggesting unity, the tale tends to come apart toward the end. The various spatial configurations do not *quite* coalesce into a convincing synthesis. On the other hand, Novalis himself clearly recognized the sort of difficulties he was getting into. In the preceding chapter of *Heinrich von Ofterdingen*, he has Klingsohr provide the following commentary to the tale: "Ich weiß selbst, daß mir in jungen Jahren ein Gegenstand nicht leicht zu entfernt und zu unbekannt sein konnte, den ich nicht am liebsten besungen hätte. Was wurde es? ein leeres, armseliges Wortgeräusch, ohne einen Funken wahrer Poesie. . . . Es ist mir [ein Märchen] erinnerlich, was ich noch in ziemlich jungen Jahren machte, wovon es auch noch deutliche Spuren an sich trägt" (I, 286–87).

The unpredictable shifts in spatial function which we have observed lead inevitably to problems of transition. The return of Eros and Ginnistan from the kingdom of Father Moon is a case in point. Following the drama in Father Moon's treasure room, Ginnistan leads Eros to a remote bath, where she seduces him; the two fall asleep in each other's arms. The narrative then turns to the adventures of little Fabel. As the latter returns from Arcturus's kingdom to the World, we encounter Ginnistan again, alone on the shore. In the longest monologue of the tale, she relates her dismay at the strange changes which she and Eros have undergone in their sleep. "Wir erwachten spät aus dem verbotenen Rausche, in einem sonderbar vertauschten Zustande," she tells Fabel (I, 305). Nowhere in her lengthy account of the events which have proceeded from her union with Eros, however, does she mention, even in passing, her return with Eros from the strange kingdom of the Moon. One might, for instance, expect something like, "When we awoke, we found ourselves back in the World again." Instead, she dwells extensively on the external and internal changes which she and Eros have undergone. That these changes have been accompanied by a sudden change in their spatial orientation is completely unproblematical for her. The return of Eros and Ginnistan to the World (or, more precisely, to what functionally represents the World) is the *self-evident* spatial correlative of their shift in abstract character. Through his union with Fantasy, Love has become the earthly Cupid. Correspondingly, he moves without transition from the ethereal kingdom of the Moon to the realm of the World. In the same way, Ginnistan's new mood of remorse and guilt automatically transplants her from her father's intoxicating dream world back to earth, where she is provided with a poetic spatial expression of her grief, a scenic portrait which might be entitled "Ginnistan on the Desolate Shore." Internal and external transformations go hand in hand here. In the semirealistic tale of Atlantis, by way of contrast, the princess and the youth awake after their night in the cave to the *feeling* that they are in a new world. They are, of course, still in the cave, and the formulation "new world" has only figurative meaning, primarily as an expression of their emotional state. There still exists a clear divergence between internal and external reality. In the Klingsohr tale, on the other hand, Eros and Ginnistan quite literally awake in a new world, but they fail to register any internal reaction to it. This acceptance of the marvelous as self-evident is an acknowledged hallmark of the folk fairy tale, and Novalis demonstrates here a certain fidelity to folk tradition. At the same time, however, Ginnistan's lack of reaction is supported by the logic of allegorical representation. As a narrative moves in the direction of allegory, the distinction between external and internal reality gradually becomes obliterated; the characters become conceptual fragments devoid of internal definition, and the external world loses its function as an adversary to this increasingly nonexistent internal world. To the extent that it appears at all, spatial structure becomes symbolic of the conceptual relationships of the figures. It is impossible, then, to ask what space as such means for an allegorical character, first of all because he no longer has the psychological apparatus to interpret it, and secondly because external space no longer has an independent significance to which he could react.

The spatial transition from Moon kingdom to World thus corresponds exactly to the internal changes in abstract character which Eros and Ginnistan have experienced. The function of these two changes is identical. This means that Novalis is demonstrating, through the *form* of his tale, the synthesis that is achieved in its *content* only at the conclusion: that is, the synthesis of internal and external reality, of mind and nature.

Still another problem is that of internal dimension. In the opening scene, Arcturus descends with his attendants from the cupola of his throne room. As he embraces his daughter, a countless host of stars fills the hall. The word "Saal" defines a closed interior space, but the image of innumerable stars drifting through the hall necessitates a readjustment of dimensions. The room expands to such cosmic proportions that it is difficult to visualize it as interior space. Similarly,

Fabel discovers an enormous realm in the depths of the earth: "Endlich kam sie auf einen freien Platz hinaus, der rund herum mit einer prächtigen Kolonnade geziert, und durch ein großes Tor geschlossen war. . . .Die Luft war wie ein ungeheurer Schatten; am Himmel stand ein schwarzer strahlender Körper" (I, 301). In broadening concentric circles we see first the plaza, then the colonnade with its gate, and finally a sky large enough to hold the counterpart of the sun. In the interior of the earth itself, a monstrous cavity opens up. Again it takes a special exertion of imaginative power to visualize the shell of the earth enclosing this vast space. Finally, the drama which Eros and Ginnistan view takes place in the treasure room of Father Moon, which is also described as a large garden. This garden, then, contains not only herds of sheep and buildings laden with tapestries, carpets, and drinking vessels, but cities and castles, deserts, mountains, plains, and finally an entire ocean. If it was difficult to envision the immense realm of the Fates in the heart of the earth, it is all but impossible to picture this colossal landscape within the confines of a garden, much less a treasure room.

This paradoxical voluminousness of interior space recalls immediately Hyazinth's endless journey into the interior realm of his own soul. Throughout his works, Novalis makes repeated metaphorical use of such terms as *inner*, *innigst*, or *innerlich* to evoke the internal world of the spirit.[41] Fichte had proposed a conception of the world as a nonego posited by the ego in its own process of self-definition. The incessant mental activity of projecting a nonego and then destroying it in order to project a larger, more encompassing nonego lent itself readily to figurative representation in terms of internal expansion. In the Klingsohr tale, this metaphorical interior extension becomes physical reality. What in the other works had been a figurative expression for the growth of the mind becomes a literal property of nature itself. Arcturus's throne room displays the same paradoxical internal vastness which had characterized Hyazinth's mind in the earlier tale. In this complex transfer of images, Novalis once again seeks to achieve a *formal* identity of mind and nature, in perfect accordance with his own demand of the fairy tale, that it intermingle "die ganze Natur auf eine wunderliche Art mit der ganzen Geisterwelt" (III, 280). Furthermore, this acquisition of mental properties by Nature is mirrored by a corresponding alteration in the representatives of the mind, which have become objectivized, not only with regard to their appearance as concrete physical entities, but also in their loss of internal, psychological definition. This does not mean, of course, that the two spheres have traded roles, that Nature has become a conscious mind and Mind an unconscious object; such an exchange would only mean a reestablishment of the original polarity on different terms. Rather we are to interpret this transfer of attributes as a partial convergence of the two spheres, an approach to identity, an "intermingling", as Novalis puts it, which breaks down the formal boundaries between subject and object.

A further—and, for our purposes, decisive—consequence of Novalis's allegorical technique is that space comes to express *temporal* situations such as stasis, progression, repetition, and regression. This provocative correlation of space and time requires special attention, and it also calls for some preliminary discussion of the role of time in Novalis's works, a topic to be taken up in Chapter 3. In the meantime, however, we shall turn our attention to the role of space in the tales of Ludwig Tieck.

II

Split Terrain
Space in the *Märchen* of Tieck

"Der blonde Eckbert"

In contrast to Novalis's tales, which are intellectually engaging but rather short on emotional appeal, the *Märchen* of Ludwig Tieck speak directly to the feelings and senses. "Der blonde Eckbert," for instance, is so lyrically evocative that some critics have been inclined to interpret it more as poetry than as prose, writing off the plot as inconsequential and meaningless.[1] While Novalis sublimated his intense emotional energies into creations of exquisite refinement, the young Tieck tended to let himself go, turning out works which sometimes reflect all too clearly the neurotic preoccupations of their creator. The two tales under consideration here, "Der blonde Eckbert" and "Der Runenberg," while easily the best that Tieck produced in the genre, are divergent enough in quality to give some indication of the unevenness of Tieck's work. As a free-lance writer, of course, he was dependent on sheer volume of output, rather than artistic excellence, for a livelihood. Also, the partisan encouragement that he as the first official practitioner of literary Romanticism received from the Schlegels may well have blunted his sense of fastidiousness, never very strong to begin with. Whatever may be said for or against the Schlegels' influence, however, it was "Der blonde Eckbert" (1796) that first drew their enthusiastic attention to Tieck. By almost any standard, this brief, uncanny tale remains a masterpiece of narrative fiction, surely one of the finest pieces of writing to emerge from Early Romanticism.

At first glance, "Der blonde Eckbert," which chronicles the gradual disintegration of a troubled mind, seems so fundamentally different from Novalis's tales that there is almost no common ground for a comparison. One of the advantages of an analysis of spatial and temporal organization, however, is that it offers a more abstract basis for comparison than an analysis of thematic material in the conventional sense. As it turns out, both "Eckbert" and the Novalis *Märchen* share a most crucial structural feature. In all of them, space is split into a polar configuration that appears as the juxtaposition of two internal spaces. In "Eckbert," precisely as in "Atlantis," a house in the woods confronts a castle. The two spatial foci serve as headquarters for opposing forces. But although the house and castle in Novalis's tale both represented incomplete, one-dimensional entities in need of—and in search of—synthesis, the confrontation in "Der blonde Eckbert" is between a state of utopian perfection and a state of dire inadequacy, and relations between the two realms are anything but pleasant.

The opening pages of "Der blonde Eckbert" are full of hints of trouble at Eckbert's and Bertha's castle. The lonely, secluded location of the little fortress; the orderly, austere, childless existence of the couple; their lack of guests and friends; Eckbert's bent toward melancholy: all of these details point to a state of withdrawal, a defensively private existence, a life pared back to the barest minimum of joy and warmth. One senses immediately the presence of an uncomfortable secret behind all this privacy. One evening Eckbert invites his only close friend, Philipp Walther, to spend the night at the castle, and in the intimate glow of the fireside, Bertha relates the strange story of her childhood.

On this particular evening, the isolation of the castle from the outside world seems more pronounced than ever:

> Es war schon im Herbst, als Eckbert an einem neblichten Abend mit seinem Freunde und seinem Weibe Bertha um das Feuer eines Kamines saß. Die Flamme warf einen hellen Schein durch das Gemach und spielte oben an der Decke, die Nacht sah schwarz zu den Fenstern herein, und die Bäume schüttelten sich vor nasser Kälte. . . . Nun ward Wein und die Abendmahlzeit hereingebracht, das Feuer durch Holz vermehrt, und das Gespräch der Freunde heitrer und vertraulicher. . . . Es war jetzt gerade Mitternacht, der Mond sah abwechselnd durch die vorüberflatternden Wolken.[2]

In almost every respect, the interior scene represents an antithesis to the external world. The castle room is warm and cozy while the night outside is wet and cold. The room is bright with the cheery blaze of the fire while the external world is only sporadically illuminated by the moon. Moreover, in contrast to the more or less stationary group around the hearth, the natural world outside is constantly in motion, an indefinite landscape of trees and clouds moving in the wind and in the eerie interplay of light and darkness. This nature is full of eyes which peer malignantly into the castle as if to keep its inhabitants under constant surveillance and to observe the revelation, at last, of Bertha's dreadful secret. To judge from the opening scene, then, Eckbert's castle represents a defensive and rather vulnerable little stronghold of internal space surrounded by the hostile external space of nature.

The second spatial focal point of the tale is the old woman's hut in the forest, where Bertha spends six years of her childhood. She first views the hut from the top of a hill: "Wir stiegen nun einen Hügel hinan, der mit Birken bepflanzt war, von oben sah man in ein grünes Tal voller Birken hinein, und unten mitten in den Bäumen lag eine kleine Hütte" (14). Like Eckbert's castle, the hut is surrounded by, and indeed even engulfed in, the world of nature; but there the similarity ends. If the castle represented a complete disjunction of inside and outside space, the interior of the hut is coordinated with the forest outside in a most remarkable way. Bertha's description of her first night in the hut makes the nature of this correspondence clear:

Ich blieb nicht lange munter, ich war halb betäubt, aber in der Nacht wachte ich einigemal auf, und dann hörte ich die Alte husten und mit dem Hunde sprechen, und den Vogel dazwischen, der im Traum zu sein schien, und immer nur einzelne Worte von seinem Liede sang. Das machte mit den Birken, die vor dem Fenster rauschten, und mit dem Gesang einer entfernten Nachtigall ein so wunderbares Gemisch, daß es mir immer nicht war, als sei ich erwacht, sondern als fiele ich nur in einen andern noch seltsamern Traum. (15)

In this initial impression, inside and outside are conjoined by sound, as the two birds sing together and the coughing of the old woman mingles with the rustling of the birches. The correspondence also extends to a visual level. The ever-changing colors of the bird's feathers and the ceaseless mobility of the old woman's face find their counterpart outside in the shimmering leaves of the birch trees. Finally, after Bertha has adjusted herself to the routine at the hut, a significant daily pattern is established: the bird sings in his cage, Bertha spins away in the hut, and the birches rustle and shimmer in the valley outside. The image that emerges is one of concentric circles of complementary activity, activity which fills time with color and sound but does not lead to change or any sense of temporal progression. The inside of the hut is totally integrated with the outside; each sphere of activity is self-sufficient but coordinated harmoniously with the others.[3] Here again we find a kind of boundless presence, in which near and far are nothing more than variations on a single theme, and in which space (representing diversity) merely affirms the essential spacelessness of unified existence. It is worth noting that Bertha herself is not at the center of this spatial scheme. The innermost circle is occupied by the magic bird in his cage, who may be taken to represent the creative heart of nature. Thus it is appropriate that Bertha's later crimes are directed primarily toward the bird: she not only displaces it from its central location in order to utilize its productivity for her own gain, but later strangles it in a paroxysm of guilt and fear.

In comparison with the conclusions of Novalis's tales, there is something rather modest and domesticated about Tieck's utopia. The notion of completion and self-fulfillment within the confines of one's own snug little circle is strongly reminiscent of Classicism, even *Biedermeier*. At the heart of this eminently Romantic tale are unmistakable signs of the cozy conservatism that Tieck was to adopt as his personal and literary style a decade or so later.[4]

By the time Bertha has finished her tale of betrayal and murder, the implications of the discrepancy between inside and outside space at Eckbert's castle have become fairly evident. The castle is a spatial image of self-protective guilt, a retreat from the existential and moral necessity of meaningful interaction between man and man, and between man and nature. Castle and hut thus function as spatial manifestations of one of the most important conflicts in the tale: on the one hand, the impulse toward independence, narcissism, isolation, and repression of guilt; on the other, the need for openness and integration.

Secondary literature is sharply divided on the problem of the ultimate significance of "Der blonde Eckbert." One well-defended view argues that the tale revolves around moral issues such as transgression, unatoned guilt, and retribution. On the other side, an equally convinced group of critics contends that ethical considerations are irrelevant in the overall context of the tale, and that Eckbert and Bertha, guilty or not, fall victim to an irrationally vindictive, a demonic force residing in nature.[5] The fact that critical opinion has taken such divergent directions suggests certain tensions in the tale itself, and I would argue that "Der blonde Eckbert" does in fact accommodate *both* readings. Critics who espouse the second interpretation usually focus their attention on Eckbert's horrifying epiphany in the concluding episode. The revelations voiced there by the old woman, they maintain, retroactively invalidate any interpretation of the tale in moral terms. Nevertheless, the ethical problems that are raised in the preceding twenty-four pages of the text are simply too prominent, and too insistent, to be dismissed out of hand as irrelevant. Whether or not Eckbert's final fate is sealed by a demonic or inscrutable force, there is no denying that he has played an active role in his own destruction.

Because the spatial scheme of the tale generally supports an ethical reading, this chapter will take up the line of interpretation advanced by the first group of critics. Later, in Chapter 4, we will consider the second viewpoint in light of the special problems that are posed by the idyll of *Waldeinsamkeit* and by the ambiguous role of the old woman in Eckbert's and Bertha's destinies.

While Valentine C. Hubbs could, as late as 1956, defend Eckbert as the innocent victim of Bertha's transgressions,[6] later studies have agreed that Eckbert is no less culpable than his sister. There are indications that he shared Bertha's greed for the jewels and married her at least partly for her money. He says, for instance, to Walther: "Ich hatte kein Vermögen, aber durch ihre Liebe kam ich in diesen Wohlstand" (21). And he murders Walther with the same impulsiveness with which Bertha murdered the bird. More important, however, are his union with Bertha and his friendship with Walther, which point to a deeper source of guilt. By marrying—not entirely unwittingly—his own half-sister and by choosing as his best friend a man in whom he found "approximately the kind of thinking to which he himself was most devoted" (9), Eckbert reveals a narcissistic need to surround himself with people who reflect his own image.[7] Bertha and Walther do not function as total human beings for him, but are reduced to mirrors that fortify him in his isolation. Thus as his mind begins to collapse, he wonders whether Bertha had ever even existed: "Jetzt war es um das Bewußtsein, um die Sinne Eckberts geschehn; er konnte sich nicht aus dem Rätsel herausfinden, ob er jetzt träume, oder ehemals von einem Weibe Bertha geträumt habe" (25).[8]

It would be wrong, however, to assume that Eckbert is fully conscious of his narcissistic impulses. Not until the cataclysmic revelations of the old woman at the conclusion is he aware of the terrible loneliness of his existence. There are signs that the marriage with Bertha has been preying on his conscience: his occasional moodiness; his hasty assurance to Walther that "unsere Verbindung hat uns bis jetzt noch keinen Augenblick gereut" (21);[9] and his anguished cry at the conclusion, "Warum habe ich diesen schrecklichen Gedanken immer geahndet?" (26). When he becomes conscious of the extent to which he has been dominated by the drive toward selfishness and isolation, he perishes in anguish. One of the truly modern, and at the same time deeply pessimistic, premises of "Der blonde Eckbert" is that the impulse toward community and integration, as well as the impulse toward self-glorification, independence, and detachment, are both imbedded in the unconscious mind.[10] Bertha's description of her internal struggle before leaving the old woman's hut is most telling: "Es war mir eng und bedrängt zu Sinne, ich wünschte wieder dazubleiben, und doch war mir der Gedanke widerwärtig; es war ein seltsamer Kampf in meiner Seele, wie ein Streiten von *zwei widerspenstigen Geistern* in mir" (18; emphasis added). In contrast, the conscious mind proves to be tragically impotent in times of crisis. The most important actions in the tale are carried out without the conscious control of the characters. Bertha, for instance, departs from her parents' house propelled by blind need: "Als der Tag graute, stand ich auf und eröffnete, fast ohne daß ich es wußte, die Tür unsrer kleinen Hütte. Ich stand auf dem freien Felde, bald darauf war ich in einem Walde" (11). In a similar fashion, Eckbert loses command of his actions when he murders Walther: "Plötzlich sah er sich etwas in der Ferne bewegen, es war Walther, der Moos von den Bäumen sammelte; ohne zu wissen, was er tat, legte er an, Walther sah sich um, und drohte mit einer stummen Gebärde, aber indem flog der Bolzen ab, und Walther stürzte nieder" (23).

Not only is the conscious mind unable to superintend the powerful impulses emanating from the subliminal self, but to a certain extent it seems actually to be directed by the subconscious. In contrast to the wonderful interplay of order and disorder that characterized the old woman's hut, Eckbert's castle seems to be a model of rational control: "Nur selten wurde Eckbert von Gästen besucht, und wenn es auch geschah, so wurde ihretwegen fast nichts in dem gewöhnlichen Gange des Lebens geändert, die Mäßigkeit wohnte dort, und die Sparsamkeit selbst schien alles anzuordnen" (9). The stable and rather Spartan regime at Eckbert's castle serves to put the lid on emotions that, once released, could engulf the loveless couple in guilt and despair; it fortifies Eckbert and Bertha in their independence and isolation. The conscious mind with its loyalty to order and control thus operates—unwittingly, of course—in the service of a corrupt subconscious. Bertha herself points out the connection between conscious awareness and guilt midway through her story: "Ich war jetzt vierzehn Jahr alt, und es ist ein Unglück für den Menschen, daß er seinen Verstand nur darum bekömmt, um die Unschuld seiner Seele zu verlieren" (17). Those critics who have been quick to blame the "demonic forces" of nature and/or the old woman for Eckbert's and Bertha's downfall overlook the very real presence of demonic impulses *within* Eckbert and Bertha, impulses that effectively sabotage every attempt to breach the walls of loneliness and mistrust.[11]

What follows in the tale proper (as opposed to Bertha's narrative) is a systematic destruction of the sanctuary of repressed guilt that Eckbert and Bertha have established. The agents of destruction are Walther, Hugo, and the old woman herself, all representatives of the world of nature, which in turn embodies an absolute and pitiless moral law.[12] If in Novalis's tales Nature was willing and eager to proceed hand in hand with Mind toward mutual perfection, Tieck presents what might be termed Old Testament pantheism: the supernatural force that manifests itself in this nature (and through the old woman) has the judgmental authority to reward the childlike and selfless and to deal out a terrible punishment to the wicked. Hyazinth's initial withdrawal from nature marks the beginning of his journey toward reconciliation on a higher and total level. In "Eckbert," the crime of withdrawal provokes a relentless persecution from the external world.

In spatial terms, the primary focus of attack is, predictably enough, the discrepancy between inside and outside which characterizes Eckbert's castle. The strategy which the external world adopts to puncture Eckbert's and Bertha's insular existence displays the intricacy of a carefully planned field campaign in psychological warfare. There are at least four distinct maneuvers. First, the state of isolation must be made more and more uncomfortable, thereby (secondly) forcing Eckbert and Bertha into a confession. Thirdly, if either one of them is so hapless as to annul the effect of the confession by reverting to suspicion and mistrust, then their suspicions are to be mercilessly confirmed. Finally, if sanity has operated in the service of isolation, it must be destroyed.

The first step is at work on the night of Walther's visit to the castle. As we have noted, the outside world on this particular evening seems more than usually agitated and menacing. Bertha's confession, which she relates at Eckbert's behest, would appear to be a response to the threatening countenance of the external world, an attempt to fortify themselves by drawing Walther into the circle: "Es gibt Stunden, in denen es den Menschen ängstigt, wenn er vor seinem Freunde ein Geheimnis haben soll, was er bis dahin oft mit vieler Sorgfalt verborgen hat, die Seele fühlt dann einen unwiderstehlichen Trieb, sich ganz mitzuteilen, dem Freunde auch das Innerste aufzuschließen, damit er um so mehr unser Freund werde" (9). In spite of the rather conspiratorial atmosphere in which it is presented, Bertha's story has the earmarks of a true confession. It represents a movement outward, an attempt at communication and responsibility, an act of humility and contrition. By the time Bertha has finished her tale, however, Eckbert's negative, secretive side has begun to reassert itself, and he hurriedly throws in a defensive lie that severely compromises any redemptive effect the confession may have had: "Unsere Verbindung hat uns bis jetzt noch keinen Augenblick gereut" (21). It is significant that Walther's mention of the dog's name—his seemingly offhand but devastating form of retribution—*follows* Eckbert's initial act of bad faith. The comment that Bertha makes after Eckbert's remark (and before Walther's parting shot) is also of interest: "Aber über unser Schwatzen ist es schon tief in die Nacht geworden" (21). It seems more than a little incongruous that she should use the word *Schwatzen* to describe a lengthy confession of betrayal and murder. Through her choice of words she makes light of something that is extremely serious, thereby departing from her former attitude of remorse and penitence.

After the other two have retired for the night, Eckbert paces back and forth, animated by a deepening sense of mistrust toward Walther: "Ist der Mensch nicht ein Tor? . . . Ich bin erst die Veranlassung, daß meine Frau ihre Geschichte erzählt, und jetzt gereut mich diese Vertraulichkeit!—Wird er sie nicht mißbrauchen? Wird er sie nicht andern mitteilen? Wird er nicht vielleicht, denn das ist die Natur des Menschen, eine unselige Habsucht nach unsern Edelgesteinen empfinden, und deswegen Plane anlegen und sich verstellen?" (21). The positive impulse toward confession is followed, then, by the negative impulse toward suspicion, withdrawal, and greed. The effect of this night in the castle is to liberate both sides of Eckbert's psyche and to bring the internal ambivalence to a head. Significantly, as the emotional forces within him are unleashed, Eckbert becomes spatially mobile. From the time Bertha's confession has concluded to the end of the tale, he is constantly in motion: "Auch Walther legte sich schlafen, nur Eckbert ging noch unruhig im Saale auf und ab (21). . . . In einem abgelegenen Gemache ging er in unbeschreiblicher Unruhe auf und ab (22). . . . Wie ein unruhiger Geist eilte er jetzt von Gemach zu Gemach, kein Gedanke hielt ihm stand, er verfiel von entsetzlichen Vorstellungen auf noch entsetzlichere (24–25)." Eckbert's desperate pacing back and forth is a reflection of the increasing lack of comfort which the internal space of his castle affords him. Soon, he who otherwise was "only rarely seen outside the walls of his castle" (9), is driven out into the external world. The last pages of the tale are characterized, in spatial terms, by Eckbert's increasingly hysterical oscillation between outside and inside space, between interaction and retreat (neither of which provides any enduring solace or satisfaction), as the two conflicting aspects of his subconscious are more and more intensely mobilized. The dynamics of this process are worth examining in some detail. After Bertha reveals that Walther's inexplicable knowledge of the dog's name is responsible for her illness, Eckbert retreats to a remote room in the recesses of the castle. Finding no peace there, he bursts out of the castle full of murderous intent of which, as we have seen, he is barely conscious. He finds Walther and kills him, far out in the hostile external space of the forest: "Es war ein rauher stürmischer Wintertag. . . . Er hatte einen großen Weg zu machen, denn er war weit hinein in die Wälder verirrt" (23). Then he flees—or, more precisely, is mindlessly propelled—back to the castle: "[Es] trieb ihn ein Schauder nach seiner Burg zurück" (23). Soon the loneliness of his existence becomes unbearable, and he emerges again from the castle in search of companionship. In a rather grim parallel to Fabel's movements in the Klingsohr tale, each successive excursion into the external world takes Eckbert further away from the seemingly protective shelter of his castle. He begins to take part in social functions in the nearby city and meets a young knight named Hugo, who makes a special point of befriending Eckbert. This latest experiment in human communication culminates again in a confession, as Eckbert reveals his dreadful secret to Hugo while the two are "out on a lonely ride" (external space). Once more, however, the confession backfires. Back in a hall in the city (an internal space), Eckbert's negative side reasserts itself, and he begins to mistrust Hugo. To his horror, he sees his suspicions affirmed, as Hugo assumes Walther's features. Half mad with fear, he races out into the night and returns to his castle.

The former citadel of moderation and rational control is by this time no longer capable of providing even the slightest comfort for his deranged mind. Isolation is unbearable, communication impossible; the two opposing directions of Eckbert's tormented psyche have *both* been defeated, and by each other. Under the illusion that he will be able to "order his thoughts again," he sets out in blind flight. Having rejected his castle once and for all, however, he delivers himself into the clutches of the external world and is drawn, with terrible consistency, directly toward the opposite spatial pole, the old woman's valley, the site of the lost paradise.[13] When Eckbert hears the bird and the dog, the last underpinnings of his sanity give way. He is, however, granted one last moment of lucidity. The old woman appears and delivers with brutal directness the insight that Eckbert has avoided all of his married life: that Bertha is his own half-sister. Having provided Eckbert with three test situations (Walther, Hugo, the peasant), three opportunities for interaction, all of which he has failed, the old woman herself must now provide him with the final and annihilating confession which he would not or could not bring himself to make. There is a cruel irony in the fact that his one interaction of pure communication—the only such interaction that Eckbert has ever known—must inevitably destroy him. As his last mental defences fall, the internal void which he has sheltered and never admitted becomes his only reality. Unable to perceive space at all, he hears only crisscrossing voices and sounds: "Eckbert lag wahnsinnig und verscheidend auf dem Boden; dumpf und verworren hörte er die Alte sprechen, den Hund bellen, und den Vogel sein Lied wiederholen" (26).[14]

The spatial indefiniteness that Eckbert experiences at his death is a far cry from the wondrous synthesis of space and spacelessness at the conclusions of Novalis's tales. There is no fusion of former polarities here, no participation of the entire community or cosmos. Eckbert's fate is agonizingly private, the culmination of a life characterized by withdrawal and the repeated failure to establish true contact with other human beings. Bertha's childhood existence in the old woman's valley, with its coordination of inside and outside space, order and disorder, is as close as Tieck ever came to a depiction of utopia. The whole movement of the tale is *away* from this state of synthesis. Initially, internal and external space are severed in the situation at Eckbert's castle. Then, gradually, external space comes to predominate exclusively. In the final scenes, Eckbert is utterly exposed to the open landscape. Although he has apparently returned to the old woman's valley, there is, appropriately, no further mention of the cozy internal space of her hut.

In comparing Tieck's employment of space with that of Novalis, it is useful to examine Bertha's journey to the old woman's valley. Like Hyazinth, Bertha runs away from her home village as fast as her legs will take her. While Hyazinth was obsessed with the desire to find the "Mother of All Things," however, Bertha's only thought is escape, headlong flight from the intolerable situation at her parents' house. Despite their differing motivations, the two figures traverse landscapes that are all but identical. As was the case with Hyazinth, Bertha's journey takes her through forests and mountains, which become increasingly wild and desolate. One morning she wakes up to find herself in a landscape that, like Hyazinth's deserts, appears to be a monstrous void: "Als ich aber oben stand, war alles, so weit nur mein Auge reichte, ebenso, wie um mich her, alles war mit einem neblichten Dufte überzogen, der Tag war grau und trübe, und keinen Baum, keine Wiese, selbst kein Gebüsch konnte mein Auge erspähn, einzelne Sträucher ausgenommen, die einsam und betrübt in engen Felsenritzen emporgeschossen waren" (12–13).

For both characters, the experience of an utterly barren landscape represents a critical turning point in their development. As we observed in Chapter 1, the spatial indefiniteness of the desert reflected a gradual settling of Hyazinth's aggressive drive, a clearing of all fragmentary scraps of knowledge from his mind, and the beginning of his facility to experience nature in its totality. Bertha's response to the barren landscape around her is rather more specific: "Es ist unbeschreiblich, welche Sehnsucht ich empfand, nur eines Menschen ansichtig zu werden, wäre es auch, daß ich mich vor ihm hätte fürchten müssen" (13). Having tasted the anguish of absolute isolation, Bertha is prepared to establish human contact again, no matter what the consequences. As if to reward her for her inner conversion, the natural world gradually becomes much more hospitable than she has ever known it to be: "Gegen Abend schien die Gegend umher etwas freundlicher zu werden, meine Gedanken, meine Wünsche lebten wieder auf, die Lust zum Leben erwachte in allen meinen Adern. . . .

Ich sah Wälder und Wiesen mit fernen angenehmen Bergen wieder vor mir liegen. Mir war, als wenn ich aus der Hölle in ein Paradies getreten wäre" (13). The mountains, once a source of terror, are now suddenly pleasant.[15] Stopping by a brook, she scoops up a drink—like Hyazinth's drink from the spring, the action suggests a sacrament with nature—and in that very moment hears the approach of the old woman. After a supper of bread and wine (a second sacrament), the old woman leads Bertha further away from the wilderness, and as the two emerge from the forest, a magnificent panorama opens before them in the sunset: "Ich werde den Anblick und die Empfindung dieses Abends nie vergessen. In das sanfteste Rot und Gold war alles verschmolzen, die Bäume standen mit ihren Wipfeln in der Abendröte, und über den Feldern lag der entzückende Schein, die Wälder und die Blätter der Bäume standen still, der reine Himmel sah aus wie ein aufgeschlossenes Paradies, und das Rieseln der Quellen und von Zeit zu Zeit das Flüstern der Bäume tönte durch die heitre Stille wie in wehmütiger Freude." (14).

In the corresponding phases of Hyazinth's journey, the landscape is described in general as becoming fuller, brighter, more substantial, while a discrete number of specific details are reintroduced. Significantly enough, Tieck's landscape also appears as a marvelous mixture of definite and indefinite space. One's first impression is not of an articulated landscape at all, but of a wash of color ("In das sanfteste Rot und Gold war alles verschmolzen"), followed then by a few details ("die Bäume mit ihren Wipfeln," "die Felder") in an indefinite setting of light ("die Abendröte," "der entzückende Schein"). One sees the vast open space of the sky and notes at the same time such an intimate detail as the leaves of the trees. The fusion of determined and nondetermined space is reinforced by similar muted combinations of sound and silence, motion and rest, and various moods (as in the oxymoron "wehmütige Freude"). In every respect, the panorama that Bertha views here is a herald of the life which she is about to lead at the old woman's hut; she too, at her own level and in her own sphere, is to integrate herself into this landscape. It is most significant, in light of the central ethical conflict of the tale, that her response to this natural spectacle is one of *selfless* awe and total immersion: "Ich vergaß mich und meine Führerin, mein Geist und meine Augen schwärmten nur zwischen den goldnen Wolken" (14).

There is, however, an important distinction in the way Novalis and Tieck use space in these passages. In "Hyazinth und Rosenblüte," the external landscape consistently corresponded to the internal situation in Hyazinth's mind; operating in unison, mind and nature developed together toward perfection. In the description of Bertha's journey, on the other hand, the natural world seems to be all but autonomous. Rather than accompanying Bertha's internal development, it directs it. The whole sequence of landscapes during her journey serves to prepare her for entrance into the old woman's valley. Bertha is transformed from an awkward, dreamstruck child to a person who is willing—and able—to take part in a community. The natural world has a decidedly pedagogical function, educating Bertha to the horrors of loneliness and rewarding her after she has learned her lesson. Unlike "Hyazinth und Rosenblüte," where nature and mind were peers, mutually dependent on each other, nature here is of a higher order than mind. As we noted earlier, the natural world in "Der blonde Eckbert" functions as the executor of an absolute moral law, whose prime commandment is an extension of Kant's categorical imperative to all of nature as well as humanity: treat each living creature not as a means, but as an end in himself. It is precisely this commandment which Eckbert and Bertha repeatedly break, in their greedy and selfish dealings with the old woman, the bird, and themselves.[16] Neither the conscious nor the unconscious mind is able to mount any kind of effective defense against the primal force that resides in nature. It is through the generosity of the natural world and the responsiveness of her still innocent soul that Bertha is permitted to participate in the harmonious community at the old woman's valley. Eckbert's castle, on the other hand, is an affront to the moral law of nature, and both Eckbert and Bertha are ultimately driven from its questionable shelter.

From the perspective of the old woman, and from the traditional standpoint of Western ethics, Eckbert and Bertha are clearly culpable, and the retribution visited on them is appropriate and just. But this ethical system presupposes, as a fundamental and necessary condition, the freedom to choose between good and evil. Eckbert and Bertha do not enjoy such freedom. Throughout the tale they are manipulated by subconscious impulses that make a mockery of free will and unclouded moral choice. On this point the ethical interpretation of "Der blonde Eckbert" founders. While an absolute and unconditional moral viewpoint will not hesitate to find Eckbert and Bertha guilty as charged, a psychologically informed reading must consider them more sympathetically and with a certain measure of forbearance—though it can scarcely exonerate them altogether. We may justifiably deplore Eckbert's and Bertha's behavior, and we may even take some satisfaction from Eckbert's final collapse, since his horror and despair are only comprehensible as the reaction of a man who has the stature to regard himself to the end as accountable for his actions.[17] But we cannot applaud the old woman's harsh tactics in bringing Eckbert and Bertha to justice, much less her insistence on exacting the death penalty for human frailty and involuntary evil.

The triumph of external forces over a weak and divided mind in "Der blonde Eckbert" is indicative of Tieck's rather eccentric position in Early Romanticism. Like his close friend Wilhelm Heinrich Wackenroder, Tieck never felt very comfortable with Fichte's and Schelling's conceptions of the mind as an endlessly creative force capable of transcending itself and transforming nature. It may well be said that Tieck experienced the crisis of Romantic subjectivity before he ever joined forces with the Schlegels, Schelling, and Novalis. His philosophical affinity with the leading spirits of the movement was at best a tenuous one.[18] Even the so-called Romantic irony of his *Der gestiefelte Kater* is more a matter of clever mischievousness than a serious attempt to juxtapose the limited and incomplete world of empirical experience with the higher world of abstract thought.[19] While Tieck was willing to acknowledge the attractiveness of Fichtean idealism, he was inclined to regard nature as a more valid source of authority than the mind. Ludwig Wandel, the hero of Tieck's short story, "Die Freunde" (1797), experiences a series of dreams which are encapsuled in each other in a manner reminiscent of Fichte's process of reflection. Unlike Hyazinth, however, who travels through the endless chambers of his dream into the "realm of the holiest," Ludwig becomes successively alienated from the external world of love and friendship and enticed into a fantasy world of self-gratification. The caveat that Tieck expresses here is not merely a compromise of his Romantic impulses for the sake of his conservative reading audience.[20] Rather it stems from his conviction, gained from personal experience, that unbridled subjectivity leads to a state of lovelessness and self-indulgence.

In "Der blonde Eckbert," however, Tieck entertains at least the *possibility* that the mind can rise above itself to create a new utopia. Here we come to the most crucial distinction between Bertha's development and Hyazinth's. Although it is possible to interpret Bertha's life in the valley of birches as a "second paradise," as Janis Gellinek has done,[21] this paradise must not be equated with Novalis's second Golden Age. To be sure, the synthesis of space and spacelessness as well as unity and diversity corresponds in many respects to the conclusions of Novalis's tales. What is missing in Tieck, however, is the participation of mind in this state of perfection. *Waldeinsamkeit* is, in effect, a second Golden Age scaled down to the dimensions of a child's mind. Nevertheless, it is to serve as a model for the adults Bertha and Eckbert. The naive synthesis of internal and external space that is presented to Bertha as a reward for her innocence and unselfishness must be reachieved on a higher level through an active process of moral will, as an accomplishment of the mature mind. Thus the qualities of openness, integration, and self-fulfillment on one's own level, which Bertha experiences in the old woman's valley, are to be transformed into the ethical categories of responsibility, generosity, repentance, and self-knowledge.[22] The natural world cannot bestow these latter qualities on Eckbert and Bertha. The most it can do is to force them into a position where they must choose for themselves and to punish them if they make the wrong decision. Again, however, we must note that the old woman's tactics, although defensible from an absolute ethical standpoint, are predicated on the erroneous assumption of free moral will in Eckbert and Bertha.

To a certain extent, Eckbert and Bertha are in the same position as Hyazinth in the second phase of Novalis's tale. Alienated from nature and from each other, they lack the ability to free themselves from a perpetual state of inadequacy. Unlike Hyazinth, however, they are incapable of recognizing and acting on the advice of the old woman in the wood, and it is questionable whether their lives could be salvaged even if they *were* to undertake the task of regeneration through confession, repentance, and self-scrutiny. The second Golden Age, in which an original harmony is recreated on a higher level through the activity of the mind, is in Tieck's tale only a remote possibility. While Novalis outlines the methods by which the new perfection is to be achieved, Tieck explores the depths of human fallibility and weakness that make this perfection unattainable.

"Der Runenberg"

The years of close association with the other Romantics restored some of Tieck's confidence in the creative power of subjectivity. In "Der Runenberg," which he wrote overnight in 1802, he was able to juxtapose an ecstatic private vision of truth with the value system of conventional social mores and to present the two options as more or less equally justified. Once again space falls into a polar arrangement, but the tension is neither dialectical (as in Novalis's tales) nor the product of a confrontation between insufficiency and a preliminary model of perfection (as in "Der blonde Eckbert"). Here the natural world itself is split into a *dualistic* configuration that supports both of the above options and at the same time presents them as irresolvably opposed. The spatial arenas of the mountains and the plains confront each other with a hostility that precludes any possibility of synthesis. Since the external organization of these two worlds bears most of the burden of

Split Terrain 53

suggesting what sort of values they represent and the means by which they exert their influence over the minds of men, it is necessary to examine the physical appearance of each of them in some detail.

The first extensive description of the plant realm is supplied near the beginning of the tale. The moody young hunter, Christian, has unexpectedly met a stranger in the forest. As the two walk together in the gathering darkness, Christian talks at length of his homeland on the plains:

[Meine Eltern und ich] wohnten weit von hier in einer Ebene, in der man rund umher keinen Berg, kaum eine Anhöhe erblickte, wenige Bäume schmückten den grünen Plan, aber Wiesen, fruchtbare Kornfelder und Gärten zogen sich hin, so weit das Auge reichen konnte, ein großer Fluß glänzte wie ein mächtiger Geist an den Wiesen und Feldern vorbei. . . . Die Ebene, das Schloß, der kleine beschränkte Garten meines Vaters mit den geordneten Blumenbeeten, die enge Wohnung, der weite Himmel, der sich ringsum so traurig ausdehnte, und keine Höhe, keinen erhabenen Berg umarmte, alles ward mir noch betrübter und verhaßter. (63–64)

Later, after his strange adventure on Rune Mountain, Christian descends dazedly to the plains on the other side of the mountains. There he is greeted by a landscape that, though he finds it quite different from his homeland (69), bears more than a passing resemblance to the landscape which he described to the stranger: "Die engen Gärten, die kleinen Hütten mit ihren rauchenden Schornsteinen, die gerade abgeteilten Kornfelder erinnerten [Christian] an die Bedürftigkeit des armen Menschengeschlechts. . . . Reizend und anlockend dünkte ihm die Ebene mit dem kleinen Fluß, der sich in mannigfaltigen Krümmungen um Wiesen und Gärten schmiegte" (69).

The all but identical descriptions of the two locales suggest a first major point about the plant realm. Wherever it appears, it assumes precisely the same form, as if in adherence to some natural mandate.[23] Only rarely does a tree or a hill mar the consistent flatness of this landscape; fields, meadows and river all conform to the law of horizontality. Moreover, the scenery is essentially static. Even the rivers seem scarcely to move; the verbs that refer to them suggest motion only indirectly, or not at all: "ein großer Fluß glänzte . . . an den Wiesen und Feldern vorbei" (63–64); "mit dem kleinen Fluß, der sich . . . um Wiesen und Gärten schmiegte" (69). Another aspect of this landscape is the principle of community: no individual meadow or field, garden or hut catches the eye, but rather a plurality of ordered, defined spatial units. Only the church, as the ideological center of the community, stands out among the various buildings. And almost all of the internal spaces—gardens, huts, and church alike—are described as being small or narrow. Within these diminutive enclosures one leads a pleasantly circumscribed existence, content with modest aspirations and a minimum of excitement. The whole spatial organization of the world of the plains reflects a commitment to order, subordination, individual limitation, community, and law.

Such principles can, and indeed must, make a claim to universal validity. By connecting the world of the plains with Christianity, Tieck seemingly grants this tidy social system the sanction of divine law.[24] At the same time, however, he establishes in the mountains a counterforce with its own supernatural backing, its own offer of salvation. The values which manifest themselves in the landscape of the mountains are not merely in partial conflict to the values of the plains, but diametrically opposed in every respect.

The panorama which Christian and the stranger view as they emerge from the forest provides a fairly clear illustration of the differences between the two realms: "In unkenntlichen Formen und vielen gesonderten Massen, die der bleiche Schimmer wieder rätselhaft vereinigte, lag das gespaltene Gebürge vor ihnen, im Hintergrunde ein steiler Berg, auf welchem uralte verwitterte Ruinen schauerlich im weißen Lichte sich zeigten" (65). There is little that is tangible or concrete in this view. Except for the sketchy description of the mountain with its ruins, all specific detail is missing. What Tieck is doing here is quite characteristic of Romantic landscape description in general: the vaster the panorama, the greater the tendency toward vagueness. Any view that extends more than a few miles is certain to be obscured by mist, haze, or twilight, or blurred into indefiniteness by unusual lighting effects, such as moonlight or—one thinks of Bertha's experience—the glow of sunset. By virtue of the obscuring medium, all irrelevant or accidental detail is erased from the landscape. The indistinct masses and shadowy half-forms that loom up in the distance give intimations of a purer, more abstract nature.[25] The world of the plains has no need of such obscurity; its substance is on the surface, so to speak. The landscape of the mountains, on the other hand, suggests the existence of a world beyond appearances, a secret realm that is accessible only to the visionary who is prepared to leave the security and comfort of human fellowship behind. Consequently, Christian's experience of the ultimate mystery of the mountain world cannot succeed in one simple step, but involves several successive stages of penetration. The first stage is represented by the turbulent landscape that greets him when he first arrives in the mountains: "Nachmittags befand ich mich schon unter den vielgeliebten Bergen, und wie ein Trunkener ging ich. . . . Bald verlor ich die Ebene hinter mir aus dem Gesichte, die Waldströme rauschten mir entgegen, Buchen und Eichen brausten mit bewegtem Laube von steilen

Abgründen herunter. . . . blaue Berge standen groß und ehrwürdig im Hintergrunde" (65). Here the scenery is suddenly full of motion and sound. Even the vegetation appears to hurtle itself down the slopes. In this highly energized landscape, the various forms of nature become self-assertive and independent, each fully engaged in its own activity. If the horizontality of the plains suggested submissiveness and subordination, the jagged verticals and diagonals of the mountains reflect a world of emphatic and vigorous self-expression. At the same time, the neatly arranged vista of boundaries and enclosed spaces in Christian's homeland yields to a disorganized wilderness, whose spatial confusion and openness act as an incitement to let oneself go, to loosen one's inhibitions, to break free of all constrictions.

If this first type of landscape produces an intoxicating sense of freedom and self-assertiveness, the second type of landscape, represented by the vista of moonlit mountains, provides a direction for the newly released psychic energies, as well as a first, tentative vision of totality. The events immediately preceding the appearance of this panorama are significant. Sitting alone and disgruntled in the forest, Christian has unthinkingly torn a root from the ground. As if in response to his action, a distant, muffled whimpering echoes from beneath the earth. Christian is about to flee, when he suddenly sees a stranger behind him, who offers to accompany him a stretch of the way. Although none of Christian's experiences in the mountains is without a certain ambiguity—what appears to be unequivocally true in the stone world is interpreted as madness or hallucination in the plains—the incident with the root may be taken to represent his permanent and irreversible break with the plant world. In contrast to his former mood of indecision, Christian's attitude toward the plains is now uniformly negative. As he walks with the stranger through the forest, he emphasizes how repugnant his homeland was to him and repeatedly professes his allegiance to the mountains. It is then, after this verbal acknowledgment of his true loyalty, that the nocturnal spectacle suddenly opens up before him: "Der fremde Mann hatte aufmerksam zugehört, indem beide durch einen dunkeln Gang des Waldes gewandert waren. Jetzt traten sie ins Freie, und das Licht des Mondes, der oben mit seinen Hörnern über der Bergspitze stand, begrüßte sie freundlich: in unkenntlichen Formen . . . lag das gespaltene Gebürge vor ihnen" (65).

The shift from one landscape to another appears to result from the creation of a new and stronger emotional bond between Christian and the mountain world. The aimless energy produced by the first landscape is now channeled into purposeful activity. Confronted at last by a visible goal, Christian sets out immediately for the eerie ruins on Rune Mountain: "Er verdoppelte nur seine Schritte nach dem Runenberg zu. . . . Seine Schritte waren wie beflügelt, sein Herz klopfte, er fühlte eine so große Freudigkeit in seinem Innern, daß sie zu einer Angst emporwuchs" (66). As he ascends the mountain, the last traces of the horizontal plant world disappear behind him, until he finds himself clinging to a sheer vertical wall devoid of vegetation, gazing through a window into the ancient castle. What he sees there is a living embodiment of the landscape that he had seen in the distance a few hours before. The grandeur of the mountains, their massive beauty and forbidding solemnity are distilled into the figure of the woman in the castle. Moreover, like the landscape that greeted Christian when he first arrived in the mountains, she is constantly in motion, striding back and forth in her majestic hall.[26] After singing a lament to the "Ancients"—the once all-powerful spirits of the stone realm, now withdrawn into the depths—she begins to undress, gradually revealing her magnificent body to Christian. Fully clothed, she had seemed to embody the external landscape of the mountains. Now, however, her appearance suggests the internal treasures of the stone realm. Christian stares spellbound at her marblelike body with its "gleaming forms": "Er wagte kaum zu atmen, als sie nach und nach alle Hüllen löste; nackt schritt sie endlich im Saale auf und nieder, und ihre schweren schwebenden Locken bildeten um sie her ein dunkel wogendes Meer, aus dem wie Marmor die glänzenden Formen des reinen Leibes abwechselnd hervorstrahlten" (68). Her act of disrobing represents a further stage of Christian's initiation into the mysteries of the mountains, but it is not the last. After pacing up and down for "a considerable time," she takes a tablet from a golden chest and stands gazing at the strange pattern formed by jewels inlaid in the tablet: "Die Tafel schien eine wunderliche unverständliche Figur mit ihren unterschiedlichen Farben und Linien zu bilden; zuweilen war, nachdem der Schimmer ihm entgegenspielte, der Jüngling schmerzhaft geblendet, dann wieder besänftigten grüne und blau spielende Scheine sein Auge" (68). The interplay of form and formlessness, the "incomprehensible figure," the shimmering lights on the tablet recall again the image of the moonlit mountains. This connection, which may at first seem rather tenuous, is then established explicitly through metaphor. As Christian gazes at the tablet, a mountain landscape of emotions wells up within him: "Er sah eine Welt von Schmerz und Hoffnung in sich aufgehen, mächtige Wunderfelsen von Vertrauen und trotzender Zuversicht, große Wasserströme, wie voll Wehmut fließend" (68). As he grasps the tablet, the magic figure itself passes into his mind; both the woman and the room suddenly disappear, and Christian stumbles down the mountain in a daze.

It is not difficult to understand the effect of this scene on Christian's later life. In spite of his resolve to reunite himself with the community of the plains, he finds himself increasingly drawn back to the mountains as the mysterious figure implanted in his mind gradually reasserts itself and overpowers his superficial commitment to the plains. On the other hand, the specific content, or substance, of Christian's experience on Rune Mountain is by no means self-evident. We have seen that the woman and the tablet represent successive condensations of the mountain landscape to increasingly more compact and essential forms. In addition, each of the figures represents a further movement into the internal space of the mountains. The tablet, for instance, lies in a chest in a room in the castle, removed threefold from the outside world.

On the basis of these observations, it seems safe to interpret the tablet, and not the woman, as containing the very essence of the mountain realm. The traditional interpretation of Christian's experience on Rune Mountain as a preeminently erotic adventure is not adequately supported by the text. While one can scarcely deny the sensual appeal of a naked woman striding back and forth, the attraction which the young and innocent Elisabeth exerts is in essence no less erotic, though her sensuality is, of course, of a rather less imposing sort than that of the *Waldweib*. In both cases, sexuality functions primarily as an indication of the kind of visceral response that the two worlds elicit. For this reason, it is difficult to differentiate the two realms on the basis of rationality as opposed to irrationality; certainly both of them demand an emotional response that is essentially irrational. Moreover, the woman herself does not represent the culmination of Christian's experience. Instead, she serves to prepare him for the much more intense, indeed overpowering, vision of the tablet. There is other evidence that the woman functions as an intermediary figure. First, her invocation of the ancients suggests that she is a priestess of the stone world, but not yet its purest essence. Secondly, she appears to be half woman, half stone, a fusion of the two opposing worlds, stone divinity become flesh. The parallel to Christ is made explicit in the few words that the woman speaks as she hands the tablet to Christian, which echo the words of Christ to his disciples at the Last Supper: "Nimm dieses zu meinem Angedenken!" (68).[27] Whether or not the woman—like Christ—is fully *equivalent* to the divinity of the mountains is, however, open to question. In her role as *Vermittler* she is capable of assuming several different forms (the two strangers, the ugly old woman) and moving freely between the village and the mountains. Again, if one interprets her as the innermost spirit of the stone world, it is disturbing that she should wander with such ease into the very heart of enemy territory.[28] Finally, we may note that the title of the tale is, after all, not "Der Venusberg," but "Der Runenberg." As crucial as the woman may be in furthering Christian's initiation into the stone world, the tablet with its runes not only equals her in importance, but actually supercedes her.

If the tablet with its twinkling stones is viewed as containing the final mystery of the mountain world, one is still faced with the problem of assigning some sort of content to this mystery. Here the text raises all but insurmountable barriers to interpretation. The signs on the tablet are incomprehensible: runes, one must assume, from a lost world. That neither Tieck nor his hero ever makes any attempt to decipher the writing into a human language can be taken as an indication that the words are untranslatable. Indeed, if one could decode them, they would in effect become community property, accessible to one and all. The whole sequence of events leading up to the first appearance of the tablet attests to the elaborate initiation rites which must precede an understanding of the mysterious script. The single most important event, and the one that sets all the others in motion, is Christian's destruction of the mandrake root, his unwitting but decisive renunciation of the plant world and its entire value system—including, of course, its language, which (like all languages) represents a codification of existing mores and values.

The essence of the mountain world is thus beyond comprehension from the viewpoint of the plains and ultimately from the viewpoint of the reader as well.[29] Nevertheless, it is possible to reach some conclusions about what this essence means for those who experience it. For instance, Christian's passive stance at the window while contemplating the tablet, together with the fact that the tablet appears to contain some sort of written information, indicates that what Christian receives there is *knowledge*, knowledge of a truth which no humanly known words can define or paraphrase. Moreover, this privileged knowledge can be received only at the price of eternal commitment to the stone realm. The mind that has been restructured to admit the secrets of the mountains can never again be permanently at home and at peace in the plains.

In the fixed and merciless polarity of the two opposing worlds no possibility of synthesis exists. Only at the very beginning of the tale does something like a medial position obtain. The young Christian sits alone on a fowling place high in the mountains, not yet finally committed to either realm. In a moment of exuberance he breaks into a hunting song, the first of three ideological statements set to music in the tale. The other two are the woman's hymn to the "Ancients" and the song that Christian's father sings in praise of the plant world. The landscape allusions in Christian's hunting song are noteworthy:

> Froh und lustig zwischen Steinen
> Geht der Jüngling auf die Jagd,
> Seine Beute muß erscheinen
> In den grünlebendgen Hainen,
> Sucht' er auch bis in die Nacht.
>
> . . . . .
>
> Seine Heimat sind die Klüfte,
> Alle Bäume grüßen ihn,
> Rauschen strenge Herbsteslüfte
> Find't er Hirsch und Reh, die Schlüfte
> Muß er jauchzend dann durchziehn. (62–63)

If the other two songs are notable for their one-sided advocacy of one world or the other, Christian's hunting song exalts elements of *both* realms. The hunter goes merrily among the rocks and rejoices as he passes through the chasms, but all the trees hail him and the woods in which he seeks his prey are alive and green. In a tale which revolves around the division of nature into plant and stone kingdoms, such details as these are surely anything but accidental. Moreover, as we noted above, the landscape which surrounds Christian here is not only diverse in its elements, but highly charged with activity and movement: the trees rustle, great clouds pass overhead, birds twitter, and the brook murmurs incomprehensible words. The mixed and highly animated character of Christian's environment corresponds to a pronounced emotional ambivalence within him, as he alternatively affirms and rejects both his homeland and his present situation.[30] Such a state of quivering excitement and indefinite longing, accompanied by sympathetic vibrations from the natural world, is highly characteristic of Early Romantic sensibility. Two decades later, E. T. A. Hoffmann was to satirize the inevitability of such situations in Romantic prose:

Es ist eine alte hergebrachte Sitte, daß der Held der Geschichte, ist er von heftiger Gemütsbewegung ergriffen, hinausläuft in den Wald oder wenigstens in das einsam gelegene Gebüsch. . . . Daß es ferner in einer romanhaften Historie keinem Gebüsch an rauschenden Blättern, seufzenden, lispelnden Abendlüften, murmelnden Quellen, geschwätzigen Bächen u.s.w. fehlen darf, so ist zu denken, daß Peregrinus [der Held von *Meister Floh*] das alles an seinem Zufluchtsorte fand.[31]

The image of the pensive youthful person alone in a turbulent landscape was so appealing to the younger generation of Romantics that it became a favorite subject for painters at the turn of the nineteenth century.[32] Nonetheless, the opening scene of "Der Runenberg" marks an important turning point in the development of Romanticism, for Christian is clearly neither delighted nor satisfied by the situation in which he finds himself. Indeed, he is very close to despair, as he admits to the stranger: "Jetzt sitze ich seit acht Tagen hier oben auf dem Vogelherde, im einsamsten Gebürge, und am Abend wurde mir heut so traurig zu Sinne, wie noch niemals in meinem Leben; ich kam mir so verloren, so ganz unglücklich vor" (65). The implication of this opening episode is that it is impossible to remain forever suspended in a state of emotional volatility and ferment, savoring the varied assortment of one's own sensations. Sooner or later one has to press toward some kind of consummation, some deeper and final commitment. Christian's dissatisfaction, frustration, and sense of entrapment in this scene herald the end of at least one aspect of Early Romanticism: its free-wheeling independence of mind and emotions and its ideological aversion to any binding allegiances. By 1802, the delight in such spiritual freedom had very nearly run its course, and Romantics were beginning to look around for other, more tangible goals for their idealism.

It is in this light that "Der Runenberg" as a whole may be placed in a much larger context. For the two spatial arenas of mountains and plains, whatever else they may mean, clearly anticipate the opposing directions of Early and Late Romanticism. The kind of experience which the mountains offer, for instance, represents a distillation of some of the most important aspects of the Early Romantic lifestyle. Here as there the emphasis is on the emancipation and flight of the individual soul—"flight" in its double meaning of both escape and air-bound ascent. The implicit elitism of the Jena circle also finds its counterpart in the mountains, where the vision of perfection is reserved for the very few who dare to leave the comfort of traditional values behind in their quest for the absolute. Moreover, the Early Romantic conception of reality is reflected in the mountain landscape itself, with its peculiar ambiguity, its multiplicity of meaning in every phenomenon—one thinks of the various masks and disguises of the *Waldweib*, the hints of her existence behind every tree, brook, and mountain.

The world of the plains, on the other hand, incorporates many of the values which the younger generation of Romantics was beginning to espouse. In the place of programmatic individualism and exuberant, even aggressive, subjectivity, a new and no less vigorous dedication to the ideals of community and state began to assert itself. With its foundation in conventional religion, its demand of individual subordination to society, its affirmation of the time-honored verities of home and hearth—in short, its allegiance to traditional objective authority—the little village on the plains sums up many of the most pressing requirements of the new generation.

Some qualifications are necessary here. Certainly it would be reckless to argue a straightforward identification of Tieck's mountain realm with Early Romanticism and the plains with Late Romanticism. In speaking of the two forms of Romantic thought, we are dealing not with existential absolutes, as is the case in Tieck's tale, but with historical directions. There are, in fact, numerous elements of continuity between the two movements. The notion of an idealized religious community, for instance, had been formulated with great eloquence in Novalis's *Die Christenheit oder Europa*, a work which is still well within the framework of Early Romanticism, despite the frosty reception that the Schlegels accorded it. The point is that such a community, and other forms of idealized objective reality, were generally considered accessible only through dizzying heights of subjectivity.[33] The later generation was far more content to accept received forms of authority, rather than transforming them through the mind or searching for new and more spectacular types of authority in the labyrinths of irrationality. "Der Runenberg" is a transitional and thoroughly ambivalent work in that it appears to assign absolute validity to *both* directions, but in such a way that neither of the two realms can be unambiguously identified as the true divine.[34]

For all this, it must be conceded that the implications of "Der Runenberg" are rather more intriguing than the tale itself. The existential conflict here is *only* suggested. It never becomes compelling, never draws the reader into the kind of intense and complicated experience that is characteristic of all substantial works of art. From one point of view, one may argue that the aesthetic weakness of "Der Runenberg" derives principally from the character—or rather lack of character—of its hero. This is not to suggest that great works of art must necessarily champion independence of mind and the nobility of free will. On the basis of such a criterion, one would be forced to condemn such works as *Oedipus Rex*, *Macbeth*, and *Woyzeck*. But if the human soul is to be reduced to a mere mechanism in the hands of fate, then one may legitimately demand that the forces that shape and direct the soul be presented with some depth or subtlety. It is precisely in the depiction of the external forces that are brought to bear on the hero that "Der Runenberg" falls short of its intended goals. We are *told* that the two spatial zones are equivalent, or very nearly equivalent, in their opposing claims over Christian's soul, but we fail to *experience* this implied equivalence. The problem is at least partially one of unequal narrative weighting. Our immediate knowledge of the essence of the mountain realm is limited primarily to the short and highly enigmatic adventure on Rune Mountain, while the more accessible world of the plains receives page after page of leisurely, detailed description. The average intelligent reader, who would tend to identify himself with the familiar ethos of the village in any event, is simply not provided with enough convincing material about the mountain realm to appreciate the latter as an effective and believable counterweight to the plains. It is this unfortunate imbalance which has led most critics to assume, against Tieck's intention I believe, that the village world represents the only true source of salvation in the tale. Ultimately one suspects that Tieck himself was more inclined to cast his sympathies with the conventional forces of community than with the impulse toward mystic solitude. It is at best a shaky dualism which he presents in "Der Runenberg." By attempting to establish the mountains as a valid existential alternative to the village, Tieck does lip service to the spirit of Early Romanticism; but his feeling for the traditional forms of society and salvation emerges finally as a truer, deeper, and more enduring affinity.

III

Waiting for Fabel
Time in the *Märchen* of Novalis

"Hyazinth und Rosenblüte"

The Romantic experience of disjunct space as symbolic of larger, more abstract polarities was inevitably accompanied by a conscious preoccupation with time and temporality. The psychological impossibility of envisioning a universe eternally divided against itself necessarily forced the Romantics to evolve a construction of history that could accommodate their vision of perfection. To a certain extent, Enlightenment thought provided a workable and convenient model, and it is not difficult to see in Fichte's philosophy a continuation of the fundamental assumption of eighteenth-century thinking: that mankind, under the guidance and inspiration of Reason, is progressing more or less linearly toward a state of perfection.[1] Fichte, of course, subjected the notion of "reason" to considerable modification, and he was concerned more with the perfectability of the individual than with that of mankind in general. His followers, notably Schelling and Novalis, directed their attention backwards as well as forwards in time, attempting to establish the whence as well as the whither of history. By grafting substantial elements of Rousseauian thought onto the Enlightenment scheme, they conceived a state of perfection at both the beginning and the end of time. The resultant triadic rhythm (harmony–disharmony–regained harmony) is one of the most familiar tenants of Early Romantic thought.[2] In addition, Herder's influential ideas on historical relativity had refined the notion of a linear development of history to encompass the rise and fall of individual cultures, each with its own distinctive and self-justifying characteristics. Implicit in such works as *Von deutscher Art und Kunst* (1773) was a bitter denunciation of eighteenth-century culture as derivative and imitative, as lacking precisely the sort of natural center of gravity that Herder found exemplified in ancient Greece and Elizabethan England.

The sense of living in an imperfect and deficient era informed Romantic thinking from the very beginning. The urgency of Novalis's dreams of a new Golden Age and the power of Tieck's fantasy of punishment (in "Eckbert") derive to a large extent from a feeling of profound personal crisis that both writers found to be symptomatic of their age in general. Yet this universal sense of dismay with the present generated two rather different responses. Novalis and the Schlegels turned to the past as a source of hope and consolation; through the contemplation of a utopian past they sought the fortitude and inspiration to create a utopian future. In Wackenroder and Tieck, on the other hand, such chiliastic notions of the future never seem to have found much resonance, as we have seen. For them the fervent longing for the past became all but an end in itself. Wackenroder's portrait of Joseph Berglinger depicts the contemporary artist as tormented and foredoomed, and Tieck's characters are either barred forever from a lost paradise or attain to a questionable new one at a terrible sacrifice ("Der getreue Eckart und der Tannenhäuser," "Der Runenberg").

It is characteristic of Novalis's orientation toward the future that the first Golden Age receives rather short shrift in his *Märchen*. Only in "Hyazinth und Rosenblüte" is there an extended description of this blissful first innocence. "Atlantis" begins with the split between science and poetry as a *fait accompli*, and "Eros und Fabel" contains only scattered references to the "old times." The second Golden Age is accorded scarcely more narrative time than the first, as we shall see. In each of Novalis's tales, the bulk of the narrative is comprised of a description of the long journey toward reintegration and the dawn of the new age. This emphatic concern with the intermediate period and with the strategies one must undertake to surmount it suggests a tentative classification of Novalis's tales as *Erziehungsmärchen*, instructional parables on the ways and means of reconsolidating a broken universe. More importantly, however, the relegation of both golden ages to a few short sentences leads one to suspect that their primary role in the tales, and in Novalis's thought in general, is to serve as philosophical foils to set off the inadequacy and anguish of the intermediate period.

Not surprisingly, then, "Hyazinth und Rosenblüte" opens at a point where discord has already become fairly conspicuous. Only after a lengthy description of Hyazinth's alienation from the other children and from nature does the narrative backtrack to the preceding stage of naive harmony. As we established in Chapter 1, this first happy state is not without danger signals of its own. One indication is the spatial separation of the two lovers at their windows and their childish, though charming, resistance to a world of nature that never tires of chortling over their love: "Da sahen [die Kätzchen] die Beiden stehn, und lachten und kicherten oft so laut, daß sie es hörten und böse wurden. . . . So riefs von allen Seiten: 'Rosenblütchen ist mein

Schätzchen!' Nun ärgerte sich Hyazinth" (I, 92). The syntax of this passage is especially revealing as concerns the relationship that obtains between Hyazinth and nature: "Wenn nun Hyazinth die Nacht an seinem Fenster stand, ... da sahen [die Kätzchen] die Beiden stehn. ... [Die Stachelbeere] ließ nun das Sticheln nicht, wenn Hyazinth gegangen kam. ... Und wenn Hyazinth ausging, so riefs von allen Seiten: 'Rosenblütchen ist mein Schätzchen!' Nun ärgerte sich Hyazinth, und mußte doch auch wieder aus Herzensgrunde lachen, wenn das Eidechschen geschlüpft kam" (I, 92). The repeated temporal conjunction "wenn" indicates not only frequency of occurrence ("whenever"), but also the simultaneous occurrence of separate activities. In this manner Hyazinth is repeatedly depicted as somewhat isolated from the events around him. Moreover, this sense of isolation is amplified by the context. All three sets of actions conjoined by "wenn" betray a very slight undertone of hostility (Hyazinth's and Rosenblüte's momentary anger at the animals, the teasing prickle of the gooseberry). The tension here derives from the secretiveness of the two lovers as opposed to the machinations of the exuberant and affectionately gossipy plants and animals. Even this innocent idyll of young love reveals a certain fateful tendency toward privacy at the exclusion of the natural world; and the seemingly harmless gap which has opened here can be closed again only with the attainment of absolute knowledge at the end of Hyazinth's journey.

The arrival of the old man from foreign lands brings the initial state of affairs to an abrupt end. In contrast to the durative character of the preceding passage, a group of verbs of perfective aspect appears, denoting a temporal succession of unique events: "Es kam ein Mann aus fremden Landen gegangen. ... Er setzte sich vor das Haus, das Hyazinths Eltern gehörte. ... Nun war Hyazinth sehr neugierig, und setzte sich zu ihm und holte ihm Brot und Wein" (I, 93). For the first time in the tale, narrative time and narrated time begin to approach each other.[3] The significance of these events, however, is reflected not only in the sudden sharpening of narrative focus, but also in their subsequent effect on Hyazinth. Immediately after the departure of the strange old man, Hyazinth begins a new way of life: "Von der Zeit an hat er sich wenig aus [Rosenblüte] gemacht und ist immer für sich geblieben" (I, 93). The events surrounding the short visit of the old man result, then, in a new state of affairs; Hyazinth's isolation from the world around him suddenly becomes acute. It is this phase of his development that is described at the opening of the tale: "Er grämte sich unaufhörlich um nichts und wieder nichts, ging immer still für sich hin, ... und dann sprach er immer fort mit Tieren und Vögeln ... Er blieb aber immer mürrisch und ernsthaft" (I, 91). The emphatic repetition of "immer" and its variant "unaufhörlich" indicates a state of obsession, of dogged, unhappy determination that leads nowhere. Hyazinth's sudden blindness to the external world following the visit of the old man is anticipated in the lizard's song, where, curiously enough, it is *Rosenblüte* who becomes blind:

> 'Rosenblütchen, das gute Kind,
> Ist geworden auf einmal blind,
> Denkt, die Mutter sei Hyazinth,
> Fällt ihm um den Hals geschwind;
> Merkt sie aber das fremde Gesicht,
> Denkt nur an, da erschrickt sie nicht,
> Fährt, als merkte sie kein Wort,
> Immer nur mit Küssen fort.' (I, 92)

This little song represents, in fact, a veiled summary of the entire tale, with the roles of the two lovers reversed. Just as the blind Rosenblütchen hurries into her mother's arms, Hyazinth impetuously sets out to find the "Mother of All Things." In both cases, the mother unexpectedly turns out to be none other than the beloved. Despite its playfulness, the song thus makes a pedagogical and prophetic point which Hyazinth, in his benighted state, is unable to recognize.

After an unspecified period of time, the second phase is in turn terminated by another decisive event: the woman in the wood casts the old man's book into the fire and advises Hyazinth to leave his homeland in search of the veiled maid. If Hyazinth's development thus far could be characterized in temporal terms as a step-wise progression of durative states bridged abruptly by sudden, decisive events, his long journey represents the loosening of time to a more and more regular flow. The initial stages of the journey are still marked by successive landscapes that divide the passage of time into clear stages: "Im Anfange kam er durch rauhes, wildes Land. . . . Dann fand er unabsehliche Sandwüsten, glühenden Staub" (I, 94). As the chaotic, hostile landscape of the first region yields to the monotony of vast deserts, Hyazinth finds the flow of time ever slower, and his internal restlessness gradually abates. Time as articulated by days, years, or distinct periods of growth begins to dissolve into indefiniteness. It becomes increasingly difficult to determine the temporal extent of Hyazinth's journey, as its corresponding spatial coordinates become more and more blurred. Up to this point, Hyazinth's progress is remarkably similar to that of K. in Kafka's *Das Schloß*. In both cases, the protagonist finds his goal becoming ever less focused as time passes increasingly more slowly.[4]

Then, however, the miracle occurs which Kafka's K. is never permitted to experience. Hyazinth's journey, rather than ending in a nameless void, begins to reverse itself: "Nun wurde die Gegend auch wieder reicher und mannigfaltiger, die Luft lau und blau, der Weg ebener. . . . Die Zeit ging schneller" (I, 94). The reversal from decelerating to accelerating time underscores the notion of a spiritual watershed which we noted in Chapter 1. More important, it establishes a significant symmetry in the course of Hyazinth's journey. From the point where the reversal occurs, time becomes in effect *two-directional*. Hyazinth's further progress through space is concurrently his return through space to Rosenblüte and his homeland. His accelerating journey forward through time brings him *backward* through time to the point of departure—and beyond. (The slowing pace of the first phase of his journey, relived backward, would of course be experienced as acceleration.) The process leading to the attainment of the second Golden Age leads simultaneously and symmetrically to the recovery of the first. One must stress again the crucial importance of the turning point in the desert. Hyazinth's wanderings do not—as most interpreters imply—constitute a linear development, or even a circular one. There is no steady accumulation of knowledge from one end of the journey to the other. Hyazinth's aggressive, headstrong attempt to find the "Mother of All Things" leads him straight to the void. Only after his impetuousness has stabilized itself to a clear, firm resolve does the true accumulation of knowledge begin. From the turning point in the desert, his progress operates in two directions at once. At the same time as he is moving forward to perfect consciousness, he is also moving backward, recovering the capacity for naive feeling that characterized the first Golden Age. The experience of the leaves that filled his heart with green colors is evidence of the increasing fusion of emotion and consciousness, as is the later conversion of waking consciousness to dream.[5]

As Hyazinth emerges from the desert, the world gradually becomes full and rich again, but no specific landscape unfolds, no single moment breaks the now accelerating tempo of time: "Immer höher wuchs jene süße Sehnsucht in ihm, und immer breiter und saftiger wurden die Blätter, immer lauter und lustiger die Vögel und Tiere, balsamischer die Früchte, dunkler der Himmel, wärmer die Luft, und heißer seine Liebe, die Zeit ging immer schneller, als sähe sie sich nahe am Ziele" (I, 94). The hastening movement of time is depicted here in the language itself, as the parallel grammatical units become successively shortened to produce a headlong series of impressions. If it was difficult in the first stages of Hyazinth's journey to ascertain how much time had passed since he left his homeland, here it is all but impossible to establish one's temporal bearings. It is clear, however, that time *has* passed, and a good deal of time. This indefinite flow of time is interrupted only once, when Hyazinth encounters the spring and the flowers. This episode, however, does not represent an abrupt turning point as did the visit of the old man or the book burning; rather it has an illustrative function. We see Hyazinth inquiring about the location of the temple, as he already has done innumerable times in the past; we see that he has finally reacquired the facility of speaking with plants and animals; and we learn that he is approaching his goal. Aside from its sacramental implications (noted in Chapter 1), the passage in no way suggests an interruption or turning point in Hyazinth's journey.

At the temple, Hyazinth's dream carries him through endless chambers whose spatial vastness implies a corresponding extension of time toward infinity. At the same time, his progress from one chamber to the next indicates continuous development and internal expansion. Gradually everything around him appears "familiar, and yet in such a splendor as he had never seen," a sign that he is approaching both goals simultaneously: "Es dünkte ihm alles so bekannt und doch in niegesehener Herrlichkeit, da schwand auch der letzte irdische Anflug, wie in Luft verzehrt, und er stand vor der himmlischen Jungfrau, da hob er den leichten, glänzenden Schleier, und Rosenblütchen sank in seine Arme" (I, 95). As in the third "Hymne an die Nacht," which closely resembles this passage in its diction as well as its syntax, the visionary moment is introduced by the repeated adverb "da," which denotes the unqualified uniqueness of this time, this place. Moment and location are unique, however, not in the sense of isolation, but in the sense of absolute extension. It is here that all space in the sense of separation vanishes, and with it the experience of time as articulated by the process of change. Hyazinth's total knowledge of the world and his own soul precludes the apprehension of a new event that, like the visit of the old man, might bring about an alteration in the final state of affairs. The tale thus concludes with a summary description of this final state: "Hyazinth lebte nachher noch lange mit Rosenblütchen unter seinen frohen Eltern und Gespielen, und unzählige Enkel dankten der alten wunderlichen Frau für ihren Rat und ihr Feuer" (I, 95). The mystical synthesis of reality and super-reality achieved in the reunion with Rosenblüte makes it clear, moreover, that the young couple has triumphed over their own mortality, and that their deaths will produce no break whatsoever in their happiness.

At this point it is useful to formulate a few general conclusions regarding the role of time in Novalis's *Märchen*. Time here is intimately linked with the experience of space, particularly space in its symbolic function of representing disparate, and mutually incomplete, spheres of existence. Temporal movement arises from the interaction or collision of two such spheres, resulting in a change of state in one or both of them. Precisely because of the isolation and disparateness of these spatial zones, interaction between them is initially experienced as sudden, unexpected, or accidental. It is here that the decisive role of chance in Novalis's thought becomes apparent. Unpredictable events are a signal that one has arrived at the interface between two levels of existence. That which initially appears disturbing and accidental is later resolved, retrospectively, into the logic of a higher law. "Aller Zufall ist wunderbar—Berührung eines höhern Wesens—ein Problem Datum des thätig religiösen Sinns" (III, 441). Vulnerability to time is a direct correlative of imperfect and immature existence. Indeed, the very *experience* of time is a symptom of existential deficiency. Concurrently, however, it is a symptom of growth. Fundamental to Novalis's optimism is the belief that any such interaction between two formerly distinct zones must inevitably bring both of them closer to a state of unity, and that the forces of cohesion are ultimately more powerful than those of disjunction. "Alle Berührung ist ein Anlaß zur Erregung der Einenden, systematisirenden Kr[raft]—i.e. der Weltseele—oder der Seele überhaupt. . . . Unwircksame Berührungen sind keine Berührungen im strengern Sinn" (III, 341).

Spatial immobility, then, signifies temporal stasis, "time-lessness" for better or worse; spatial movement results in temporal progression. Novalis was to formulate this theoretical insight explicitly in the *Allgemeine Brouillon*: "Zeit und Raum entstehn zugleich und sind also wohl Eins, wie Subject und Object. Raum ist beharrliche Zeit—Zeit ist fließender, variabler Raum—Raum—Basis alles Beharrlichen—Zeit—Basis alles Veränderlichen" (III, 427–28).

Significantly, the most abrupt transitions in Hyazinth's development occur at the beginning of the tale, where they mark the first collisions between internal and external reality. Subsequently the transitions become less and less abrupt, the interactions less turbulent. After the turning point in the desert, there can no longer be any talk of distinct partitions of sudden, unique events bridging distinct static periods. Hyazinth's development becomes, instead, a smoothly accelerating process of change, in which the quickening of time signifies a continually more rapid interaction between the two spheres of mind and nature. The reunion with Rosenblüte, finally, marks the point of complete fusion between the two levels of reality, after which any further experience of time in the sense of substantive change is absolutely precluded. If Hyazinth's journey signified a continual expansion and enrichment of present experience, the final apotheosis represents a boundless present, eternally and universally complete. As was the case with space, time does not disappear altogether. Instead of representing progression through various stages of (decreasing) inadequacy, however, it now provides the opportunity of novelty and diversion within an essentially unchanging state. Later, in the Klingsohr tale, Novalis went to some lengths to ensure that the final condition not be thought of as a static, tedious timelessness. Here only the reference to the countless grandchildren indicates that temporality has its place in the second Golden Age, as a source of abundance, diversity, and variation.[6]

"Arion" and "Atlantis"

In comparison with "Hyazinth und Rosenblüte," the tale of Arion is relatively uncomplicated in its temporal structure. Here there is no trace of acceleration or sudden change from one state to another, but only a simple narrative arch which rises to a turning point (the poet's song) and then falls again. Yet the tale is not without temporal idiosyncracies of its own. The opening section of the tale is marked by adverbs such as "einmal," "bald," and "da," which introduce specific stations of the journey across the sea. The implied horizontal progress of the ship over the water serves to underline this temporal succession spatially. At the song of the poet, however, the linear horizontal development of the journey is suddenly sliced perpendicularly, as the narrator describes the vertical reverberation of the song from the sky to the sea. This sudden intrusion of vertical coordinates effectively brings the horizontal movement to a halt, and thus, in an indirect way, momentarily stops the flow of time. Novalis reinforces the illusion of timelessness here by causing the sun and the stars to appear simultaneously in the sky, thus erasing the temporal distinction between night and day. When the poet's song is finished, this brief pocket of timelessness yields once again to the successive flow of events marked by "da," "nach kurzer Zeit," "nach einiger Zeit," and "einmal." The passage of time here, however, forks into two separate tracks. The description of the poet's miraculous escape and recovery of the treasures is followed by a flashback relating the murderous struggle of the seamen and the wreck of their ship. In effect, the rescue of the poet and the self-inflicted punishment of the evil seamen occur simultaneously; they are complementary manifestations of a single process of justice.

On a thematic level, the poet's recovery of his treasures signifies to a large extent his recovery of the past: "[Die Kleinode] waren ihm als

Erinnerungen glücklicher Stunden und als Zeichen der Liebe und Dankbarkeit . . . wert gewesen" (I, 212). The monstrous deed of the seamen, which threatened to separate the poet not only from the past, but from life itself, has been annulled. By means of his retrieved treasures, the poet is reunited, at least symbolically, with the happy hours of his past. The tale thus reveals, in condensed form, the familiar triadic rhythm from harmony to disruption (caused by covetousness and selfish hostility) to a final state of renewed harmony. While Hyazinth, however, underwent this development in his own person, the poet is an essentially static figure, unchanged from beginning to end, despite his momentary travail with the seamen. On closer scrutiny, the triadic development of "Arion" may be seen to derive from the conflict between two forms of *timelessness*: on the one hand, the positive timelessness of abundance and harmony, the Golden Age which is embodied and recreated in the song of the poet; on the other hand, the negative, empty timelessness which threatens the poet after his encounter with the seamen. Selfishness and greed have a distinct temporal dimension here. As forces of disunity and chaos they polarize reality, creating a state of separation and deficiency. In other words, they lead to a *fixation* of time at an inadequate level of existence. In this sense, the evil seamen clearly anticipate the Scribe and the Fates in "Eros und Fabel," as we shall see.

After the poet's song, the competing forces of unity and disunity go to work simultaneously. The continuing effect of the song ensures the recovery of the jewels (through the grateful sea monster), just as the continuing effect of the seamen's greed ensures their ultimate destruction and death. Again one may note Novalis's fundamental optimism: the process leading to a reestablishment of unity is inevitably sovereign over the process leading to chaos and disintegration. The three stages of the tale emerge, then, as a period of harmony, a period of competition between the two opposing forces, and a period of renewed harmony. Since the concluding state is in no significant way an ascent to a higher phase of reality than the first state, however, "Arion" must be considered something of an anomaly among the tales of Novalis.

"Atlantis," like "Hyazinth und Rosenblüte," begins with a lengthy exposition of an existing state of affairs, or more precisely two simultaneous but separate states of affairs. The first of these is the splendid life at the court of the old king. Predictably, durative and iterative verbs dominate this section of the narrative, and the verbs themselves are enclosed in clusters of five or six nouns. The second sentence of the tale is indicative of this heavily nominalistic style, whose purpose is to evoke a static, self-perpetuating condition rather than action leading to a change in state: "Es gebrach weder den täglichen Festen an Überfluß köstlicher Waren des Gaumens, noch an Musik, prächtigen Verzierungen und Trachten, und tausend abwechselnden Schauspielen und Zeitvertreibungen, noch endlich an sinnreicher Anordnung, an klugen, gefälligen, und unterrichteten Männern zur Unterhaltung und Beseelung der Gespräche, und an schöner, anmutiger Jugend von beiden Geschlechtern, die die eigentliche Seele reizender Feste ausmachen" (I, 213). The peaceful, harmonious life at the court is the result of a passionate devotion to the spirit of poetry and song. The king and his bards have established an artificial world that owes its seeming timelessness in large measure to the supertemporal nature of the poetry it creates: "Frieden der Seele und innres seliges Anschauen einer selbst geschaffenen, glücklichen Welt war das Eigentum dieser wunderbaren Zeit geworden" (I, 214). Although the situation at the court reflects any historical period in which art takes leave of its mimetic function and becomes an end in itself, it is possible to see here a critique of Enlightenment literature in particular. From the Romantic point of view, eighteenth-century poetics seemed restrictive and legalistic, a codified system that encouraged stylistic formulas, rhetorical finesse, and a prissy adherence to acceptable subject matter. Like the poetry of the king's bards, such literature is quite capable of producing an illusory sense of serenity and self-sufficiency. Nevertheless, its effect is one of surface brilliance, an elegant deception that attempts to mask an underlying hollowness and sterility.

The king's attempt to circumvent the inexorable flow of time by founding a poetic utopia is threatened, moreover, by purely physical processes: "Der König ward immer älter" (I, 214). In the heart of this seemingly static state of affairs, a temporal development is in progress which threatens ultimately to plunge the whole kingdom into leaderless chaos. In addition, the king's aging is accompanied by the parallel, and equally disastrous, development of his regal pride. Novalis depicts the course of this development up to the time of the story by means of the pluperfect tense and intensifying adverbs such as "allmählich" and "immer mehr": "Das Gefühl des Abstandes hatte [die Prinzen aus anderen Ländern] allmählich verscheucht. . . . Der König war bei aller Milde beinah unwillkürlich in ein Gefühl der Erhabenheit geraten. . . . Ihr hoher, einziger Wert hatte jenes Gefühl in ihm immer mehr bestätigt. . . . In dem Zauberspiegel ihrer Kunst war ihm der Abstand seiner Herkunft von dem Ursprunge der andern Menschen, die Herrlichkeit seines Stammes noch heller erschienen" (I, 215). If the king's increasing age makes his daughter's marriage more and more desirable, his increasing pride makes it ever more unlikely. The serene illusion of timelessness at the court is thus undermined by two mutually reinforcing developments that, if allowed to run their course, will inevitably lead to the destruction of the kingdom. It is not difficult to see a parallel here between the exaggerated pride of the king and the selfish greed of the seamen in "Arion." Common to both cases is a certain note of arrogant self-assertion, an unjustified claim to power or grandeur which not only impedes positive progress but actually works to stop time at an imperfect level of reality. It is worth noting that these forces of disunity become much more explicit and virulent in the later tales than in "Hyazinth und Rosenblüte," while the source of salvation is narrowed down to the single force of poetry.

Concurrent with the life at the court, a second state of affairs exists at the house of the old man. Father and son live in peaceful isolation, devoting themselves to the study of nature. No internal development threatens their existence, but they, too, as members of the kingdom, are jeopardized by the passage of time and the increasing likelihood of the king's death without an heir.

Following this double exposition, the narrative proper begins with a specific temporal datum: "Eines Tages hatte die Prinzessin . . . sich allein zu Pferde in den Wald begeben" (I, 216). As was the case with the arrival of the old man in "Hyazinth und Rosenblüte," the temporal uniqueness of this "eines Tages" derives from the interaction between formerly discrete spatial zones and a resultant change of state in each of them. After a brief, temporally compressed depiction of the ride of the princess through the forest, narrative time broadens suddenly to record in detail the simultaneous reactions of the youth, the princess, and the old man at the crucial moment of first encounter. Novalis achieves the effect of simultaneity here by means of the word "gleich," which counteracts the impression of consecutive action and draws the reader back twice to the moment of the princess's appearance in the doorway, each time with a shift in view point:

Der Sohn war gegenwärtig, und erschrak beinah über diese zauberhafte Erscheinung eines majestätischen weiblichen Wesens. (I, 216)

Es fiel ihr, gleich beim Eintritt, der mit tausend seltenen Sachen gezierte Hausraum, die Ordnung und Reinlichkeit des Ganzen, und eine seltsame Heiligkeit des Ortes auf. (I, 216)

Der Alte hielt sie gleich für eine zum Hof gehörige Person. (I, 216)

Following this extended description, narrative time is again compressed with relation to narrated time: "Nach einigen Gesprächen mit beiden, dankte sie auf die lieblichste Weise für die freundliche Bewirtung" (I, 217). By framing the temporally enlarged moment of encounter with two segments of relatively compressed time, Novalis effectively indicates the extraordinary impact of this moment on each of the three characters; and the very intensity of their responses may be taken as evidence both of their existential disparity and their inherent disposition toward union.

The narrative then splits into a similar three-way tracking of the time stretch following the princess's departure:

Dem Alten, der Prinzessin, und dem Jüngling war die einfache Begebenheit des Tages gleich wichtig. Der Alte hatte leicht den neuen tiefen Eindruck bemerkt, den die Unbekannte auf seinen Sohn machte. (I, 217)

Die Prinzessin hatte sich nie in einem ähnlichen Zustande befunden, wie der war, in welchem sie langsam nach Hause ritt. (I, 217)

Der Jüngling hatte sich gleich nach ihrem Abschiede in den Wald verloren. An der Seite des Weges war er in Gebüschen bis an die Pforte des Gartens ihr gefolgt. (I, 218)

After following the youth through a sleepless night, the narrative switches back to depict the separate but simultaneous agitation of the princess and her subsequent return to the forest in the morning. At her sudden reencounter with the youth, the two time tracks converge again, resolving the considerable structural tension which the narrator has engendered by the use of shifting view points and the repeated backtracking of time. As we noted in Chapter 1, this convergence also represents a preliminary resolution of thematic tension, as the princess and the youth are united symbolically in the image of a jewel wrapped in a poem.

At this point, the dynamics of simultaneous but separate actions yield to a linear development of time. The youth and the princess now proceed together on a course of mutual development indicated by the verb "werden": "Der Jüngling ward unvermerkt ihr Begleiter bei diesen Spaziergängen.... Sie beobachtete ein unverbrüchliches Stillschweigen über ihren Stand, so zutraulich sie auch sonst gegen ihren Begleiter wurde.... Sie ward bald einheimisch in dem wunderbaren Hause" (I, 220). The developing intimacy between the representatives of the two worlds soon reaches its culmination. Once again, the decisive moment is introduced by the perfective temporal adverb "eines Tages": "Eines Tages, wo ein besonders kühner Schwung sich seiner Seele bemächtigt hatte, und die mächtige Liebe auf dem Rückwege ihre jungfräuliche Zurückhaltung mehr als gewöhnlich überwand, so daß sie beide ohne selbst zu wissen wie einander in die Arme sanken, und der erste glühende Kuß sie auf ewig zusammenschmelzte, fing mit einbrechender Dämmerung ein gewaltiger Sturm in den Gipfeln der Bäume plötzlich zu toben an" (I, 221). The intricate syntax of this sentence serves to coordinate three events temporally: the kiss, nightfall, and the storm. In most of Novalis's works—and particularly, of course, in the *Hymnen an die Nacht*—night functions as a symbol of a unified existence. The storm reflects, on an external level, the mounting passion of the two lovers. The simultaneous occurrence of these events indicates not a causal reaction (which would be successive), but rather an invisible correlation between human affairs and nature. One might dismiss this passage as a predictable instance of pathetic fallacy, but the situation is in fact more complicated. The sudden correspondence between man and nature here reflects precisely what is taking place on the allegorical level: that is, the union of Nature and Mind in the embrace of the two lovers.

The outbreak of the storm is followed by a rapid succession of events (the flight through the forest, the discovery of the cave, the erotic union of the lovers), which conclude the first major phase of the tale. It can scarcely be considered coincidental that the temporal structure of this first phase closely resembles that of "Hyazinth und Rosenblüte" as a whole. In both tales, an exposition of coexistent but disparate spatial arenas is followed by a series of decisive events that lead to an accelerating interaction and mutual change of state in the two formerly discrete zones. The effect here is not unlike that of a ball which bounces faster and faster as it approaches a state of full rest. In both tales, moreover, this accelerating interaction is the direct result of an ever more powerful love, the energizing force of attraction, which leads directly to a state of complete union.

It now remains for this personal union to be integrated into a more universal context, a process that occurred automatically in "Hyazinth und Rosenblüte." Following the night of love in the cave, the original tension of simultaneous but separate affairs between the court and the house is resumed. While the princess and the youth live peacefully at the house of the old man, life at the court falls into a dreary pattern, as the poets raise songs of lament and the king vacillates between self-reproach and a proud sense of martyrdom. The narrative lingers to such an extent over the description of this state that the whole section gains the appearance of a second exposition. Finally the spell is broken: "Eines Abends, da es gerade jährig wurde, da sie verschwand, war der ganze Hof im Garten versammelt" (I, 224). The return of the princess on the anniversary of her disappearance has the same effect as Hyazinth's reunion with Rosenblüte: the new life is to pick up precisely where the old one left off, albeit on a higher level of reality. The king himself feels this sense of renewal: "Es dünkte ihm das traurige Jahr nur ein schwerer Traum zu sein" (I, 224).

As the assembly in the garden stands in a silent, motionless tableau which anticipates similar configurations in "Eros und Fabel," the youth suddenly appears with his lute and sings two lengthy songs, both of which relate, on different planes of abstraction, the ultimate triumph of love and poetry. The first song spells out the history of the world, the second the wondrous fate of a nameless poet who wins a king's daughter. The theme thus proceeds temporally in ever smaller concentric circles. The unsung third song is the reality of events in the tale itself, and the king is indirectly implored through the parallelism of the songs to complete the grand design on his own level. This is by no means the only occurrence of thematic parallelism on different temporal levels in the works of Novalis. We shall encounter it on an even more impressive scale in "Eros und Fabel," and it informs the entire narrative structure of *Heinrich von Ofterdingen*. At the heart of this technique is the religious conception of ritualistic action as a means of gaining access to the supertemporal meaning of existence.[7] For Novalis such ritual was not merely symbolic. Precisely as Christian communion represents not an imitation, but an actual reenactment of the Last Supper, the kingdom of Atlantis shares in the final cosmic unity *in advance* through the ritual of love and forgiveness. The underlying structural and thematic similarity of Novalis's works is not the result of an impoverished imagination, but of a profoundly religious one, which sought to reiterate the ritual process toward triumph over death on as many levels as possible, from the abstract realm of "Eros und Fabel" to the poetized personal experiences of the *Hymnen an die Nacht*.

The two songs that the youth delivers are thus anything but idle variations on a theme. Like all decisive events in Novalis's works, they lead in a series of temporal stages to an alteration in the existing state of affairs in the garden; and as usual the temporal development is represented by means of spatial choreography. During the first song, the stationary crowd begins to regroup around the youth, and at the end of the song the king himself moves to the youth and embraces him. The youth then begins his second song, the events of which are related in the historical present, a device that is to facilitate the transition from poetic present to actual present time in the garden. The song is divided into eleven stanzas. The first five of these depict the despair of the poet at the lack of reward for his songs, and the last five relate his success in winning both the heart of the king's daughter and, finally, the forgiveness of the king himself. At the pivotal sixth stanza, which anticipates the events of the following stanzas in a dream vision which appears to the despairing poet, the narrator interrupts the youth's song to relate certain occurrences that take place in the garden during the course of the song. First, the veiled princess and her child appear, accompanied by the old man. Secondly, the king's eagle suddenly dives down from the treetops and drops a golden headband on the youth's head. If the first event involves the appearance of the princess at the precise moment of her first mention in the song, thus establishing a temporal correlation between poetic and empirical reality, the action of the eagle represents an instantaneous affirmation of this correlation. Moreover, the princess's first appearance in the poem is by way of an oblique reference ("die treuste Hand") in the *dream*. It is this reality twice removed that is immediately affirmed by the symbolic action of the eagle. Significantly, the eagle, as a representative of nature, bestows a token of the king's favor on the youth before the king himself is prepared to do so. Like the solicitous plants and animals who attempt to show Hyazinth "the right way," the eagle in "Atlantis" demonstrates one of the fundamental premises of Romantic thought: the assumption that the natural world, by virtue of its purely instinctive and unconscious existence, is much closer to a state of perfection than man in his present murky condition of incomplete and unreliable consciousness. Thus Arcturus, in the Klingsohr tale, is able to prophesy the ultimate happy ending long before the characters at the House have any idea of the future course of events. This conception of nature as existing on the very threshold of perfection emerges even more clearly from the temporal organization of "Eros und Fabel," as we shall see presently.

The conclusion of the youth's second song is followed by a rapid series of events: the youth removes the veil, the princess falls weeping to the feet of the king and holds the child up to him, and the youth kneels at her side. At the formation of this ceremonial tableau, which brings all of the principal figures within inches of complete spatial union, time seems to stop: "Eine ängstliche Stille schien jeden Atem festzuhalten. Der König war einige Augenblicke sprachlos und ernst" (I, 229). The king decides abruptly to forgive his daughter and to accept the youth as his heir. This short and highly charged penultimate state yields to another rapid succession of events that close the last remaining spatial gap: the king embraces the princess and the youth, lifts the child toward heaven, and greets the old man. On a realistic level, the harmony and the order of the kingdom have been renewed for at least two generations. On a mystic level, the kingdom through its ritual action has transcended earthly time altogether to exist forever in a state of peace and tranquillity: "Der Abend ward ein heiliger Vorabend dem ganzen Lande, dessen Leben fortan nur *ein* schönes Fest war" (I, 229).

In general terms then, the temporal structure of "Atlantis" from the depiction of the uneasy year at the court to the conclusion bears a striking resemblance to that of the first part of the tale. Once again, decisive events bridge and introduce ever shorter time spans in an accelerating step-wise progression to the conclusion. Each successive temporal phase brings the figures of the tale closer to a state of spatial unity. In effect, "Atlantis" is comprised of two separate but related tales with very much the same temporal structure. The first relates the development toward union on a personal level, the second the development toward social and, by implication, cosmic unity.

"Eros und Fabel"

The process which in "Atlantis" was accomplished in two parallel steps unfolds in "Eros und Fabel" with one mighty sweep. The ultimate personal union of Eros and Freya caps a revolution that embraces all creation. This simultaneous development on both a personal and universal level derives primarily from the allegorical nature of the tale. Abstractions such as Love, Fantasy, and Wisdom constitute aspects of the individual psyche as well as supertemporal concepts whose gradual development may span several millennia.

Thus the long night mentioned at the beginning of the tale encompasses a whole series of temporal planes superimposed on each other: "Die lange Nacht war eben angegangen" (I, 290). First, this long night is the stretch of time of man's estrangement from nature, the hundreds and thousands of years in which the mysteries of nature are obscured from the forces of mind and consciousness. It is the era of death and the dark powers of the Fates and, paradoxically, the period of the sun's domination over the affairs of men. Secondly, however, it may be interpreted as the "dark night of the soul" on a purely individual basis, in which case it might extend to no more than a few years (as in "Atlantis"). Thirdly, in terms of the imagery of the tale, it is the long polar night of about four months that Arcturus's kingdom must endure by virtue of its location at the North Pole. Finally, it is the stretch of time from Eros's infancy to the destruction of the sun, a period which in terms of *apparent* narrated time appears to last no more than a day and a half. The reader is most acutely aware of the simultaneous operation of at least two time levels when Fabel returns to the House after leaving Eros and Ginnistan. In the time of her absence, the House has fallen into ruin. The steps have crumbled, and thistles grow in the windows. Yet from the time of her departure from the House, we have followed Fabel through a tight succession of events described *in continuo*, which appear to add up to no more than a single day, much less the hundreds of years which have left their mark on the House. The reader is faced with the sudden need to readjust his temporal thinking. What seemed like minutes on the abstract level of Fabel's allegorical adventures amounts to years on the level of earthly time which the House experiences by virtue of its location in the World. Similarly, the time which elapses until her second return to the House appears to encompass only a few hours, partly because of the increasing ease with which she bridges spatial gaps, and partly because a good portion of this period is taken up by dialogues in direct quotation, which represent the closest approximation possible between narrated time and narrative time. Neither these movements from one place to another nor particularly these dialogues add up to the time stretch which the House has undergone in its continued process of aging: "[Das Haus] war zu völligen Ruinen geworden. Efeu umzog die Mauern. Hohe Büsche beschatteten den ehmaligen Hof, und weiches Moos polsterte die alten Stiegen" (I, 311).[8] In both instances the unexpected extent of decay serves to reorient the reader to the temporal magnitude of the process which Fabel is carrying out.

These interlocking levels of time, in which days are simultaneously months, years, or centuries, serve to break down the primacy of "objective time" which can be measured in clearly defined units.[9] From an absolute standpoint, the boundaries of time known to man—hours, days, years—are purely arbitrary; they owe their existence to the accident that the earth takes a certain amount of time to rotate on its axis and a certain greater amount of time to revolve around the sun. The ultimate fall of the sun in "Eros und Fabel" represents, among other things, the destruction of this arbitrary time system. For Novalis, the movement of the sun has nothing whatsoever to do with real time, but represents a condition of *premature timelessness* marked by the mechanical, unchanging alternation between night and day.[10] This unwavering predictability of the sun is responsible for locking the minds of men into a static, mechanistic conception of the universe, exemplified by Newtonian physics. True time is measured not by chronological duration, but by change and progression. In a sense, the "objective" time of the physicists is objective only in that it is equally irrelevant for all beings. Each individual develops according to his own temporal amplitude, irrespective of clock time. Thus an identical process toward unity may be observed in the seeming minutes of the action in the windows of Arcturus's palace, the hours of Father Moon's drama,[11] the year of "Atlantis," the indefinite years of Hyazinth's quest, and the century-days of Fabel's ceaseless activity. In the *Allgemeine Brouillon*, Novalis notes that a true chronology must recognize each individual as occupying his own sphere, his own scale in time: "Kronologie ist die Lehre von der *Zeitlängenbestimmung* eines Factums—eines zeitlichen Individuums. Die Zeit ist hier, als ein unermeßlicher Meridian zu betrachten—worauf jedes zeitliche Individuum seine Sfäre, seine Skala hat" (III, 340). The superimposed temporal levels which simultaneously constitute the "long night" represent, then, an emancipation from the lockstep of objective time. They are equated *not* according to duration, but according to the identical processes which unfold within them, each occupying its own dimension in time.

Like the other tales of Novalis, "Eros und Fabel" opens with two concurrent but disparate states of affairs. At the North Pole lies the kingdom of Arcturus, temporally as well as physically frozen. In the circular mountain belt lies the House, whose occupants are either posed in a silent tableau or are involved in iterative activities characterized by temporal adverbs such as "immer," "zuweilen," or "beständig." What little action there is at the northern kingdom is restricted to the very beginning of the tale and has an illustrative function. The bluish light that Freya emits, for instance, is intended to symbolize the northern lights, and the effect of her electric spark on the Old Hero suggests thunder and lightning: "Seine Rüstung klang, und eine durchdringende Kraft beseelte seinen Körper. Seine Augen blitzten und das Herz pochte hörbar an den Panzer" (I, 291–92). These actions have no effect on the ensuing course of events, but serve rather to establish Arcturus's kingdom as the seat of Nature. Similarly, the dance of the stars in the throne room does not represent a unique event, but is rather like a motion picture that may be run repeatedly with identical results. In fact, as we have seen in Chapter 1, it provides a general scenario for the tale as a whole as well as for the miniature reproductions in Arcturus's windows and Father Moon's treasure room. The only event with direct repercussions on the development of the tale is the casting of the Hero's sword into the World. Even this event, however, has no immediate effect on Arcturus's kingdom, where the various figures in effect simply sit back and wait for the ice to melt. Freya (as we later learn) falls asleep, and Arcturus and his councilors assume the fixed configurations of the northern constellations: "Der König saß umringt von seinen Räten, als Fabel erschien. Die nördliche Krone zierte sein Haupt. Die Lilie hielt er mit der Linken, die Waage in der Rechten. Der Adler und Löwe saßen zu seinen Füßen" (I, 304).[12] In contrast to the substantial and dramatic transformations that the representatives of Mind (notably the Father, the Mother, Eros, and Ginnistan) undergo in the course of the tale, the kingdom of Nature experiences no essential changes except for the process of melting. As crucial as this process is, it is relatively simple in comparison with the complicated maneuvers which Fabel must carry out in order to transform the various forces of Mind. As with the eagle in "Atlantis," the implication here is that Nature is inherently closer to a state of perfection than Mind. While Arcturus's kingdom takes one step *backward* (by melting), the figures at the House must take a whole series of complex steps *forward* in order to achieve a state of perfection.

This circumstance should not, however, obscure the fact that the frozen condition of Arcturus's kingdom and the initial state of affairs at the House are complementary aspects of a single phenomenon. An imperfect Mind, composed of a distracted Heart, a lascivious and frivolous Fantasy, immature Love, and a Sense which can perceive only fragmentary data, is responsible for the emergence of such a figure as the Scribe. And it is above all the Scribe—this epitome of Enlightenment philosophy at its worst—who has banished the realm of Nature to the eternity of a perpetual motion machine.[13] In accordance with the dialectics of Schelling's *Naturphilosophie*, thesis (imperfect Mind) and antithesis (frozen Nature) evolve from an original synthesis by a single reciprocal process.[14]

As with "Hyazinth und Rosenblüte" and "Atlantis," the narrative proper begins with the first interaction between the separate spheres of reality. Once again, it is a measure of their disparity that this interaction is sudden, unexpected, accidental: "Auf einmal brachte der Vater ein zartes eisernes Stäbchen herein, das er im Hofe gefunden hatte" (I, 294). The arrival of the sword splinter from Arcturus's realm causes an immediate, dramatic change in the baby Eros: upon touching it, he suddenly matures to a young man. In terms of the rather clever magnetic imagery of the tale, the charge that Freya has conducted into the Old Hero's sword polarizes Eros with respect to his future bride. The energy he receives via the sword splinter produces, as it were, a proper charge distribution, so that both poles of the magnet are now equally balanced: on the one hand, a full-grown maiden, on the other, a full-grown youth. Later, consistently enough, the premature and false discharge of this energy with Ginnistan results in his reconversion to a baby. If in "Atlantis" the instantaneous maturation of a character was still expressed figuratively,[15] here it is a literal event.

As was the case with space, time in "Eros und Fabel" cannot be said to exist independently of the characters. Eros's sudden internal development is accompanied by an equally sudden acceleration of external time, so that his outer appearance keeps pace with his change of character. Once again we note the formal identity of internal and external reality, which is achieved thematically only at the conclusion of the tale. Critics who have been quick to take Novalis to task for his bent toward allegory have always failed to consider that allegory is the only form of narrative that accomplishes this synthesis of ideas and matter, mind and nature.[16] For Novalis, allegorical representation was not a mere tool in the service of simple-minded didacticism, as it often enough becomes in the hands of lesser writers. He saw in allegory the most perfect formal expression of the ideal toward which all of his tales strive thematically.

Given this theoretical justification, however, one may still object that the intended synthesis of mind and matter is rather too heavily weighted on the side of mind. Despite its delicacy and charm, the Klingsohr tale is so dominated by abstractions that its connection with immediate, empirical reality can only be assumed, not experienced. If one of the primary aims of Romantic literature was to combine "the individualisation of the general with the universalisation of the individual,"[17] it must be conceded that "Eros und Fabel" accentuates the latter half of the formula at the expense of the former half.

The precipitous growth of Eros results in a regrouping of the various figures at the House, as we have seen in Chapter 1. While mature Love and Heart embrace, Sense seizes the opportunity to steal away with Fantasy, and both Wisdom and petrified Reason depart. The first effect of the sword splinter, then, is a tentative consolidation of several of the representatives of Mind; but the absence of Sophie suggests a certain lack of good judgment in this consolidation. The second effect of the splinter holds greater promise. Drawn by the magnetic attraction of Freya, Eros sets out with Ginnistan for Arcturus's realm. This seemingly reasonable plan, however, leads immediately to disaster. While Eros reverts to childhood in the arms of Ginnistan, the Scribe terrorizes the House, laying the Mother and Father in chains and driving away Sophie and Fabel. The situation here corresponds roughly to Hyazinth's state of mind under the domination of the old man's book. And it is at this point of greatest disunity that the synthesizing activity of Fabel begins. From here to the end, the tale consists of a steady, linear succession of events, as Fabel darts from one realm to another. Wherever she goes, she finds a static state of affairs, usually defined by a tableau; her sudden appearance repeatedly causes an alteration in the existing state or the inauguration of a totally new state. In successive trips to the World, she calms the restless Eros and sings him to sleep in the arms of the now motherly Ginnistan, awakens the giant Atlas, brings the sacramental ashes of the Mother to the waiting motionless group around the altar of the House, and finally leads Eros to Arcturus's palace to waken Freya and usher in the final state.[18] Thus while Fabel's tale unwinds in a continuous sequence of events, the World progresses step-wise from one prolonged state to another. The similarity of this latter plot line to that of Novalis's earlier tales should be obvious. There is, however, one important exception: from the time of Fabel's first departure from the House to the conclusion, all events are viewed from her moving standpoint. The events which occur in the World while Fabel is in the realm of the Fates or at Arcturus's palace remain almost totally nondetermined, and, more important, it is impossible to determine them, even hypothetically. If a character in a realistic (as opposed to allegorical) narrative leaves Stuttgart by train and arrives in Hamburg later in the day, the reader may assume that the train went by way of Bonn or by way of Kassel. Either route is possible but not, strictly speaking, significant. It is quite another thing to postulate Sophie's actions during the interim of her absence, or the return of Eros and Ginnistan to the House. Since every action, every spatial movement in the Klingsohr tale is imbued with allegorical significance, the reader is no longer permitted to fill in the nondetermined passages at will. The plot line of the tale thus contains certain *lacunae*, completely indefinite stretches of time that can neither be considered empty nor tentatively filled in with postulated events. No doubt this circumstance is partly responsible for the confusion that has prompted critics to label the tale incomprehensible. "Hyazinth und Rosenblüte" and "Atlantis" display no such gaps in time. Despite their miraculous events, they are grounded on the reality of the physical world, and the reader may arbitrarily posit fill-in material for the indefinite passages without seriously altering or manipulating the meaning of the tales.

Whatever may happen in the World during Fabel's absence, each time she returns, she discovers matters at an impasse. Her sudden appearance—precisely like the book burning in "Hyazinth und Rosenblüte" or the first arrival of the princess at the old man's house in "Atlantis"—breaks the impasse and furthers the progression of events toward the final resolution. If she were *not* to appear, one can only assume that Ginnistan, Eros, Sophie, and the slumbering Father, for example, would remain in a ceremonial tableau at the House through all eternity. Here we come to the most crucial problem of time in Novalis's works. His characters do not fear death per se as an existential terminus; nor do they fear time as a source of alienation and change. Rather they face the threat of the dead-end situation, the impasse, the paralysis of an unchanging and unfulfilled existence. Hyazinth's obsession with the old man's book is a similar blind alley, as is the sterile and incomplete life at the court at the beginning of "Atlantis," where the imminent danger of the king's death threatens to turn an inadequate state of affairs into a disaster. It is not time per se, then, that is a problem in Novalis's works, but rather premature timelessness. The experience of time itself is unequivocally positive. In the Fichte studies (1795–96), Novalis explicitly identifies the dynamics of an ideal philosophical system with the nature of time: "Das Universalsystem der Filosofie muß, wie die Zeit seyn, Ein Faden, an dem man durch unendliche Bestimmungen laufen kann—Es muß ein System der mannichfachsten Einheit, der unendlichen Erweiterung, Compass der Freyheit seyn" (II, 289–90).

If time as a fundamental medium of cognition is compared here with a thread of infinite extension, it is precisely the function of the Fates to snip this thread short in the middle of its development. Significantly, the Fates are shown to be in close league with the Scribe, who in his own way strives for a premature stoppage of time. His writings, for instance, represent a codification of imperfect and incomplete observations, as the passage with the sword splinter makes clear: "Der Schreiber ward bald des Betrachtens überdrüssig. Er schrieb alles genau auf, und war sehr weitläufig über den Nutzen, den dieser Fund gewähren könne. Wie ärgerlich war er aber, als sein ganzes Schreibwerk die Probe nicht bestand, und das Papier weiß aus der Schale hervorkam" (I, 294–95). Moreover, by locking up the Mother and Father, he enforces spatial immobility, which, as we have seen, is a correlative of temporal stasis. The implicit parallel between the Scribes and the Fates becomes most apparent, however, in the description of the subterranean realm of the Fates, which is one of the most original and brilliant pieces of imagery in Novalis's works: "Alle Figuren waren hier dunkel. Die Luft war wie ein ungeheurer Schatten; am Himmel stand ein schwarzer strahlender Körper. Man konnte alles auf das deutlichste unterscheiden, weil jede Figur einen andern Anstrich von Schwarz zeigte, und einen lichten Schein hinter sich warf; Licht und Schatten schienen hier ihre Rollen vertauscht zu haben" (I, 301). A black sun! With terrible consistency, the symbol of a mechanistic universe continues to shine even in the land of Death. There is no hint of transcendence here, no trace of elevation or development through death, but only a reversal of the fatal polarity of light and darkness. This is the purgatory of those who die too soon, suspended eternally at an unfinished level of existence; it is the image of unfulfilled death as the counterpart of unfulfilled life. *True* death is characterized by transition and progression, and as such is wholly positive: "Alles ist von selbst *ewig*. Die Sterblichkeit—Wandelbarkeit ist gerade ein Vorzug höherer Naturen" (III, 436).

It is Fabel's mission, then, to effect this positive death by lifting the other characters to ever higher planes of perfection.[19] While she accomplishes her tasks without the slightest trace of exhaustion or indecision, the fact that the development of the other figures is so utterly dependent on her activities is a sign that Novalis was becoming increasingly aware of, and concerned about, the problem of temporal stasis. Here, as nowhere else in his poetic works, one can clearly sense the approaching crisis of Romantic progressivity. As Helmut Schanze has pointed out, Novalis's philosophical orientation was gradually shifting away from a belief in the unbounded freedom of the ego, as he progressed from Fichte to Hemsterhuis and finally to the medical theories of the Scottish physician John Brown.[20] The dependence of the mind on external stimuli was already evident in "Hyazinth und Rosenblüte," as we have seen. In the Klingsohr tale, however, the single effective source of mediation between the external and internal worlds is the synthesizing activity of poetry. The other components of the mind repeatedly become grounded in a state of imperfection. The abstract setting of "Eros und Fabel" serves to illuminate more than the intricate process of fusion between mind and nature. It also, perhaps unwittingly, lays bare the ultimate tenuousness of Novalis's optimism. Following his death in 1801, both Friedrich Schlegel and Tieck reverted to traditional forms of authority, and the new movement which arose in Heidelberg had a decidedly more conservative bent than Jena Romanticism. While the ideal of progressivity was maintained by Hegel, Schubert, and (occasionally) E. T. A. Hoffmann, it was never again to find such clear and affirmative literary expression as in the works of Novalis.

The full burden of propelling the mind through its successive stages of development falls, then, on Fabel. As in the earlier tales, the terraced progression from one state to another accelerates through the course of the narrative. The temporal gap between each successive stage is more or less a function of the time it takes Fabel to cross from one realm to the next. Initially her passage is relatively slow. She descends "for a considerable time" before reaching the land of the Fates. Her next three journeys are shorter, and she soon reaches her destination:

Sie kletterte schnell hinauf, und kam bald vor eine Falltür, die sich in Arcturs Gemach öffnete. (I, 304)

Fabel hatte bald das Gestade erreicht. (I, 305)

Sie sah bald von weitem die hohe Flamme des Scheiterhaufens, die über den grünen Wald emporstieg. (I, 307)

Thereafter no temporal adverb at all is provided to describe the duration of her journey. In terms of narrative time—and of narrated time—she arrives at her goal almost as soon as she sets out:

[Sie] ging auf die Trümmer des Altars zu, und räumte sie weg, um die verborgene Treppe zu finden, auf der sie mit ihrem Tarantelgefolge hinunterstieg. Die Sphinx fragte: "Was kommt plötzlicher als der Blitz?" (I, 308)

Fabel schlich sich zur Leiter und begab sich zu Arctur. "Monarch", sagte sie,"die Bösen tanzen, die Guten ruhn." (I, 308)

Her increasing speed is also reflected in the verb "eilen," which occurs twice in the closing stages of her mission:

Fabel entfernte sich, und eilte dem Hause zu. (I, 311)

Sophie sagte: "Eros, eile mit deiner Schwester zu deiner Geliebten. Bald seht ihr mich wieder."
 Fabel und Eros gingen mit ihrer Begleitung schnell hinweg. (I, 312)

The reader's sensation of accelerating time is repeatedly held in check, however, by passages such as the awakening of Atlas or the sacramental ceremony around the altar, in which narrative time suddenly broadens with respect to narrated time. We have noted in Chapter 1 how the proliferation of spatial detail in "Eros und Fabel" threatens to obscure the architecture of the tale. Here too, the need to linger over passages of considerable allegorical import impedes the temporal flow of the tale to such an extent that it is no longer possible to experience the kind of mounting excitement that characterized "Hyazinth und Rosenblüte."

On the other hand, it seems fairly evident that such considerations as reader excitement and the quickening of narrative suspense were relatively unimportant to Novalis. Indeed, he goes to some trouble to *counteract* any suspense as to the ultimate outcome of events. Throughout the tale, a whole series of prophetic events point to a happy finale. The song of the bird in Arcturus's throne room, the course of the moon drama, and Fabel's song in the kingdom of the Fates all point directly and with considerable specificity toward the final events. Arcturus's forecast at the conclusion of his card game is equally direct but more vague: "Es wird alles gut" (I, 293). Minor details such as the movement of the figures in the windows of Arcturus's palace and the appearance of the Phoenix through a crack in the Fates' cave presage the ending indirectly. In a similar vein, Fabel's first speech to Arcturus indicates the stages of her activity in advance: "Dreimal werde ich bitten, wenn ich zum vierten Male komme, so ist die Liebe vor der Tür" (I, 304). In none of these cases is there the slightest reason to doubt the authority of the speakers or the signs. The effect of all these prophecies is to make the reader absolutely certain of the outcome of the tale from the very beginning, and thereby to channel his attention to the mechanics of the process by which the final resolution is achieved. This technique belies the popular—and tenacious—notion that the Romantics' eyes were directed only toward the vast and shimmering reaches of the beyond. Novalis not only outlines a program for reachieving the Golden Age, but sees to it that the reader's attention is securely fastened on the *process* of this program rather than engaging itself in speculations as to the outcome.

Once again, however, with all due admiration for Novalis's good intentions, one may legitimately object that the pedagogical functions of the tale are rather uncomfortably wed with its aesthetic needs as a literary work of art. The sheer volume of material that Novalis incorporates into the closing phases of the tale produces such a slackening of narrative momentum that the reader, however attentive or well-disposed, simply begins to lose interest. In this last great work before his death, Novalis shows disturbing signs of losing control of his materials, of permitting the ingenious detail to supercede the requisites of the work as a whole. As brilliant as it is, "Eros und Fabel" betrays evidence of a literary mind in crisis. Here for once—and not only for once—the Romantic drive for totality fails to be adequately reconciled with the Romantic drive for unity.

At the conclusion, some sense of temporal momentum is regained as the various figures converge, singly or two by two, to form a grand ensemble at Arcturus's palace. For the first time, a number of spatial movements toward unity occur without the explicit direction of Fabel: Father Moon appears with his court, Sophie descends from the cupola with Arcturus, and the kingdom of the Fates rises up into the courtyard. These seemingly unmotivated developments reflect Novalis's thesis that the final elements of synthesis fall into place *automatically* once certain conditions are met:

Die *Anstrengung* überhaupt bringt nur, als indirecter, vorbereitender Reitz, eine Operation zu Stande. In der rechten Stimmung, die dadurch entstehn kann, gelingt alles von selbst. Der Mangel an mehreren, zugleich gegenwärtigen Ideen etc. rührt von Schwäche her. In der vollkommensten Stimmung sind alle Ideen gleich gegenwärtig—In dieser ist auch keine *Passion*, kein Affect möglich—In ihr ist man wahrhaft im Olymp—und die Welt zu unsern Füßen. Die Selbstbeherrschung geht in ihr von selbst von Statten. *Kurz alles scheint von selbst zu geschehen*—wenn das *rechte Medium* vorhanden ist—wenn das *Hinderniß gehoben wird*. (II, 609).

Once again, total spatial unification signifies the end of time in any normal sense of the word. One should not assume, however, that the characters are to settle down into a static eternity of perfection at the conclusion. Instead, the final condition is to be understood as a *synthesis of temporality and eternity*. In the *Allgemeine Brouillon*, Novalis postulates such a state as the highest ideal of self-consciousness: "Selbstb[ewußt]S[eyn] im größern Sinn ist eine Aufgabe—ein Ideal—es wäre *der* Zustand, *worinn* es keine Zeitfortschreitung gäbe[,] ein zeitloser—*beharrlicher* immer gleicher Zustand. (Ein Zustand, ohne Vergangenheit und Zukunft. und doch veränderlich.) Im ächten S[elbst]B[ewußt]S[eyn] wechselten wir blos—aber ohne *weiter* zu gehen" (III, 431). This state "without past and future, and yet changeable," may appear to be a purely theoretical construct that eludes empirical comprehension.[21] Nevertheless, the attempt to express such a state symbolically through its near equivalents in earthly experience produced some of the most familiar Romantic images, as we shall see in the case of Tieck. In "Eros und Fabel," the reintroduction of time into an essentially timeless state is accomplished through the *arts*, as the former agents of empirical temporality become converted into games or artistic instruments. Thus the realm of the Fates becomes a stage for Father Moon's dramas, Fabel uses the Fates' spindle to spin her own endless song, and the senseless polarity of darkness and light that characterized the sun's domination is banished into the black and white format of a chess board. Through these devices, time is experienced symbolically rather than directly; it becomes created reality rather than imposed necessity. The crucial mediating function of art, which we have noted repeatedly in the figure of Fabel, is here again apparent. In the world of change and transition, art offers a glimpse of timeless perfection, while in the world of timeless perfection it provides a diverting illusion of change.

The narrative concludes with the erotic union of Eros and Freya and Fabel's triumphant song. Strictly speaking, however, these events do not yet constitute the last step. Following the end of the narrative itself, the whole group is to follow Sophie into the temple to live there eternally and "guard the secret of the universe." It is characteristic of the gradual descent of the narrative perspective from Klingsohr's initial ominiscient viewpoint to the level of events in the tale itself that the entry into the temple and subsequent life there are presented as an (infallible) forecast by one of the characters, rather than as a summary report by the narrator on the order of the concluding lines of "Hyazinth und Rosenblüte." The distance between the narrator and the narrated events has vanished, and with it the sense of these events as past, even with respect to a fictional narrator. By the time Fabel returns to Arcturus's palace for the last time, our consciousness of the cozy group around the hearth at Schwaning's house has completely faded. It would be a severe shock, in fact, if after Fabel's final song the narrative were to turn back to this mundane situation with, for instance, a laudatory comment from Heinrich. What has happened here is a loss of the narrative *frame* that Enlightenment poetics would have favored and demanded. The concrete viewpoint, the carefully controlled and emphatically human perspective of the eighteenth century, gradually disappears in the course of "Eros und Fabel," until the reader is finally left suspended in a state of timeless abstraction, face to face, as it were, with the absolute. Only the quotation marks at the conclusion of Fabel's song remain as the last vestige of a narrative frame. A modern writer might have been tempted to discard even this imperceptible reminder of authorial presence:

> Gegründet ist das Reich der Ewigkeit,
> In Lieb' und Frieden endigt sich der Streit,
> Vorüber ging der lange Traum der Schmerzen,
> Sophie ist ewig Priesterin der Herzen." (I, 315)

IV

Between "Waldeinsamkeit" and Community
Time in the *Märchen* of Tieck

"Der blonde Eckbert"

Thoreau's observation that one cannot kill time without injuring eternity[1] would have pleased German Romantics. For the young Tieck in particular, whose brilliant imitative talents betrayed a certain lack of personal stability, the problem of boredom and misused time became something of a private obsession. In his first great novel, *William Lovell*, he presented ennui as the most conspicuous symptom of a superfluous and wasted existence. One year later, in "Der blonde Eckbert," the tedium and melancholy of a misspent life were no longer punishment enough in themselves. Here Tieck produced a supernatural agency, an injured eternity, capable of exposing unguessed depths of loneliness and alienation beneath the surface symptoms of monotony and discontent.

As one might suspect, the two spatial foci in "Der blonde Eckbert"—that is, Eckbert's castle and the old woman's hut—are characterized by two very different kinds of temporal experience. As a description of the situation at Eckbert's castle, the expression "killing time" is especially apt, for the life of the lonely couple is marked by estrangement from past, present, and future. The present reveals itself as an empty tedium, whose colorlessness, mediocrity, and depression seem to be reflected even in Eckbert's physical features: "Er war ohngefähr vierzig Jahr alt, kaum von mittlerer Größe, und kurze hellblonde Haare lagen schlicht und dicht an seinem blassen eingefallenen Gesichte" (9). Once again, durative verbs ("leben," "wohnen"), iterative temporal adverbs ("gewöhnlich," "selten," "häufig"), and the iterative conjunction "wenn" are employed to describe an essentially static condition:

Er lebte sehr ruhig für sich und war niemals in den Fehden seiner Nachbarn verwickelt.... [Eckbert und Bertha] klagten gewöhnlich darüber, daß der Himmel ihre Ehe mit keinen Kindern segnen wolle.... Nur selten wurde

Eckbert von Gästen besucht, und wenn es auch geschah, so wurde ihretwegen fast nichts in dem gewöhnlichen Gange des Lebens geändert. . . . Nur wenn er allein war, bemerkte man an ihm eine gewisse Verschlossenheit, eine stille zurückhaltende Melancholie. (9)

If the present is experienced as a cheerless, unchanging continuum, the future appears equally bleak, for the couple has no children who could relieve the monotony of their old age and afford them some sense of renewal. Finally—and most crucially for the development of the tale—they are estranged from the past. Eckbert's lack of knowledge of Bertha's past and his own is revealed dramatically at the end of the tale; Bertha's alienation from her childhood is evident from the very beginning. Despite her admonition to take her narrative seriously, the whole setting in which the story of her past is unfolded is one of convivial detachment. The fireside coziness, the late hour, the cameraderie of the three friends all contribute to an atmosphere of comfortable congeniality in which the terrible events of Bertha's past seem remote and less than real. At one point in her tale, Bertha herself remarks on the sense of temporal distance between her present condition and the past: "Ihr lächelt! wir sind jetzt freilich alle über diese Zeit der Jugend hinüber" (17). Moreover, her characterization of the tale as mere "chatting" (21) betrays, as we have noted earlier, a reluctance on her part to confront and come to grips with the guilt of her youth. Although, on the one hand, Bertha's tale is intended as an honest confession, on the other it represents an attempt to consign the past to storytelling time. This ambivalence in motives only deepens and compounds the guilt of the unhappy couple.

If Eckbert and Bertha appear to be suspended in an empty, sterile present which denies the past and ignores the future, the valley of birches and its inhabitants represent the ideal of perfect timelessness, an eternal summer of abundance and tranquillity. The old woman and her pets are immune to death. The dog that Bertha has left to starve and the bird that she strangles reappear unscathed at the end of the tale, and the old woman in the guise of Walther survives Eckbert's murderous assault. For these figures, the passage of time simply does not exist. While Bertha uses the past tense to relate the story of her youth, Walther pointedly refers to her experiences with the *present* tense: "Edle Frau, ich danke Euch, ich kann mir Euch recht vorstellen, mit dem seltsamen Vogel, und wie Ihr den kleinen *Strohmian* füttert" (21).[2]

There is, however, a remarkable and important element of change in this utopian eternity:

Indem ich [die Alte] so betrachtete, überlief mich mancher Schauer: denn ihr Gesicht war in einer ewigen Bewegung, indem sie dazu wie vor Alter mit dem Kopfe schüttelte, so daß ich durchaus nicht wissen konnte, wie ihr eigentliches Aussehen beschaffen war. . . . in der Nacht wachte ich einigemal auf, und dann hörte ich die Alte husten und mit dem Hunde sprechen, und den Vogel dazwischen, der im Traum zu sein schien, und immer nur einzelne Worte von seinem Liede sang. Das machte mit den Birken, die vor dem Fenster rauschten, und mit dem Gesang einer entfernten Nachtigall ein . . . wunderbares Gemisch. (15)

Here again we encounter Novalis's ideal condition without past and future, and yet changeable. The strange fluidity of the old woman's face, the changing colors of the bird's feathers, and the tremulous mixture of sound in the night reflect a condition of endless variation, a synthesis of temporality and eternity in which infinite changeability produces no essential change. It was primarily this aspect of "Waldeinsamkeit" which caught the imagination of the Early Romantics and launched a whole series of literary clichés. From Bertha's experience at the old woman's hut derive the all but inexhaustible stores of gurgling brooks, rustling leaves, mill wheels, spinning wheels, and flickering flames that fill the pages of Romantic literature. Like the Indian ragas that recently captivated a new generation of quasi Romantics, these visual and auditory effects superimpose an interminable stream of variations and modifications on a basically unchanging foundation. The resultant blend of time and timelessness may well be termed one of the most characteristic aspects of Romantic experience.

As we saw in Chapter 2, this serene, harmonious utopia is reserved for the childlike and selfless. It is Bertha's undoing that the biological necessity of growing up introduces a totally foreign element of time into her existence at the old woman's hut. In addition to the shimmering continuum of activities at the hut, a process of genuine, irreversible change becomes evident, demarcated by the adverbs "jetzt" and "nun":

Vier Jahre hatte ich so mit der Alten gelebt, und ich mochte ohngefähr zwölf Jahr alt sein, als sie mir endlich mehr vertraute und mir ein Geheimnis entdeckte. . . . Sie trug mir jetzt das Geschäft auf, in ihrer Abwesenheit diese Eier zu nehmen. (16)

Es war mir jetzt lieber, wenn ich allein war, denn alsdann war ich selbst die Gebieterin im Hause. (17)

Ich war jetzt vierzehn Jahr alt, und es ist ein Unglück für den Menschen, daß er seinen Verstand nur darum bekömmt, um die Unschuld seiner Seele zu verlieren. (17)

The advent of puberty produces on the one hand a longing for erotic adventure that the pleasant domestic solitude of the hut cannot satisfy, and on the other hand a fatal understanding of the options of escape.

The exigencies of human temporality thus lift Bertha out of the idyllic timelessness of the valley; and each successive act of self-liberation on her part leads to a greater degree of temporal estrangement. Following her hasty departure from the valley, she returns to her home village only to find that her parents have died. The possibility of establishing some sort of continuity with her former existence is thus immediately destroyed. The only remaining link with the past is the magic bird, whose insistent reproach acts as a voice of conscience, pleading with her to make her peace with the past through repentance and acceptance of her guilt. This, however, she is unwilling or unable to do. Rather than confronting the past and reassimilating it through atonement—her only hope of regeneration in the present—she takes the easy way out and strangles the voice of conscience.[3]

At this point, Bertha finds that the present, too, has become poisoned: "Jetzt wandelte mich oft eine Furcht vor meiner Aufwärterin an, ich dachte an mich selbst zurück und glaubte, daß sie mich auch einst berauben oder wohl gar ermorden könne. —Schon lange kannt ich einen jungen Ritter, der mir überaus gefiel, ich gab ihm meine Hand—und hiermit, Herr Walther, is meine Geschichte geendigt" (21). The person who cannot come to grips with his own guilt is all the more inclined to project it onto other people. This psychological insight provides the most important key to Eckbert's and Bertha's actions in the latter part of "Der blonde Eckbert" and, at the same time, accounts for their temporal alienation: the unassimilated and unredeemed past leads inevitably to anxiety and estrangement in the present. Thus Bertha is consumed with the fear that the servant, like herself, could steal and murder to gain possession of the jewels. Furthermore, the curious abruptness with which Bertha changes the subject here, moving without transition from her fear of the servant to her marriage to Eckbert, suggests a hidden connection between the two topics. It would appear that Bertha fled into matrimony with Eckbert as a means of self-protection, in order to bring to a halt the widening aura of mistrust around her and her increasing sense of isolation. The union of Eckbert and Bertha is at best a stopgap existence, an empty monotony whose single virtue is that it prevents matters from getting any worse. But it also prevents matters from getting any better. The couple remains suspended in an unchanging state of inadequacy, withdrawn from the world and from their own pasts.

It is illuminating to compare the second phase of Bertha's development with Hyazinth's. Both characters leave an idyllic but limited situation in search of a higher ideal, in Bertha's case the handsome storybook knight, in Hyazinth's the "Mother of All Things." In the famous paralipomenon to *Die Lehrlinge zu Sais*, Hyazinth lifts the veil of the virgin to find "—Wunder des Wunders—sich selbst" (I, 110). Bertha, too, finds herself in the knight she marries (Eckbert)—but the difference between the two tales is enormous. In finding himself, Hyazinth achieves the highest state of self-knowledge, which is simultaneously absolute knowledge of the universe. Hence in the final version Novalis could substitute Rosenblüte as the embodiment of the wholly internalized external world. What Bertha finds, on the other hand, is pensive, impoverished Eckbert, her narcissistic double, whose lack of self-knowledge is as great as her own. Rather than joining together to form a perfect, all-encompassing unity, they merely reaffirm each other in their mutual inadequacy.

Up to now we have viewed the temporal estrangement of Eckbert and Bertha as the result of their inability to accept the painful consequences of self-awareness. If this were the only point to "Der blonde Eckbert," the tale would amount to little more than an elaborate and ingenious parable illustrating Plato's dictum, "Know thyself." The greatness of "Der blonde Eckbert" derives, however, from a deeper-lying ambiguity: while Eckbert and Bertha are unquestionably blameworthy, the moral authority that judges and condemns them is by no means infallible itself. Midway through her narrative, Bertha drops an incidental remark that proves in the end to be of unexpected and crucial significance. Speaking of her dreams of princes and knights, she tells Eckbert and Walther: "Wenn ich mich so vergessen hatte, konnte ich ordentlich betrübt werden, wenn ich wieder aufschaute, und mich in der kleinen Wohnung antraf. Übrigens, wenn ich meine Geschäfte tat, bekümmerte sich die Alte nicht weiter um mein Wesen" (18). The old woman's exclusive concern for the externals of Bertha's life (that is, her domestic activities) rather than for her internal development accounts for the angry and uncomprehending question that the old woman hurls at Eckbert at the conclusion of the tale: "Warum verließ sie mich tückisch? Sonst hätte sich alles gut und schön geendet, ihre Probezeit war ja schon vorüber" (26). Whatever this trial period may have been—the old woman is probably referring to the four years before she revealed the secret of the jewelled eggs to Bertha—one thing is very clear: the real trial period was *not* past. Bertha failed the final test, that of resisting the inclination toward greed and egocentricity that her adolescence imposed on her. That the old woman in her role of teacher and guardian is unaware of this internal struggle betrays a fatal irony: the moral authority that wields the power of life and death over Eckbert and Bertha is omnipotent, but not omniscient. Possibly this circumstance is responsible for the instinctive feeling of many readers that Eckbert and Bertha are not entirely guilty despite their repeated acts of betrayal and murder. By placing the witch in the role of law-giver, Tieck inverts the moral scheme of the folk fairy tale and produces an ethical confusion that is utterly alien to the traditional tale. The *Volksmärchen* presents a "naive emotional ethic,"[4] a predictable and clear-cut system of justice in which the hero is automatically rewarded and the villain automatically punished. In "Der blonde Eckbert," however, the hero is punished for reasons which are largely beyond his conscious control, and the traditional villain becomes the agent of moral order—but of a moral order that is devoid of compassion and understanding. The old woman judges and condemns Bertha and Eckbert from her own viewpoint of reality, which is founded on the temporal situation in the valley of birches and has no provision for the contingencies of human temporality. Her only advice to the child Bertha is a vague platitude about the danger of leaving the right path (17), scarcely the kind of firm and explicit moral backing that Bertha needs in her struggle with selfishness and greed.[5]

In the figure of the old woman one may detect traces of the negative theodicy that occasionally emerged in Early Romanticism as an emphatic reversal of the conception of a universe ruled by harmony, order, and love. Tieck's *William Lovell* and *Die Nachtwachen des Bonaventura*, to name the most familiar and extreme examples, culminate in the recognition of a god who is neither rational nor loving, but "incompetent and malevolent to boot."[6] While elements of this unhappy conception of God may certainly be found in the old woman, it would nevertheless be stretching the point to characterize her out of hand as irrational and demonic. Eckbert perishes, after all, because his own conscience acknowledges the validity of the old woman's accusations. Nevertheless, she is a flawed magistrate of justice. Though she enforces the laws of community, responsibility, and self-awareness, she herself is too remote, too preoccupied, too often out in the woods, as it were, while Bertha is left to her own devices. Through her unrealistic assessment of Bertha's character, the old woman implicates herself, however slightly, in the chain of betrayals and murders—and Bertha is the one who must take the punishment.[7]

In light of these shortcomings on the part of the old woman, it seems to me that the idyll of "Waldeinsamkeit" is in need of somewhat closer scrutiny than it has traditionally received. Of the critics who have written on "Der blonde Eckbert," two of the most perceptive, Virginia L. Rippere and Gerhard Haeuptner, contend that the period of Bertha's stay at the hut represents some sort of preparation for her future life. Rippere views the domestic routine at the hut as Bertha's "adaptation to life in society,"[8] and Haeuptner interprets the idyll as a period of latency in which the productive tension of "waiting and yet waiting for nothing" must not be resolved too soon.[9] These assertions are, however, very much open to question. It may be argued that Bertha's existence in the valley in fact prepares her for nothing more than further existence in the valley. Certainly this seems to have been the intention of the old woman, whose lack of provision for Bertha's future growth is revealed on three accounts: her assumption that Bertha's trial period is over; her disregard for Bertha's internal development once the ostensible trial period has been absolved; and, finally, her dumbfoundedness at Bertha's departure. Furthermore, it seems to me that Bertha's existence at the hut provides a questionable model for her future "socialization," to use Rippere's term. Despite the generally useful social training that Bertha receives (for example, the domestic crafts and the power of self-limitation), it is nevertheless a rather special sort of society in which she finds herself.[10] The word "Waldeinsamkeit" combines, after all, two distinct elements: it denotes both isolation and forest, the experience of lonesome solitude and the knowledge of secure enclosure in the arms of nature. For the young Tieck, the "introvert who tried to play the extrovert,"[11] Bertha's life at the hut must indeed have seemed like a vision of paradise, where one could enjoy the bliss of loneliness and still be comfortably integrated into a snug little society. There is no evidence in the text, however, that the routine at the hut is intended to serve as training for Bertha's future life in a more realistic society. Although the idyll of "Waldeinsamkeit" does not absolutely preclude the possibility of a happy, fruitful adult life, it does not provide for a transition to adulthood either. In the final analysis, it too is a dead-end situation, a self-contained little wonderland for the very old and the very young. Because of the lack of guidance from the old woman, Bertha never achieves true maturity, but spends the remainder of her life in a state of emotional adolescence, constantly fleeing from her childhood.[12] There is thus a good deal of unwitting irony in her aside to Eckbert and Walther in the midst of the description of her adolescent daydreams: "Ihr lächelt! wir sind jetzt freilich alle über diese Zeit der Jugend hinüber" (17).

Despite her inadequacy at this crucial juncture in Bertha's life, however, the old woman consistently maintains her function of upholding the laws of interpersonal trust, communication, and responsibility, and it is in this capacity that she returns, many years later, in the guise of Walther. Viewed in rough outline, the temporal structure of "Der blonde Eckbert" takes the form of three test situations, bridged by indefinite stretches of time and capped by the final condemnation and execution. As we have seen in Chapter 2, each of these test situations consists of an attempt at confession or human interaction which is invariably foiled by Eckbert's (or Bertha's) withdrawal and mistrust. The first, Bertha's narrative of her past, comprises about two-thirds of the text. The second, Eckbert's ill-fated friendship with Hugo, covers no more than a page and a half. The final test, the interlude with the peasant, takes up a scant three sentences. This increasing compression of narrative time is primarily responsible for the all but dizzying sense of acceleration which marks the concluding pages of the tale. In spatial terms, each of these episodes represents a penetration and destruction of the defensively insular existence that Eckbert and Bertha have established at their little castle. At the same time, the two most important interactions—those with Walther and Hugo—involve a breakdown of the corresponding temporal insularity in which the couple has lived. The confessions that Walther and Hugo provoke may be viewed as an attempt to reintegrate the past into the present. When Eckbert asks Hugo "if he could possibly love a murderer" (24), he implicitly acknowledges that his present existence and his past deeds cannot be divorced from each other, and that Hugo must accept him not only for everything he is at the present, but for everything he has been and done. Moreover, the confession as an act of trust and humility reestablishes the moral covenant that was violated through Eckbert's suspicion and hatred toward Walther. From a temporal standpoint, the confession thus has two aspects: it consolidates the past with the present under the sign of guilt, and it provides for redemption of the present through renewed recognition of moral law. In their role of furthering friendship to the point of confession, Walther and Hugo serve as Eckbert's mentors; they are closely related to the figure of the emissary in the eighteenth-century *Bundesroman*.[13] Despite the seemingly vindictive nature of their mission, it must not be overlooked that they offer Eckbert his only hope of returning to a moral community of trust and generosity. And it is Eckbert himself who repeatedly dooms this project through an immediate reversion to bad faith: by hastily assuring Walther that he has had no cause whatsoever to rue his marriage to Bertha; by sensing a conspiracy between Hugo and the elderly knight; by attempting to buy the good will of the peasant with a monetary tip. It is only *after* these acts of bad faith that the punishment sets in, and the punishment, appropriately enough, consists of an immediate objective verification of Eckbert's sense of doubt and suspicion.

The division of the tale into three test episodes provides another parallel with the folk fairy tale, in which the hero is often subjected to three identical or very similar contests.[14] As in the folk tale, these episodes are distinctly isolated in the flow of narrated time. Between the murder of Walther and the friendship with Hugo, for instance, lies a stretch of time which is characterized only by the indefinite expression "for a long time": "Eckbert lebte nun eine lange Zeit in der größten Einsamkeit. . . . Die Ermordung seines Freundes stand ihm unaufhörlich vor Augen, er lebte unter ewigen innern Vorwürfen" (23). Similarly, the duration of time between the experience with Hugo and the beginning of Eckbert's journey remains totally nondetermined, although one may assume from the state of Eckbert's mind that it lasts no longer than a few days. By means of these indefinite connecting stretches, the episodes become dissociated from each other and more or less independent. Each represents a fresh attack and a tentative close, as the same process repeats itself threefold.

As was the case with the witch figure, these parallels to the folk fairy tale only serve to underscore the fundamental difference between Tieck's tale and the naive folk narrative. In the latter, the hero invariably wins all three contests and is rewarded with glory and fame; Eckbert, on the other hand, undergoes a triple failure and execution. Moreover, the opponent against whom he contends is nothing so satisfyingly tangible as a six-headed troll, but rather his own dimly sensed drive toward egocentricity and isolation. Walther and Hugo function only as instigators of this internal contest and as prosecuting judges. Eckbert's folly is precisely that he takes them to be his actual opponents. If the battle lines here are vaguely drawn, the system of rewards and punishments is no less confusing. Although the hero of the folk tale is to receive the hand of the princess if he wins and ignominious death if he loses, "Der blonde Eckbert" depicts only the consequences of defeat. There is little assurance that Eckbert would be rewarded if he were to triumph over his self-delusion and his inclination toward withdrawal. Indeed, his "ascent" to complete self-knowledge and objectivity at the conclusion of the tale produces an unbearable burden of guilt. No matter which way the contest falls, Eckbert must lose. Prolonged self-delusion is impossible; self-knowledge is annihilating. In the end, the tests themselves are not tests at all, but punishment for a life in which too few questions are asked and too may apprehensions ignored.

It is the grim role of the old woman, then, to subject Eckbert and Bertha to these foredoomed tests, to offer them possibilities of redemption which they are incapable of fulfilling: the idyll of "Waldeinsamkeit" for Bertha, the friendship with Walther and Hugo for Eckbert. And the horrible alternative to redemption is damnation. The middle ground, the uneasy balance of semiexistence that Eckbert and Bertha have established at their castle, must be destroyed in any event. From beginning to end, the tale consists of a relentless stripping away of the false securities of Eckbert's and Bertha's existence and a revelation of the roots of their alienation.

Through a gradual shift in narrative perspective, the reader is forcefully maneuvered into experiencing this process along with Eckbert and Bertha, as they move from the illusion of security to the desperate loneliness of their deaths. The opening paragraphs are full of lean, simple prose provided by a knowledgeable (though not, strictly speaking, omniscient) narrator who is so much in control of his materials as to permit himself a lengthy aside to the reader:

Es gibt Stunden, in denen es den Menschen ängstigt, wenn er vor seinem Freunde ein Geheimnis haben soll, was er bis dahin oft mit vieler Sorgfalt verborgen hat, die Seele fühlt dann einen unwiderstehlichen Trieb, sich ganz mitzuteilen, dem Freunde auch das Innerste aufzuschließen, damit er um so mehr unser Freund werde. In diesen Augenblicken geben sich die zarten Seelen einander zu erkennen, und zuweilen geschieht es wohl auch, daß einer vor der Bekanntschaft des andern zurückschreckt. (9–10).

Despite the ominous ring of this generalization, the reader feels himself to be in the congenial presence of an intelligent, reliable observer who invites him to share in the contemplation of an enduring psychological truth.

This comfortable sensation of elevation above the subject matter at hand is maintained as Bertha assumes the narrative voice in her fireside account of the events of her past. The perspective of the hearth was a familiar convention in eighteenth-century fiction, where it was used to create considerable authorial distance and the opportunity for ironic commentary on the part of the narrator. In "Der blonde Eckbert," however, the irony eventually doubles back on the narrator herself; for her apparent detachment from the events of her past proves in the end to be illusory. With Walther's mention of the dog's name, the past unexpectedly becomes present reality, and at the same time both past and present become too enigmatic to bear. If a genuine confession reunites past and present for the sake of clarity, objectivity, and renewed moral resolve, Bertha's abortive confession is rewarded by a wedding of present and past that defies reason, maims consciousness, and throws Bertha back upon herself to die alone and helpless. It is not guilt that ultimately kills Bertha, but the knowledge that a stranger knows her history better than she herself, that her existence has been integrated and understood on terms that are utterly incomprehensible to her: "'Lieber Mann', fing sie an, 'ich muß dir etwas entdecken, das mich fast um meinen Verstand gebracht hat, das meine Gesundheit zerrüttet. . . . Wie hängt dieser Mensch dann mit meinem Schicksal zusammen? . . . Ein gewaltiges Entsetzen befiel mich, als mir ein fremder Mensch so zu meinen Erinnerungen half'" (22).

Following the collapse of Bertha's credibility as an observer of her own past, the reader finds himself increasingly drawn into Eckbert's immediate experience. With this narrowing of narrative perspective, the analytic and generalizing voice of the omniscient narrator gradually vanishes.[15] What remains is a direct confrontation with the maze of uncertainties that fill Eckbert's mind. In contrast to the opening of the tale, there is no longer any sense of relaxed, leisurely reflection or self-assured elevation above present and past experience. As the existential props of wife, friends, and home are knocked out from under him one by one, Eckbert finds it increasingly impossible to reach beyond the immediate present for some sort of explanation of his predicament. His ceaseless spatial mobility reflects a frantic attempt to escape this entrapment in a meaningless present and to reestablish himself in a new setting, a new perspective, from which everything might yet make sense: "Wie ein unruhiger Geist eilte er jetzt von Gemach zu Gemach, kein Gedanke hielt ihm stand, er verfiel von entsetzlichen Vorstellungen auf noch entsetzlichere, und kein Schlaf kam in seine Augen" (24–25). Ultimately this frenzied mobility degenerates into blind flight. Despite Eckbert's pathetic hope that traveling will help him to "order his thoughts" (25), the headlong dash through space serves only to divest his present experience of any meaning other than pure motion.

It is in the midst of this darkest and most hopeless subjectivity—which the reader has been forced to share—that the terrible epiphany occurs, a flash of objectivity eclipsing anything that the narrator himself or any of the characters has been able to offer. Here at last is the explanation that provides Eckbert with the meaning of his existence, but that meaning is precisely that his existence has been utterly senseless, that his present condition of desperate loneliness represents, indeed, the essence of his entire life. In the light of the old woman's revelations, the opening state of seeming objectivity, clarity, and control is retroactively exposed as a fraud. All in all, it is not a very edifying conclusion. If the interactions with Walther and Hugo have suggested the possibility of revitalizing the present by coming to terms with the past, the final episode reveals the past as beyond redemption and the present therefore as doomed to meaninglessness. One can, in fact, scarcely avoid the conclusion that the old woman has unnecessarily tormented Eckbert by confronting him with Walther and Hugo. If he has condemned himself for once and for all through his greed and unwitting incest in marrying Bertha, why then must he be forced again and again to reaffirm his guilt with Walther and Hugo? The old woman seems bent upon flattening Eckbert before she adminsters the final *coup de grâce*, a rather sadistic procedure for the agent of moral justice. Once again one is struck by the ethical ambiguity of "Der blonde Eckbert." It is true that Eckbert is guilty on a number of counts, ranging from greed to withdrawal and self-delusion, but the objective truth that is to serve as his punishment is withheld too long, and for reasons that reflect badly on the ostensible upholder of the law. Small wonder, then, that so many readers have expressed misgivings or even outright indignation at the conclusion of the tale. After having followed Eckbert through his unhappy attempts to find friendship and security, one is justifiably incensed at the revelation that these attempts are foredoomed and futile, that all the best intentions in the world cannot save Eckbert from the final calamity. All too often, critics have charged Tieck with shabby sensationalism or arbitrary manipulation of the plot to supply a "neat" ending.[16] On a deeper level of response, however, their dissatisfaction derives not from Tieck's supposed inadequacy as a storyteller, but from his pessimistic theology, which admits no hope of deliverance from original sin and presents man as a helpless victim of the merciless and fallible agents of moral order.[17]

The problem of time and temporality emerges, then, as one of the central concerns of this difficult and complex tale. A brief summary of the role of time in "Der blonde Eckbert" will, I think, be useful before we proceed to Tieck's later tale. The idyll of "Waldeinsamkeit" represents a utopian situation in which temporality and eternity, becoming and being, are fused. This synthesis is most clearly evident in the old woman's face, the bird's feathers, and the whispering birches, which assume endlessly varying forms without experiencing any essential change. Beyond the reaches of the old woman's valley, the synthesis of time and eternity is not so easily achieved. It is, indeed, the misfortune of human existence that the two components of the synthesis may become disconnected, so that one or the other may be experienced, but not both simultaneously. And as separate experiences, they spell existential impoverishment. Change devoid of continuity leads to confinement in the immediate present and the loss of one's temporal bearings. Bertha's adolescence, for example, propels her into a process of change that cuts the past out from under her and threatens to poison the present. Conversely, timelessness devoid of change leads to stagnation and monotony, as is the case with Eckbert's and Bertha's barren life at the opening of the tale. This fatal disjunction of time and timelessness is not, however, a necessary and inevitable consequence of human existence. While the possibility of renewed synthesis is never realized in the course of the tale, it is at least implied in the repeated test situations. Continuity in the midst of growth and change is still possible, one may assume, if the past is acknowledged and assimilated into the present, if, to be more specific, one accepts the burden of his own identity and recognizes that past guilt must remain present reality until it is resolved through repentance and permanent conversion to moral action.

In contrast to the original synthesis of time and timelessness, which Bertha was able to accept passively, the new, and higher, synthesis can be achieved only through an act of moral will, an active reintegration of one's personality in time. Correspondingly, as we noted in Chapter 2, the naive synthesis of inside and outside space is to be reachieved on a higher level through an integration of one's inner self with the external world of nature and other human beings. Rather than attempt this difficult and uncompromising self-appraisal, Eckbert and Bertha settle for the more bearable of the other two alternatives. Because time and change without continuity result in existential chaos, they establish the artificial timelessness of their own dreary "Waldeinsamkeit" at Eckbert's castle. When they are put to the test, moreover, it becomes increasingly evident that they are fundamentally incapable of achieving a true synthesis. As we observed earlier, both Eckbert and Bertha are split between two opposing drives that operate at a subconscious level. The one drive dictates responsibility, generosity, and selflessness—the conditions for renewed synthesis—while the other leads to greed, self-protectiveness, and withdrawal. It is the downfall of Eckbert and Bertha that this second drive, which eludes all conscious supervision and control, consistently dominates their actions, beginning with Bertha's flight from the valley and culminating in their narcissistic marriage and their ill-fated friendships with Walther and Hugo. Yet, and I think the point is worth emphasizing, Eckbert and Bertha are not necessarily Everyman. There is nothing in the tale to justify the gloomy assumption that all men are similarly predisposed toward lovelessness and greed. Thus it is difficult to accept the moral that Ralph Tymms derives from the tale: "If any conclusion can be drawn from the story, it is that man is perhaps happiest, and certainly most free from delusion, if he keeps to himself, and avoids both friends and spouse; if not, he will risk deception and, consequently, subsequent disillusionment, by becoming involved in the greed of others (the fateful aggression against nature and its riches, which must be horribly punished by the unspecified dark powers of fate, or nature)."[18]

"Der Runenberg"

Despite her failure to recognize and accommodate the natural rhythm of human life, the old woman in "Der blonde Eckbert" still functions, by and large, as the representative of a unified natural world. Her counterpart in "Der Runenberg," the mysterious *Waldweib* who reappears throughout the tale in various guises, represents a domain whose restricted character is unquestionable. Here the rift between "Waldeinsamkeit" and human temporality has become absolute. The woman of the forest presides over a world that not only fails to acknowledge the validity of organic growth, but denies it emphatically. The confrontation between stone realm and plant realm is not least of all a confrontation between two distinct and antithetical modes of temporal experience.

What the plant world has to offer in the way of temporal experience is most clearly stated in the song Christian's father sings near the end of the tale:

> Sieh die zarten Blüten keimen,
> Wie sie aus sich selbst erwachen,
> Und wie Kinder aus den Träumen
> Dir entgegen lieblich lachen.
>
> Ihre Farbe ist im Spielen
> Zugekehrt der goldnen Sonne,
> Deren heißen Kuß zu fühlen,
> Das ist ihre höchste Wonne:
>
> An den Küssen zu verschmachten,
> Zu vergehn in Lieb und Wehmut;
> Also stehn, die eben lachten,
> Bald verwelkt in stiller Demut.
>
> Das ist ihre höchste Freude,
> Im Geliebten sich verzehren,
> Sich im Tode zu verklären,
> Zu vergehn in süßem Leide. (79)

The point of the song is, of course, that human beings should follow the example of the plants, shaping their lives around the pivotal and ecstatic moment of blossoming. Everything which precedes this moment is mere preparation and play; the awakening buds are no more than half-conscious, smiling "like children in their dreams." And even these dreamy smiles are already directed, as if mesmerized, toward the Sun, under whose hot and insistent kisses the buds ultimately open into a state of rapturous self-fulfillment—and self-sacrifice. The culmination of their brief existence is simultaneously the beginning of their decline. Consumed and transfigured through the moment of fullest blossoming, they wither away, releasing their spirit in the form of intoxicating fragrance:

> Dann ergießen sie die Düfte,
> Ihre Geister, mit Entzücken,
> Es berauschen sich die Lüfte
> Im balsamischen Erquicken. (79)

The sun may be viewed here as the radiant life-force that informs, quickens, and finally consumes the flowers. At the point of most complete saturation with this life-force, the purpose of their existence is fulfilled, and they die willingly, even passionately. It is characteristic of the unorthodox piety of the plains that there is no suggestion here of Christian transcendence or a heavenly reward following death.[19]

In contrast to the organic cycle of growth, maturation, and decay—about which I will have more to say presently—the stone realm represents a world of changeless forms. The motif of supertemporality appears in several different aspects. The most obvious of these is the nature of stone itself, which may wear away or crumble, but remains substantially unaltered through the passage of time. Further, most of the beings and objects that populate the mountains are described as old or ancient, and in a positive sense that would scarcely be possible in the plant world. It is difficult, for example, to imagine anyone speaking reverently of an old flower.[20] The ancient ruins on Rune Mountain shimmer in the moonlight (65); Christian expects to discover many a wonder from olden times on the mountain (66); the Stranger promises Christian that he will find ancient friends there (66); Christian peers through the window into an old spacious hall (67); and the mysterious woman sings longingly of the ancients, the deities of the mountain realm who have retreated from sight (67). The insistence with which the words "old" and "ancient" are repeated in these three pages, as well as the evident emotional impact that they exert on Christian, indicates that the adjectives have considerably more than a neutral, descriptive meaning. Oldness, the resistance to the passage of time, provides an intimation of *timelessness*. The ancient forms offer Christian a first glimpse into a world in which temporality is little more than an illusion. In the figure of the woman in the castle, the motif of timelessness becomes explicit: "Sie schien nicht den Sterblichen anzugehören, so groß, so mächtig waren ihre Glieder, so streng ihr Gesicht" (67). Much later in the tale, the tablet that this unearthly beauty hands Christian appears utterly unchanged, in pointed contrast to the deterioration that he and Elizabeth and their friends have undergone in the nine or ten years of his life in the village:

"Jahre sind verflossen, daß ich von hier hinunterstieg, unter die Kinder hinein; die damals hier spielten, sind heute dort ernsthaft in der Kirche; ich trat auch in das Gebäude, aber heut ist Elisabeth nicht mehr ein blühendes kindliches Mädchen, ihre Jugend ist vorüber, ich kann nicht mit der Sehnsucht wie damals den Blick ihrer Augen aufsuchen: *so habe ich mutwillig ein hohes ewiges Glück aus der Acht gelassen, um ein vergängliches und zeitliches zu gewinnen.*" (78; emphasis added)

It would appear, then, that the stone realm is intended to represent a world of perpetuity, the plant realm a world of temporality as manifested in growth and decay. In fact, the situation is rather more complicated. There is an element of timelessness in the plant world itself: although the life of the individual organism is transitory and brief, the species endures unchanged. Sixteen years before *Die Welt als Wille und Vorstellung*, Tieck entertained Schopenhauerian assumptions: the individual is merely the fleeting phenomenon in which the timeless Idea of the species manifests itself. Thus one tulip produces another tulip; Christian becomes a gardener like his father. This subordination of the individual to the collective, which we have already noted in the spatial organization of the plant world, is implicit in the sermon that Christian hears upon arriving in the village. The priest speaks not only of the preservation of the human race through the annual harvest, but derives the eternal nature of Holy Communion itself from the fact that God's love perpetually supplies a fresh source of sustenance in bread: "Der Gesang war eben beendigt und der Priester hatte seine Predigt begonnen, von den Wohltaten Gottes in der Ernte: wie seine Güte alles speiset und sättigt was lebt, wie wunderbar im Getreide für die Erhaltung des Menschengeschlechts gesorgt sei, wie die Liebe Gottes sich unaufhörlich im Brote mitteile und der andächtige Christ so ein unvergängliches Abendmahl feiern könne" (70). In this context, the idea of bread from heaven is given a rather pragmatic twist: the preservation of the species mankind is ensured through the preservation of the species wheat. To judge from the priest's sermon and the later pronouncements of Christian's father, the Christian piety of the village seems quite generally to be contaminated with reminiscences of pagan vegetative cults.[21]

There is, however, another element of timelessness in the plant world, quite apart from the participation of the individual in the eternal species.[22] The ecstasy that the plants experience in blossoming represents a momentary transcendence of individuality very similar to the "cosmic moments" which Gotthilf Heinrich von Schubert was to describe—with a diction that frequently echoes the song of Christian's father—in his *Ahndungen einer allgemeinen Geschichte des Lebens*, a few years after the publication of "Der Runenberg": "Alle Dinge, wenn sie in der glühendsten Vermählung mit dem Ganzen, ein Universum geworden sind, werden von einem mächtigen Lebensathem ergriffen, und dieses Ergriffenwerden, das Nachklingen jenes ewigen Wehens erscheint ihnen als höchster Genuß. Sie vergehen, oder die individuelle Kraft in ihnen wird geschwächt, je mächtiger sie ein Ganzes, ein Organ des Weltgeistes werden."[23] Through the climactic experiences of blossoming or reproduction, the individual, plant or man, is united with the eternal life-force. The temporal arc of organic growth peaks precisely at the instant in which temporality is transcended and the living creature partakes of timelessness.

By the same token, the stone world itself accommodates a certain measure of temporality. As was the case with "Waldeinsamkeit," the rustling of the trees, the murmuring of the brook, the changing configurations of the clouds provide a diverting sense of variation and novelty in this world of essentially unchanging forms. Time here is expressed first of all through movement, usually of a periodic kind. Thus the woman in the castle is described as moving back and forth:

Er sah dem Scheine nach, und entdeckte, daß er in einen alten geräumigen Saal blicken konnte, der wunderlich verziert von mancherlei Gesteinen und Kristallen in vielfältigen Schimmern funkelte, die sich geheimnisvoll von dem wandelnden Lichte durcheinanderbewegten, welches eine große weibliche Gestalt trug, die sinnend im Gemache auf und nieder ging. (67)

Er wagte kaum zu atmen, als sie nach und nach alle Hüllen löste; nackt schritt sie endlich auf und nieder. (68)

Similarly, the magic tablet itself oscillates between blinding radiance and soothing color tones: "Zuweilen war, nachdem der Schimmer ihm entgegenspielte, der Jüngling schmerzhaft geblendet, dann wieder besänftigten grüne und blau spielende Scheine sein Auge" (68). This quality of projecting quite different appearances at different times is reiterated in the figure of the *Waldweib*, who manifests herself variously as a majestic woman, a strange man, an ugly old woman, and even, in her most diffuse form, as the trees and streams of the forest. If the characteristic experience of time in the plant world was a linear, irreversible development through maturation and decay, time in the stone world is an illusion produced through the play of external forms, which may repeat themselves or reverse the sequence of their appearance or, as is the case with the leaves of the trees or the water of the brook, assume an endless variety of configurations through constant motion. In any event, there exists a reality beneath or within the animated surface phenomena that does *not* change: the tree remains the same despite the movement of its leaves; the brook remains a brook no matter what diverse forms the ripples and currents that flow through it may momentarily assume; and the tablet itself presents a figure that remains fixed and immutable despite the kaleidoscopic colors and lights that it emits.

In effect, then, *both* realms offer a fusion of time and timelessness. In the temporal world of organic life, timelessness is achieved through participation in the eternal species and through brief but ecstatic union with the life-force. In the timeless world of inorganic nature, temporality is achieved through the unending variation and movement of external forms. It is crucial to an understanding of the tale to recognize that each of the two realms can assert a claim to totality; each of them approaches a state of synthesis, but from opposite directions.

It is this correspondence between the plant world and the stone world, moreover, which makes it possible for Christian to assimilate himself temporarily into life on the plains, despite his inner allegiance to the mountains. He returns to the plains, after all, at noon on the day of the harvest feast, in the period of fullest fruition and at the very moment when the whole community is gathered in a timeless ritual of gratitude and joy. Sitting in the church, he falls in love with Elisabeth, who herself is the image of a flower in full bloom: "Sie war schlank und blond, ihr blaues Auge glänzte von der durchdringendsten Sanftheit, ihr Antlitz war wie durchsichtig und in den zartesten Farben blühend" (70). Notwithstanding his resolution to banish the "godless feelings" of the previous night from his mind, Christian is drawn to the plant world by the same lure of timeless experience that had presented itself to him in the castle on Rune Mountain.

After the birth of their child Leonora, however, Christian gradually begins to sense the temporal implications of life in the plant world:

Christian wurde zwar zuweilen etwas ernster, indem er das Kind betrachtete, aber doch kam seine jugendliche Heiterkeit immer wieder zurück. . . . Nach einigen Monaten fielen ihm aber seine Eltern in die Gedanken, . . . es ängstigte ihn, daß er Vater und Mutter seit so langer Zeit ganz hatte vergessen können, sein eigenes Kind erinnerte ihn, welche Freude die Kinder den Eltern sind, so beschloß er dann endlich, sich auf die Reise zu machen und seine Heimat wieder zu besuchen. (71).

The sight of his youthful baby troubles Christian because it suggests to him that his own youth is passing. In a first attempt to establish some kind of temporal continuity in his life, he decides to visit his homeland and regain contact with his own past.

In terms of the spatial logic of the tale, it is fitting that this search for continuity and permanence should lead Christian back toward the mountains. Scarcely is he out of the village when the theme of transitoriness and loss of youth becomes explicit: "Da kam ihm der Gedanke, daß seine Jugend vorüber sei, daß er eine Heimat gefunden, der er angehöre, in die sein Herz Wurzel geschlagen habe; er wollte fast den verlornen Leichtsinn der vorigen Jahre beklagen" (72). Before he reaches the mountains, however, he unexpectedly meets his father, that eloquent apologist for the plant world, and together they return to the plains. As they talk, Christian regains his sense of satisfaction with life in the village.[24]

Five uneventful years pass. Then a mysterious stranger appears in the village, stays for several months at Christian's house, and finally departs for the mountains, leaving a sum of money in Christian's safe-keeping. Significantly, Christian's first statement concerning this money contains a reference to time (or, more precisely, timelessness): "Diese Summe könnte uns recht glücklich machen . . . für uns und unsere Kinder wäre *auf immer* gesorgt," he tells his apprehensive father (74; emphasis added). His fascination with the money rapidly becomes an obsession, an *idée fixe* that preoccupies him continuously, breaking down the natural rhythm of day and night and superimposing itself on every experience: " 'Ja,' sagte Christian, 'ich verstehe mich selber nicht mehr, weder bei Tage noch in der Nacht läßt es mir Ruhe; seht, wie es mich jetzt wieder anblickt, . . . das ruft mich, wenn ich schlafe, ich höre es, wenn Musik tönt, wenn der Wind bläst, wenn Leute auf der Gasse sprechen; scheint die Sonne, so sehe ich nur diese gelben Augen,' " (74–75). Like the internalized figure of the tablet within Christian, to which the gold corresponds and to which it directs its appeal, the metal exerts a fascination that is at once ceaseless and infinitely diverse. Christian hears the gold calling in the wind, in the sound of music, in the indistinct sounds of people talking outside. In response to this characteristic call of the mountain realm, the suppressed internal reality gradually rises to the level of conscious realization. Christian is able now to confront his shocked and frightened father with a description of the mysterious sign, the governing constellation within him that takes possession of his cognitive abilities and transforms all external reality into its own fixed image: "Dann kann ich sie nur denken und fühlen, und alles umher ist verwandelt, oder vielmehr von dieser Gestaltung verschlungen worden" (76). At the same time, his aversion to the plant world becomes emphatic. The very essence of this world, he claims, is "die schrecklichste Verwesung" (77). Standing on the hill above the village and observing the harvest festival in precisely the same routine that he had seen years before, but with different participants, Christian finally recognizes that the timelessness of the plant realm is maintained at the cost of the individual; that the individual is granted only a brief and illusory sense of timelessness; and that in fact only the *tradition*, impersonal and mechanical, is truly immune to time: "So habe ich mutwillig ein hohes ewiges Glück aus der Acht gelassen, um ein vergängliches und zeitliches zu gewinnen" (78). This conscious articulation of the temporal distinction between the two realms serves as the decisive and final turning point in Christian's zigzag course of development. He yearningly enters a nearby wood, rediscovers the tablet, and then disappears once and for all into the forest.

What awaits him there is by no means clear from the context of the tale. Does Christian's inner conversion to the timeless stone world assure him of immortality, or must he, too, ultimately succumb to death? It is difficult to dismiss the first possibility out of hand. Given the mysterious and, for normal human understanding, utterly incomprehensible nature of the stone world, there is little reason to contend that he could *not* be subsumed into its timelessness. It is, after all, a world of supernatural events and figures. On the other hand, Christian's father characterizes him at one point as a flower that only grows in the mountains (73), a designation that suggests that Christian is as mortal as the rest, despite his internal affinity for the stone realm. While the other utterances of the father scarcely commend him as a reliable observer of Christian's character and motivations, this one statement is reinforced at the conclusion of the tale by Christian himself, who reappears near the village wearing a wreath of green foliage around his head, an evident analogy to Christ's wreath of thorns. The implication would appear to be that Christian considers himself a martyr to the plant world, a man whose true allegiance is to the timeless realm, but who must pay the price of having been born a mortal. In any event, it is possible, I think, to establish at least one thing with some degree of certainty. Although the inhabitants of the plains live in time, anticipating, experiencing, and remembering one brief, climactic period of full happiness and vitality, Christian enters into a continuous, unbroken (and therefore, within the span of his lifetime, *time-less*) state of rapture, perceiving both the play of external forms and the profound and mysterious essences which underlie these external forms. Whether or not entrance into this state permits him to transcend his own mortality must remain a moot point.

It is well known that "Der Runenberg" evolved from discussions on natural philosophy and geology between Tieck and his friend Henrik Steffens.[25] To a perceptive contemporary reader, however, the juxtaposition between stone world and plant world may have recalled not only Steffens, but also the *Philosophical Enquiry into the Origin of our Ideas of the Sublime and the Beautiful* (1757) by the English philosopher and statesman Edmund Burke. Burke derived his aesthetic categories of the sublime and the beautiful from emotional responses on the part of the viewer (or reader). Objects that give rise to the passions of fear and astonishment he termed sublime, while objects which generate the passions of tenderness and pleasure were designated as beautiful. The specific attributes that Burke assigned to the sublime immediately call to mind Tieck's mountain world: obscurity, power, vastness, magnificence, difficulty, extreme light and dark, and sudden transitions between sound and silence, brightness and darkness.[26] Moreover, the mind, when confronted with the sublime, "is so entirely filled with its object, that it cannot entertain any other, nor by consequence reason on that object which employs it,"[27] an apt description of the irrational hold the stone world takes on Christian's mind, extinguishing all thought and memory of the plains. The beautiful, on the other hand, is characterized by smallness (one thinks of the small church, the narrow gardens, the small huts), smoothness, delicacy, and harmony of the various parts comprising the whole,[28] qualities that may be applied not only to the plains community as a whole, but also, specifically, to the girl Elisabeth, in whom much of the appeal that the plant world exerts on Christian is embodied in concentrated form. Most significant for our discussion of time in "Der Runenberg," however, is Burke's conception of the sublime as effecting the passions of *self-preservation* and the beautiful as effecting the passions of *self-propagation*.[29] Thus the mountain landscape as such immediately calls forth the impulse to sustain oneself, to enter into a kind of private timelessness. By the same token, the plains promote by their very nature the impulse toward procreation and the subordination of the individual to the species.

There is, of course, little or no justification for the assumption that Tieck went to work on "Der Runenberg" with an eye toward illustrating Burke's aesthetic categories. Burke was, to be sure, very well known in Germany. Kant himself had contrasted and provided further examples of the sublime and the beautiful in an essay written in 1763, and most of the first book of the *Kritik der Urteilskraft* (1790) was devoted to a clarification of Burke's categories. Schiller had further elaborated the contrast in two essays, "Vom Erhabenen" (1793) and "Über das Erhabene" (1795). Moreover, Tieck as a passionate Anglophile could scarcely have avoided encountering Burke's ideas in English, either directly or in the works of imitators such as Alexander Gerard or Hugh Blair. Nevertheless, it would be safer to assume that

Burke's categories were incorporated unconsciously into "Der Runenberg," as long-familiar ideas that lent themselves naturally to a depiction of two diametrically opposed psychological states. What is particularly interesting and important here, however, is the modification that these ideas underwent in Tieck's hands. Although Burke viewed his categories as options of aesthetic response that any sensitive and well-balanced individual could find equally appealing, in "Der Runenberg" these categories acquire epistemological implications: to experience the sublime presupposes a mentality radically different from the mentality that is capable of experiencing the beautiful. Indeed, the two dispositions can no longer permanently coexist within the same individual. The traditional aesthetic responses have suddenly become means of cognition, roads to knowledge, and to very different *kinds* of knowledge. The sublime and the beautiful, once mere options of taste, confront each other here as epistemological alternatives in absolute opposition. In this sense, too, Tieck anticipates the later generation of Romantics, for whom intense aesthetic responses were to become problematic and insidious, beguiling the mind and recasting its variable modes of perception into compulsive responses. The supernatural beauty of Venus in Eichendorff's *Das Marmorbild* momentarily transfixes Florio and estranges him from his beloved, but merely human, Bianca. E. T. A. Hoffmann's mines of Falun, sublime in the most gruesome sense of the word, enthrall the hapless Elis Fröbom, who succumbs to the unearthly majesty of the *Bergkönigin* and goes to his death petrified, literally as well as figuratively. The Early Romantics were in general disinclined to explore the psychological effects of aesthetic experience, though they were scarcely unaware of aberrant responses to literature and the other arts. As was so often the case, Tieck's personal instability and uncertainty led him to a precocious understanding of the dangers latent in Romantic attitudes—in this instance, the danger of losing oneself altogether in an aesthetic frame of mind. In "Der Runenberg," Tieck touches on the problem obliquely; the later writers were to take it up on an explicit basis.

Up to this point, we have considered time in "Der Runenberg" largely from a thematic perspective. For the sake of a more complete comparison with the *Märchen* of Novalis and "Der blonde Eckbert," it will be useful to glance briefly at the temporal organization of the tale.

It should be apparent, from everything that has been said thus far, that time in "Der Runenberg" is articulated primarily by Christian's passage from one spatial zone to the next, and that the structure of the tale may be broken down into an alternation between his contrasting mental states. Thus the narrative opens with an extended description of a state of acute discontent and emotional volatility, as the young hunter ponders his life in the mountains and his former life on the plains and finds himself unable to affirm either existence unequivocally. This opening state is brought to an abrupt end by Christian's unwitting act of aggression against the plant world (his ripping out of the mandrake root) and the sudden appearance of the stranger. There follows a transitional passage characterized by spatial movement to the top of the mountain, which may be further divided into two distinct phases: 1) the movement through the dark passage of the forest, during which Christian's internal realignment toward the stone world becomes evident through his retelling of his life story; and 2) following this confession, the sudden emergence from the forest and Christian's ascent alone to the distant ruins. As we have seen in Chapter 2, this terraced succession of increasingly more intense mental states is continued at the top of the mountain. Christian's passion rises by distinct stages as the woman strides back and forth, first fully clothed, then naked, and finally reveals the tablet to him. It must be emphasized that the tablet itself does not appear and disappear in one brief, climactic instant, but provides Christian with a rather prolonged state of delirious excitement.

Up to this point the temporal structure of "Der Runenberg" is similar to that of Novalis's tales and the first phase of Bertha's story in "Der blonde Eckbert." The narrative consists of a sequence of clearly articulated states bridged by sudden events that represent instantaneous points of contact between two simultaneous but separate states of affairs. The final state is one of unity between the formerly disparate spheres (in this case, Christian's mind and the innermost essence of the mountain world). What follows is typical for Tieck—and unthinkable for Novalis. The ecstatically achieved unity is quickly lost and an illusory existence assumed. Bertha marries Eckbert, Christian awakes to find himself far from Rune Mountain and returns to the plains to marry Elisabeth. From this point onward, the temporal structure of the tale is defined, generally speaking, by two processes that operate simultaneously. On the one hand, Christian acquires a family and grows older (following the temporal model of the plant world, as we have seen). On the other hand, this linear development is punctuated intermittently by the reemergence of Christian's truer self and, in each case, by a counterattack on the part of Christian's father. Precisely as in "Der blonde Eckbert," the intrusion of the supernatural stone world into Christian's life occurs three times: first, during his journey back toward his homeland, when the eyes and hair of the woman in the castle suddenly appear to him in the brooks and trees;

secondly, through the arrival of the stranger and his subsequent deposit of the gold with Christian; thirdly, through the reappearance of the wondrous tablet. As was the case with Eckbert (and a similar case could be made for "Der Tannenhäuser"), one attack is not enough. The human soul so stubbornly maintains its self-delusions, so tenaciously resists purification, that it must literally be pummeled into a recognition and acceptance of its true nature. Here again a comparison with Novalis is instructive. Fabel, it will be recalled, appears three times before Arcturus in the course of the Klingsohr tale. Her visits, however, by no means represent repeated, and initially unsuccessful, attempts at conversion, as would be the case with Tieck. Instead, she delivers in each instance a brief report of the progress she has made and gathers the materials for the next phase of her mission. Each visit marks a waystation in the continuing and uninterrupted progress toward final unity. In Tieck's tales, on the other hand, every such visit (or, one is tempted to say, visitation) from the "other world" begins the whole process anew; the only essential difference from one instance to the next is in the intensity of attack and counterattack.[30] In this respect, Tieck's tales are remarkably similar to the *Märchen* of E. T. A. Hoffmann, in which the hero repeatedly ascends to a visionary recognition of the ideal world, only to fall back into a state of clouded consciousness. We have noted above that "Der Runenberg" marks the transition between Early and Late Romanticism; here is further evidence of Tieck's affinity with the later phase.

For Novalis's heroes, to be sure, the road to perfection is difficult and usually contains one major setback, but this setback is in fact only apparent and emerges in the end as a crucial step in the development of the hero. Thus the visit of the old man estranges Hyazinth from Rosenblüte and destroys Hyazinth's naive relationship to the natural world around him, but at the same time it represents the first phase of his progress toward a total unification of mind and nature. Similarly, the Scribe's imprisonment of the Mother and the Father appears at first to be a terrible defeat for the forces of unity, but in fact it sets the stage for the immolation of the Mother, the annihilation of the Sun, and the melting of Arcturus's realm. It is evident that Tieck never felt much at home with the optimistic faith of Novalis, Schelling, and the Schlegels in a steady advancement toward perfection through reflection and multiple processes of synthesis. Novalis was, of course, too intelligent not to occasionally question the foundations of his own optimism.[31] Indeed, in the Klingsohr tale and particularly in the plans for the continuation of *Ofterdingen* one begins to sense a need to maintain this optimism through dogged determination—and with increasingly questionable means. Tieck's doubts, however, were much more pronounced from the beginning. For him, and for the later generation, the mind is of such refractory substance that it constantly denies its own best impulses, constantly regresses to a false consciousness characterized by qualities such as greed, egotism, self-deception, or pride. In general, the way homeward is considerably more problematic with Tieck than with Novalis. Eckbert enters the lost paradise only at the cost of his sanity and his life, because he has repeatedly proven himself incapable of reachieving the synthesis of time and timelessness on a higher and more mature level, through an ethical act of self-integration. Christian succeeds in regaining the lost paradise, but at the sacrifice of his original homeland and all human society.

Despite these and other contextual differences, "Der blonde Eckbert" and "Der Runenberg" are essentially similar in their temporal structure. Each is divided into two principal phases. The first describes the ascent by stages to an ideal state and the subsequent loss of this state. The second is comprised of three subsections that mark the repeated intrusions of representatives of the other world into the inauthentic existence of the hero, culminating in his return, for better or worse, to this world. Despite these similarities, however, the later tale has a very different temporal "feel" than "Der blonde Eckbert," and this difference derives primarily from the way in which the second phase is handled. While the narrative time devoted to each visit of the old woman (as Walther, Hugo, and the peasant) is progressively foreshortened so as to produce an all but frenzied sense of acceleration in the final pages of the earlier tale, the corresponding section of "Der Runenberg" moves at a much more leisurely pace. Each successive intrusion of the mountain realm serves as the occasion for an extended debate between Christian and his father. While the function of these debates is, as one senses rather too clearly, to acquaint the reader with the antithetical values of the stone world and the plant world, at the same time the prolonged discussions effectively obscure the temporal movement of the tale. In the midst of all the talking, the reader gradually loses sight of the dynamic process that Christian is undergoing. To be sure, we are told that his mind is reverting by stages to the viewpoint of the mountains, and a close examination of the text reveals that progressively less narrated time elapses between each intrusion of the stone world.[32] But we fail to experience this acceleration. It must be emphasized that structure has two distinct aspects: quite apart from its function as a meaningful organization of narrative materials, it also serves the important purpose of shaping and directing the reader's emotional responses. While the altercations between Christian and his father permit a cerebral understanding of

Christian's increasing alienation, their effect on the temporal structure of the tale is such that the reader is barred from any direct emotional participation in Christian's accelerating process of realignment with the mountain world. The narrative goes slack precisely at the point where it should pick up speed.

These observations reinforce what was said at the conclusion of Chapter 2. One finds in "Der Runenberg" a preponderance of philosophical ideas that do not rise effortlessly out of the situation and the plot, but are tacked onto the tale explicitly and with much too evident intention. One could, of course, level the same charge of top-heaviness against the Klingsohr tale, but there the conceptual interplay is so extraordinarily intricate that one becomes intellectually engaged in spite of oneself and is willing, for the moment, to overlook the almost total lack of immediate, sensual appeal. By way of contrast, the themes and implications of "Der blonde Eckbert" are, in a complex fashion, bound up with the action of the tale and rarely become overt. To put it another way, one moves from an immediate response to a deeper understanding of the tale, rather than moving from a conceptual understanding to a belated response, as is the case with "Der Runenberg." Although Tieck's later tale is anything but the "formloser Brei" that Richard Benz (who should have known better) considered it,[33] it is not exactly a taut piece of craftsmanship either. Whether this failing is a result of the haste with which the tale was written, or whether it derives from Tieck's half-conscious attempt to emulate the philosophical profundity of Novalis's tales, is difficult to say. In any event, the structural weaknesses of "Der Runenberg" should not obscure its undeniable strengths. For all its literary shortcomings, the tale brilliantly sums up the Romantic ambivalences between affirmation of community and the attempt to realize a personal vision of perfection, and between the ecstasy of temporal existence and the search for timeless essences.

V

Space, Time, and the Romantic Fairy Tale

In the preceding chapters, we have considered the tales of Novalis and Tieck with attention to the distinctive ways in which spatial/temporal patterns operate within each tale. This method of close, selective analysis is successful on its own terms and needs no special defense. Nevertheless, it does run the risk of a certain myopia with regard to historical context. The tales of Novalis and Tieck do not represent isolated experiments in the craft of the *Kunstmärchen*, but stand at the beginning of a vigorous tradition that lasted well into the nineteenth century, supported by the creative talents of almost every major writer from Goethe to Mörike. In this concluding chapter, it seems pertinent and useful to enlarge on the insights of the first four chapters by directing our attention to spatial and temporal patterns in the Romantic fairy tale at large.

It must be understood at the outset, however, that an investigation of space and time cannot pretend to accomplish a comprehensive survey of the Romantic *Kunstmärchen*. Most of the tales do in fact demonstrate a profound concern for the ways in which spatial and temporal experience defines and delimits human existence, and it will be possible to classify these tales into two major groups according to their organization in terms of space and time. But we are forced to exclude tales such as Brentano's *Italienische Märchen* and *Rheinmärchen* and Platen's "Der Rosensohn," in which time and space are simply too unimportant to serve as criteria for contrastive analysis.[1] If tales of this type are to be accounted for in a general classification of the literary fairy tale, it will be necessary to devise more inclusive categories than spatial or temporal organization. Our aims are not that ambitious. Within the framework of this study, it will suffice to approach the problem on approximate terms; to establish, in other words, the extent to which Novalis's and Tieck's use of space and time is *generally* characteristic of the Romantic fairy tale.

The tradition of the literary fairy tale neither began nor ended with Romanticism. Nevertheless, it was within the context of Romantic poetics that the fairy tale received its most spectacular promotion and justification as a form of literary art. "Das Mährchen ist gleichsam der Canon der Poësie" (III, 449): Novalis's well-known pronouncement has a characteristically apodictic ring but reflects well enough the sentiments of his contemporaries. Because the arguments that Novalis advanced in support of the *Kunstmärchen* have considerable bearing on structural elements such as space and time, we must briefly consider these arguments before we approach the tales themselves.

According to the triadic scheme of history that the Romantics evolved, or rather took over, with some important modifications, from Neoplatonic tradition,[2] the folk fairy tale was a remnant of the primal unity-in-chaos, the first Golden Age of natural anarchy in which man and nature coexisted in unconscious harmony. It is not surprising, then, that theoretical deliberations on the fairy tale often went hand in hand with a critique of contemporary existence. As early as 1798, in one of the fragments designated "Denkaufgaben," Novalis observed: "Es liegt nur an der Schwäche unsrer Organe und der Selbstberührung, daß wir uns nicht in einer Feenwelt erblicken. Alle Mährchen sind nur Träume von jener heymathlichen Welt, die überall und nirgends ist" (II, 564). Two central ideas are contained in this brief notation: first, the assumption that our true homeland, the fairy-tale world, is everywhere present, both within us and in nature itself; but that the insensitivity and lethargy of our senses, as well as our lack of genuine *self*-contact, withhold this world from our view, our immediate and conscious experience. The second important point here is the explicit association of the fairy tale with dreams: the idea that the fairy tale, like the dream, liberates us from the habitual and mechanical patterns of rational thought and confronts us with a realm of fancifully disconnected images, images whose meaning and relationship affect us profoundly but elude any sort of clever logical analysis.

In a later fragment from the *Allgemeine Brouillon*, Novalis extends this thought: "In einem ächten Märchen muß alles wunderbar—geheimnißvoll und unzusammenhängend seyn—alles belebt. . . . Die Zeit der allg[emeinen] Anarchie—Gesezlosigkeit—Freyheit—der *Naturzustand* der *Natur*" (III, 280). In other words, the fairy tale reflects not only a dream state, but nature itself, that is, "nature in its natural state," not yet subjected to the awkward and reductive ordering mechanisms of the mind. It is the nature that children perceive from their privileged viewpoint: "Der frische Blick des Kindes ist überschwenglicher, als die Ahndung des entschiedensten Sehers" (II, 564), Novalis notes immediately preceding the first fragment quoted above. In this gaze of the child, this "frische[r] Blick" that apprehends everything and comprehends nothing, the world reveals itself as a harmonious chaos. And it is precisely this harmonious chaos that is in turn captured in the naive narrative of the folk fairy tale: "Ein Mährchen ist eigentlich wie ein Traumbild—ohne Zusammenhang—Ein *Ensemble* wunderbarer Dinge und Begebenheiten" (III, 454). The experience of the fairy tale restores us to that dreamlike or childlike state of unstructured cognition in which reality is not yet intellectually coordinated or classified, not yet diminished to conform to conceptual expectations.

All this talk of disconnected images and "allgemeine Anarchie" may seem to be fairly remote from what we remember of "Snow White" or "Little Red Riding Hood." Among other things, Novalis's observations would appear to deny the very existence of a *plot* in the folk fairy tale. Significantly, however, his characterization of the fairy tale as nothing more than "ein *Ensemble* wunderbarer Dinge" is modified a few lines later with the remark: "Sonderbar, daß eine abs[olute], wunderbare *Synthesis* oft die Axe des Märchens—oder das Ziel desselben ist" (III, 455). This explicit acknowledgment of plot organization in the fairy tale is by no means an isolated flash of insight. Earlier Novalis refers to the most fundamental structural element of the fairy tale—the element of transformation—and documents his observation with several specific examples.[3] The inconsistency here of denying structure in one breath and readmitting it in the next is resolved through an analogy to music: "Ein Mährchen ist . . . Ein *Ensemble* wunderbarer Dinge und Begebenheiten—z.B. eine *musicalische Fantasie*—die Harmonischen Folgen einer Aeolsharfe—die *Natur selbst*" (III, 454). Music, with its intricate acoustical mathematics and rhythmic patterns, is anything but unstructured, even in the form of improvisation and free fantasizing. But these structures are altogether nonconceptual. What delights us in music is the play of purely formal devices: repetition, variation, emergence of dominant themes, movement toward anticipated or unexpected resolution. Similarly, when Novalis speaks of "Natur im Naturzustand" or "ächte Naturanarchie" (III, 438), he is scarcely suggesting a state of senseless chaos. Rather, as he indicates in numerous other fragments, nature is formally organized through and through—but organized in a way that resembles the laws of music. Both nature and music are emotionally suggestive but so enormously complex that the conscious mind is simply incapable of interpreting its experience of them. And so, too, the fairy tale: the terms "Anarchie," "Ensemble," "Gesezlosigkeit" do not denote a senseless and discordant conglomeration of narrative elements, but a *seemingly* disconnected configuration that evokes the emotional resonances of music, and in which all the components—characters, setting, plot structure—are essentially devoid of symbolic meaning or conceptual relationships. In the Grimm version of "Hänsel und Gretel," for instance, the children are guided to the witch's house by a beautiful snow-white bird. One could, however, quite easily substitute a little brown mouse or a butterfly for the bird without altering the meaning of the figure, for its meaning does not extend beyond the structural function of leading the children to the gingerbread house.[4]

Up to this point, we have been dealing, of course, primarily with the *folk* fairy tale. Like the tones produced by the Aeolian harp, the original fairy tale is an art form produced by and expressing nature itself; the human soul that transmits the folk narrative is analogous in every respect to the passive but wonderfully responsive strings of the wind harp. For this reason, the folk fairy tale betrays no marks of personal artistic intention, no stylistic signature of an individual author—a view that was to serve Jakob Grimm very well a decade later, when he was pressed to justify the literary gaucheness of his *Kinder- und Hausmärchen*. The anonymous authorship of the folk fairy tale bespeaks a time of rudimentary harmony between nature and the soul of man, a time referred to popularly as the First Golden Age (though Novalis himself occasionally prefers the simpler and less grandiose term, "die erste Periode"). The ambitious task of the *literary* fairy tale, on the other hand, is to create an image of the *second* Golden Age, using the folk fairy tale as a model but suffusing the naive materials of the folk tale with intellectual significance. "Ein höheres Mährchen wird es, wenn ohne den Geist des M[ärchens] zu verscheuchen irgend ein *Verstand*—(Zusammenhang, Bedeutung—etc.) hinein gebracht wird" (III, 455). The folk tale is thus to be enhanced, in the alchemical sense, through the admixture of spirit, which succeeds in maintaining all the diversity and multiplicity of the earlier form but integrates the chaos into an intelligible unity, a "vernünftiges Chaos," as Novalis terms it in an earlier fragment (III, 281). In other words, the literary fairy tale operates in two directions: it restores "der frische Blick" of the child while at the same time permeating this gaze with the informed and expansive wisdom of old age, the wisdom that not only hears the incoherent music of nature but divines the mysterious logic behind this music. What is by-passed in the conversion of folk fairy tale to literary fairy tale is precisely that medial stage of limited consciousness, that complacent and self-assured realism that Novalis found so objectionable in Goethe's *Wilhelm Meister*.

This emphatic rejection of realistic narrative had important consequences for the spatial and temporal structure of the literary fairy tale. In imitation of the folk tale, space was no longer under any obligation to correspond to the reality of everyday experience. Instead, through the process of spiritualization described above, the curiously disordered and fantastic landscapes of the folk tale were transformed into symbolic reflections of psychic events and situations. Effortless motion from one location to another could express the unpredictable leaps of associative thinking; confinement in a glass mountain or a witch's hut could represent an impoverished or obsessed state of mind. While the external space of the folk tale obeyed a logic of its own that had nothing to do either with realism or with symbolic patterns, the landscapes of the Romantic *Kunstmärchen* lost their autonomy. They became mirrors of intellectual and emotional states within the fairy-tale hero (as in "Hyazinth und Rosenblüte" or "Der blonde Eckbert"), or they were pressed into service as elaborate allegorical configurations (as in the Klingsohr tale).

Similarly, the disjointed quality of time in the folk fairy tale became, in the literary reworking, an expression of the ways in which human subjectivity alters and shapes temporal experience. One of the peculiar charms of the folk fairy tale lies, for instance, in its isolation of episodes. The hero may undergo the same ordeal three times without bothering to draw any parallels whatsoever from one experience to another, or without even displaying an iota of curiosity about the repetition.[5] In "Der blonde Eckbert," this charm takes on a sinister character. Eckbert, too, is put to the test in three separate but closely related episodes. His inability to recognize and learn from the repetition stems, however, from a psychological and existential disorder that cripples and finally destroys him. In a similar way, the *Kunstmärchen* appropriated the folk-tale motif of instantaneous transformation to express the extraordinary variability of human consciousness. In the tenth Vigil of E. T. A. Hoffmann's *Der goldne Topf*, for example, the evil hag Liese suddenly turns into a hideous beet after her defeat at the hands of the Archivarius Lindhorst. This metamorphosis, like the monumental battle preceding it, is best interpreted as a visionary experience on the part of the student Anselmus. The competing forces in his own soul assume vivid, if hallucinatory, form: the representative of poetic vision (Lindhorst) engages in mortal combat with the agent of earthly complacency and petty aspirations (Liese). Following the destruction of Liese, Anselmus's liberated consciousness immediately retranslates the entire struggle to a higher dimension by exposing Liese's essence as a tuberous vegetable and Lindhorst's true identity as a salamander-prince. The folk fairy tale frequently records the transformation of ordinary human beings into plants and princes, but no folk tale would ever make such a transformation dependent on the clairvoyant hallucinatory experiences of the hero. In Eichendorff's "Der Zauberring" from *Ahnung und Gegenwart*, to take another example, the wedding guests metamorphose into ghastly phantoms before the horrified eyes of the bride. Here again, the physical transformation reflects an abrupt alteration of perception. As the hour of her marriage to the spectral Prince of the River approaches, the bride is made to realize that she has long since surrounded herself with a company of spiritually destitute individuals who live solely for self-gratification, and whose loveless existence is scarcely distinguishable from her own wasted life. As was the case with Anselmus's vision, the transformation reveals the essence.

These observations are not intended as more than a preliminary demonstration of the ways in which spatial and temporal patterns from the folk tale were incorporated into the imaginative scheme of the *Kunstmärchen*. Before we can attempt a general classification of the Romantic fairy tale, we must take a closer look at the kinds of folk narrative that the Romantics used as models for their literary fantasies.

In the process of assembling a definitive and all but exhaustive collection of German folk tales, Jakob and Wilhelm Grimm found it useful, indeed necessary, to distinguish between *Volksmärchen* and *Volkssagen*. Both forms of oral tradition deal with supernatural events and characters; in terms of structure and narrative strategy, however, the two forms are fundamentally different. Max Lüthi, elaborating on the distinction proposed by the Grimms, views the fictional world of the *Sage* as *tiefenhaft*, that of the *Märchen* as *flächenhaft*.[6] What appeals to us in the fairy tale is precisely its one-dimensionality, its insistence on placing all options and possibilities of human existence on the same brilliantly illuminated plane.[7] Fairy-tale heroes lack psychological definition and complexity of character; possibilities of psychic conflict are projected outward onto other figures who interact alongside each other. Horizontal distribution takes the place of vertical layering. In addition, the dimension of otherworldliness vanishes altogether. Supernatural characters and objects are never experienced as uncanny or especially remarkable; if they cause distress or anxiety, it is the same order of distress as that produced by an evil stepmother or an envious sibling. In other words, all of the narrative resources of the fairy tale work toward a single ingenious goal: to fragment and isolate the controlling factors of human existence and to redistribute them so that they interact on a common abstract plane. The one-dimensionality of the hero, his freedom from psychological complexity and environmental constraints, is simultaneously his salvation. His very isolation enables him to align himself universally with figures from every sphere of human existence. He triumphs not because he embodies exceptional virtue or valor, but because he, as the hero, is the chosen one ("der Begnadete")[8] who effortlessly and *inevitably* establishes exactly the appropriate contact at exactly the appropriate moment.

The world of the *Sage*, on the other hand, is multidimensional, equivocal, and frequently tragic. Unlike the active and serenely unreflective hero of the fairy tale, the protagonist of the *Sage* inclines toward pensiveness, introspection, and emotional excitability. He is acquainted with internal contradictions and ambivalence. When he encounters supernatural figures, he reacts with terror, fascination, or rapture—or a combination of all three. The hero of the *Sage* is presented, moreover, not as a lonely visionary, but as an ordinary human being existing within the well-defined social structures of family and village. The *Sage* takes special pains, in fact, to describe the communal environment of the hero, if only to contrast this familiar and seemingly secure territory with the other dimension, the numinous forces that inhabit the nearby lake or mountain or field or forest. The supernatural figures are frequently related to the landscape from which they emerge. What appears as a harmless boulder or bush may in reality be a malicious dwarf, and a distant sparkling wave on a lake may suddenly turn into a seductive mermaid. These figures represent the uncanny side of nature, the unknown and unknowable forces that assault the incautious traveler and occasionally invade even the safe precincts of village and household. The price of contact with the numinous realm is high: the protagonist of the *Sage* often suffers terrifying and irrevocable mutilations of body or spirit. Yet the *Sage* is not primarily concerned with making a cautionary point. The collision between ordinary mortals and supernatural forces has a distinctive and timeless allure. The *Sage* fascinates us not merely by demonstrating the appalling consequences of such a collision, but also by confirming a universal human need: the thirst to seek out and experience the unknown, however terrifying the risk.

The Romantic poets were far too astute in matters of literary analysis to have overlooked the obvious distinctions between the *Volksmärchen* and the *Volkssage*. If they had shared the philological fervor of the Grimms, they might well have designated a sizeable number of their literary fairy tales as *Kunstsagen*.[9] The problem of terminology is not particularly troublesome in any event. What matters here is the striking difference, in terms of space and time, between the fairy tales that appropriated elements of the *Volksmärchen* and the fairy tales that were derived largely from the *Sage*.

We may designate the tales of the first group as allegorical *Märchen*, because these narratives exploit the one-dimensional world of the folk fairy tale to demonstrate the interaction of conceptual forces. With its distribution of isolated figures from every sphere of existence on a single common plane, the folk tale contains an inherent, but always latent, capacity for allegory. In the literary tale, this capacity is fully and emphatically developed. If, for instance, the Prince and the Princess of the *Volksmärchen* function as nothing more than stylized representatives of the universal Boy and the universal Girl, in the *Kunstmärchen* they become questing Mind and dormant Nature (in the Klingsohr tale), or grumpy Introspection and distraught Humor (in the tale of King Ophioch and Princess Liris from E. T. A. Hoffmann's *Prinzessin Brambilla*). In its crudest and least imaginative form, allegorical technique assigns each character a single, unmistakeable conceptual meaning. Most of the Romantic fairy tales successfully avoid this mechanical one-to-one correspondence between figure and concept by multiplying the number of referential meanings associated with each character. Moreover, with very few exceptions, allegorical *Märchen* are set into the framework of longer, more realistic narratives. As imbedded tales, they serve as an abstract, distilled reflection of the processes at work in the larger context.[10] This technique works very much to the advantage of the fairy tales themselves. Through an intricate system of cross reference to the main text, the allegory attains a density of allusiveness that it could not support if it stood alone.

As interpolated tales, the allegorical *Märchen* have a distinctly pedagogical character. They are narrated by figures of superior and undisputed authority: the elderly cleric in Goethe's *Unterhaltungen deutscher Ausgewanderten*,[11] the poet Klingsohr in *Heinrich von Ofterdingen*, Archivarius Lindhorst in *Der goldne Topf*, the magician Celionati in *Prinzessin Brambilla*, the sophisticated merchants who relate the tale of "Atlantis." In each case, the wise narrator invites the members of his audience to reexamine their lives from the higher, abstract plane of the fairy tale, an interpretive task that frequently requires mental powers bordering on divination.

The instructive force of the allegorical *Märchen* derives not merely from its abstract frame of reference, but, more importantly, from its depiction of an ideal process leading to ontological unity and perfection. In this regard, the temporal scheme of Novalis's *Märchen* is characteristic of the allegorical fairy tale in general. All of these tales represent procedural models, idealized blueprints that specify the steps to be taken, the hazards to be overcome, the sacrifices to be endured in order to achieve a reintegrated existence or perfect consciousness. Inevitably, as in Novalis's tales, the temporal pattern is one of terraced states created by the alignment and successive recombination of conceptual forces. The allegorical *Märchen* does not hesitate to identify the sources of temporal regression or stasis. Again and again, it is smug complacency, arrogance, pride, oafish stupidity, or self-delusion that work to stop the flow of time and perpetuate an inadequate state of affairs. In the context of a movement that supposedly abandoned ethical concerns in favor of an airy aestheticism,[12] these villanies may seem surprisingly conventional. The Romantic indictment of human weakness was, in fact, neither fainthearted nor radically new. The unconventional aspect of the Romantic allegorical tale lies in its conviction that the various forces of inertia and regression are to be combatted not through recourse to orthodox religion or enlightened social agencies, but through the individual mind operating solely on its own extraordinary resources of imagination and intellectual vitality.

In terms of spatial organization, the allegorical *Märchen* usually opens with a state of polarity, expressing the opposition of mind and nature or conflicting aspects of the mind. In keeping with what Jean Paul called the pervasive magnetic metaphor of Early Romanticism,[13] both poles are charged with attractive energy; both represent dynamic forces capable of transformation and in search of synthesis. In general, spatial patterns in the allegorical *Märchen* serve to demonstrate the assumption that the drivewheels of the universe are propelled by recurrent systems of oppositions which can, and must, be brought to interact in a productive and harmonious way.

It is difficult to bring the complicated spatial movements of the allegorical tale under a single formula. As a rule, however, the development is toward larger and progressively more cohesive clusters as the various conceptual forces assemble and reassemble themselves. Here again, the allegorical tale imitates the principles of the natural sciences. In their alternate dispersal and convergence, expansion and contraction, the interacting conceptual figures suggest centripetal and centrifugal force in physics as well as diastolic and systolic movement in biology. As we have seen in Chapter 3, the implicit analogy between the physical processes and the mental operations of analytic and synthetic reasoning points to a fundamental correspondence between mind and nature. The goal of the various spatial movements in the allegorical tale is a state of *conjunction*, in which the corresponding forces are finally situated in alignment with each other rather than in senseless and stymied opposition. The favored image for this concluding state, a ring of concentric circles, expresses a condition of abundance and controlled vitality, a paradoxical condition of articulated spacelessness that admits the diversity, but affirms the essential unity, of all spheres of existence.

Within this generalized scheme of the allegorical *Märchen* there is considerable individual variation. Goethe's "Märchen," for instance, contains such a wealth of alchemical, historical, philosophical, and even autobiographical allusions that one cannot assign distinct conceptual meanings to the various figures without encountering serious contradictions. Nevertheless, familiar patterns of spatial disjunction and temporal stasis emerge: the River slices the landscape in half, separating the kingdom of the lily from the temple of the four kings and creating a general sense of spatial disorientation;[14] the temple itself is buried beneath the earth of eternal darkness; the lily, whose touch kills the living and restores the dead to a cheerless half-life, reigns over a barren land in which plant growth is restricted to a gloomy graveyard horticulture of pines and cypresses. On both sides of the river, time is experienced either as entrapment in an immutable state or as a source of decay and death. Whatever the various figures mean in a conceptual sense, it is apparent from the beginning that their spatial separation and temporal vulnerability are maintained by an extraordinarily complex network of restrictions: laws of interaction and immobility, obligation and exemption, effectiveness and impotence.[15] Significantly, the temporal and spatial movement of the tale begins with the *collision* of two laws. The will-o'-the-wisps give the ferryman gold in payment for their passage across the river, but the river accepts only organic matter, and the will-o'-the-wisps cannot take the gold back. The gold is thus free to circulate, and wherever it goes (principally in the body of the green snake) it functions consistently as a symbol of positive metamorphosis. From the beginning, everything depends on prophetic insight that is able to capitalize on the dislodged order of restrictions and intermesh the laws in a new way so that they finally become productive as sources of unity and cohesiveness. Significantly, it is the figures most closely associated with gold—the snake, the old man with the lamp, the first king—who display such insight. Their calm, deliberate assessment of events and situations provides the other figures with the direction they need in order to make judicious use of their individual powers at precisely the appropriate moment. The prophetic phrase, "Es ist an der Zeit," rings out no less than five times as a reminder that the decisive moment has finally arrived, the moment of liberation from the deadlock of mutually self-defeating restrictions. Despite a number of setbacks produced by thoughtless or impulsive behavior, the various figures are increasingly united in a spirit of collective enterprise that works to suspend the former inflexible laws of spatial separation.[16] While the Romantic fairy tale typically centers on the transformation and extension of consciousness within an individual hero, the Classical bias of

Goethe's "Märchen" is apparent in its assumption that the regeneration of the individual ultimately depends on the transformation of the entire community through enlightened and selfless cooperation.

The two most ambitious fairy tales of E. T. A. Hoffmann, *Der goldne Topf* and *Prinzessin Brambilla*, are actually miniature novels set on a more or less realistic plane. Each contains not one but two complementary allegorical *Märchen*, myths of redemption that are to be reenacted by the confused and comically sublunar hero. In *Der goldne Topf*, the tales relate a succession of mythic cycles, beginning with nothing less than the origins of the universe and leading down, in progressively larger segments, to the realistic level of the tale as a whole. The spatial and temporal dynamics of this process are fairly intricate and vary from one cycle to the next. In each instance, however, the upper spirits of light and fire work in collaboration with the lower spirits of earth to create ever higher and more complex forms in the hierarchy of being. The creature touched and animated by the upper spirits abruptly becomes agitated and spatially mobile, often the point of losing all connection with the earth. In this vulnerable and alienated state it is entrapped by dark forces associated with the earth but independent of the benevolent earth-spirits.[17] The dark forces cannot undo the transformation caused by the spirits of light. Instead, they seek to contain the newly transformed creature in a perpetual state of inadequacy and estrangement. In the final phase of the mythic cycle, a cosmic battle erupts between the spirits of light and the forces of limitation. The latter, defeated but not annihilated, retreat to their subterranean lairs; the liberated creature emerges newly transformed, in full and secure possession of its higher state.

With each repetition, this process becomes more elaborate, reaching a remarkable degree of symbolic density and allusiveness at the level of Anselmus's experiences in Dresden. Here the spirit of light and fire is embodied in the Archivarius Lindhorst, who promotes and directs Anselmus's development toward poetic consciousness. The forces of limitation reside in the malevolent matchmaker Liese, who attempts to ensnare Anselmus in the world of Philistine contentment with its maddeningly good-natured intolerance of anything beyond the bounds of common sense. Hoffmann enriches the significance of this opposition, moreover, by providing Lindhorst and Liese with complementary artifacts. In the sanctity of Lindhorst's azure library sits the gleaming golden pot, in whose mirrored interior Anselmus comes to view the wondrous diversity of nature in the place of his own reflection. At the desolate crossroads at midnight, Liese sets up a very different sort of pot, a sinister cauldron with curious reflecting properties of its own. When Veronika, Anselmus's hopeful bride-to-be, peers into the cauldron, she sees not her own image, but a prettified Anselmus scaled down to the spiritual level of Veronika's petit-bourgeois aspirations. The cauldron locks Anselmus into Veronika's limited reflection; the golden pot triumphantly confirms the identity of Anselmus's elevated soul with the marvels of nature. These central images of temporal stasis as opposed to triumphant temporal progression are representative of the symbolic range of *Der goldne Topf* as a whole, and it is in images such as these that the more profound and subtle implications of the tale are to be sought. The imbedded narratives, despite their occasional allegorical character, serve less to clarify the events on the real level than to give these events mythic stature.[18]

In *Prinzessin Brambilla*, Hoffmann comes closer to the spirit and technique of Novalis and Goethe. The imbedded tales of the kingdom of Urdargarten not only provide a mythic subtext, but prove to be nearly indispensable to the task of sorting out and interpreting the events in the principal action of the narrative. Despite Hoffmann's open hostility toward the abstract techniques of allegory, the first tale in particular invites an allegorical reading. Its principal characters are King Ophioch of Urdargarten and Princess Liris of Hirdargarten. Their origins in separate but adjoining kingdoms suggest the conceptual tensions of Novalis's "Atlantis" and the Klingsohr tale, while the similarity of the names Urdargarten and Hirdargarten points to an underlying and concealed affinity between the two figures. In the marriage between Ophioch and Liris, two conflicting aspects of human temperament are brought into uneasy alignment: a morose sense of individuality, self-doubt, and aimless yearning (Opioch) and an all but pathological cheeriness that vents itself in incessant and utterly undifferentiated laughter (Liris). Predictably, the coexistence of two such incompatible figures results in a temporal deadlock. The entire kingdom of Urdargarten remains suspended in a state of irritable divisiveness, until the magician Hermod produces a wondrous spring ("die Urdarquelle") in whose reflection thought is transformed into perception; solipsistic self-examination and unfocused hilarity yield to the visionary realization that the self, for all its inevitable and often humorous limitations, undeniably *exists*, and exists moreover within the totality of nature. Gazing into the "Urdarquelle," whose endless depths reflect the vast blue sky above, Ophioch and Liris are united in the true and earnest humor of irony, which reconciles heaven and earth and all the divided creatures in between. In addition to the horizontal axis represented by Ophioch and Liris, the spatial scheme of the tale contains a vertical axis occupied at one end by Hermod in his tower, at the other end by the unidentified earth-goddess who animates the "Urdarquelle." It is the mysterious forces on the vertical axis who are ultimately responsible for engineering the redemption of Ophioch and Liris. In contrast to the tales of Novalis and Goethe, there is no methodical, sequential development leading up to the final resolution. The spiritual awakening of Ophioch and Liris occurs abruptly, and it is accomplished with a good deal of cabalistic hocus pocus. At the pivotal moment, Hoffmann's tale retreats into fanciful mystification. Although the significance of the transformation is explicitly spelled out,[19] the process leading to the transformation remains shrouded in occult obscurity.

On the other hand, it was surely not Hoffmann's intention to fashion an allegorical blueprint clearly outlining the steps to perfection. The story of Ophioch and Liris, like the following tale of Princess Mystilis and the multi-colored bird, provides just enough abstraction to bring the bewildering events on the real level into preliminary focus. The inlaid tales are intended primarily as a stimulus to interpretation, not as the final key that unlocks the mysteries of the tale as a whole. While the *Märchen* of Goethe and Novalis appeal to a certain intellectual cunning that can identify the complete range of allegorical associations and transfer them intact to the larger context, Hoffmann's tales rely on the reader's imaginative powers to supply what the embedded stories deliberately withhold.[20] The very lack of allegorical precision in the story of Ophioch and Liris gives the tale a peculiar opalescent quality, a general allusiveness that succeeds in clarifying not only the interaction of the real-life protagonists Giglio and Giacinta, but also the internal conflicts within each of these two figures. In further contrast to Novalis and Goethe, moreover, the clarification here is aimed almost exclusively toward the reader. Neither Giglio nor Giacinta hear the story of Ophioch and Liris, and there is little evidence that Giglio understands what he hears of the Mystilis tale. Like Ophioch and Liris, Giglio and Giacinta are essentially passive figures, maneuvered into their own redemption by forces they never quite understand. The allegorical *Märchen* retains its instructive character here, but it no longer serves as an incentive to individual initiative and active control over one's fate. It was perhaps only in the context of Early-Romantic progressivity that the allegorical tale could insist on the freedom of the individual to take charge of his own destiny. In the growing fatalism of Late Romanticism, Hoffmann could still—sporadically—endorse the notion of an ideal process leading to a happily integrated existence. He takes the control of this process out of the hands of his protagonists, however, and entrusts it to enigmatic overseers such as Celionati, whose invisible influence is constantly at work prompting Giglio and Giacinta to reenact the myth—whether they are aware of it or not.

In the tale of the enchanted castle from Eichendorff's *Das Schloß Dürande* (1835/36), the technique of the embedded allegorical tale is further modified by the disappearance of the wise narrator and the reduction of the tale itself to a mere fragment. Despite these limitations, or precisely because of them, Eichendorff's tale makes a pedagogical point of its own. It concerns a princess held captive in an enormous, deserted castle, whose ornate but lifeless splendor recalls the gloomy majesty of a baroque sarcophagus. The single entrance to the castle is securely locked and guarded by a giant who paces back and forth before the gate like the pendulum of a grandfather clock. The implied connection between a perpetual state of deficiency and a mechanical conception of time is familiar from Novalis's "Eros und Fabel." In the case of Eichendorff's tale, however, the specific allegorical meaning of the clock imagery becomes apparent only through cross reference to the themes of the novella as a whole. The giant represents a tyrannical political order that succeeds in embalming anachronistic social forms while it effectively eliminates vitality and innovation. The enchanted castle, with its soundless and stultifying opulence, is in fact only a slight exaggeration of the interior spaces throughout the novella, which reflect the oppressive conventions of an outlived society. When the giant falls asleep one night, the violent noise of his snoring shatters the museumlike stillness of the castle and momentarily quickens the artificial forms of weather vane, statues, and tapestries to a semblance of natural life. The awakening voices of nature call out to the princess to flee from her captivity. As the giant begins to stir from his slumber, she hastily leaps over his legs and approaches the abyss that lies before the castle, where she sees a knight rowing by on the moonlit river. At this point, the young narrator, Gabriele, breaks off the tale. Through the open window of the cloister where she and Sister Renate are sitting, she catches sight of a man rowing past in a light boat. The imbedded tale is interrupted at the point where it intersects most precisely with the reality of the frame story, and its continuation must be inferred from the events that follow on the real level.[21] Shortly following this episode, Gabriele flees from the protective seclusion of the cloister in search of her lover, Graf Dürande. The quest takes her directly into the upheaval of the French Revolution, and the two lovers are reunited only to meet their deaths together. Unlike the authoritative narrators of earlier imbedded tales, Gabriele does not fully understand the implications of the story she tells. While she empathizes with the loneliness of the captive princess, she fails to recognize the ominous significance of the polarity between the enchanted castle and the abyss. If the castle represents the oppressive order of the *ancien régime*, the abyss suggests, in retrospect, the bloody historical alternative of the Revolution in all its anarchic horror. By unwittingly reenacting the fairy tale through her descent into the abyss, Gabriele demonstrates a tragically limited awareness which is shared in various forms by all three of the principal figures in the novella, and which ultimately sends all three to their deaths. Moreover, the significance of the abyss extends beyond the Revolution to irrational impulses in general. Gabriele, her brother Renald, and the young Graf Dürande fail above all to recognize that the power of love can be as incalculable, and as disruptive, as the terrible forces of the Revolution.[22] It is the lure of erotic fulfillment that causes Gabriele to break off her tale impulsively, and at the very point where it begins to sound a note of warning. In Eichendorff's novella, the inlaid tale no longer identifies a detailed master plan for personal or societal transformation. To be sure, it describes a one-step process of liberation, but it no more than hints at the consequences of this liberation. In the end, the tale serves chiefly to characterize the narrator herself, as a complex and subtle mirror of her discontent, her repressed fears, and finally her vulnerability to her own intense emotions.

With Eichendorff's tale we approach the concerns, though not yet the narrative technique, of the second major group of Romantic fairy tales, those derived from the *Sage*. These tales may be designated as psychological *Märchen*. In contrast to the allegorical tale and the folk fairy tale, supernatural events, characters, and situations in the psychological *Märchen* are explicitly experienced as supernatural. They represent emanations from an uncanny otherworld that terrorize, fascinate, or enrapture the protagonist, but which never in any event leave him indifferent. The psychological tale significantly complicates the format of the *Sage*, however, by linking the supernatural forces with the peculiar mental disposition of the hero. While the numinous figures of the *Sage* demonstrate a strangeness so radical and complete as to defy interpretation, in the literary tale such figures can usually be identified through their appeal to specific, and often destructive, psychic situations in the hero.[23] The psychological *Märchen* reaffirms the Romantic belief in a hidden affinity between mind and nature, but it views this affinity as problematic, even sinister. The human mind is no longer capable of rational self-supervision, but proves instead to be perilously susceptible to states of derangement or obsession. At the same time, the external world, through its association with the darker aspects of the psyche, takes on an ambiguous and frequently malignant character. The psychological tale is inclined to mistrust not only the stability and wholesomeness of human nature but the benevolence of nature in general. By centering on the fate of particularly vulnerable human beings, the psychological *Märchen* makes a cautionary statement with strong ethical overtones. The fairytale figures may be, as they are in "Der blonde Eckbert," so susceptible to the dark forces within and outside of them that they can no longer defend themselves in any effective way. Nevertheless, their fate serves as a deterrent example for ordinary human beings who still exercise some measure of control over their destinies.

As with the allegorical tale, the typical spatial configuration of the psychological *Märchen* involves an opposition between two contrasting modes of existence. Located at one pole is the human community, with its shared values, its safeguards against extreme or erratic behavior, its various individual compromises, its uneasily maintained sanity. At the other pole lies the realm of the supernatural, which is characteristically situated in a remote and primitive area—as remote and primitive, in fact, as the submerged levels of the human psyche to which the supernatural extends its dubious appeal. The haunted zone in the distant forest, the mountains, or the overgrown meadow represents only a sort of central headquarters for the numinous forces. Their influence penetrates the defences of the community and threatens it from within. In Fouqué's *Undine*, the cistern in Huldbrand's courtyard gives the water-sprites, and ultimately the avenging figure of Undine herself, immediate access to the very heart of his castle.[24] The ball just outside the city of Lucca in Eichendorff's *Das Marmorbild* is such a maze of masks and mirrors that Florio can no longer distinguish between the maiden Bianca and the apparition of Venus. Ännchen's handsome vegetable garden, in Hoffmann's *Die Königsbraut*, provides an entrée for King Daucus Carota I, a vile earth-spirit who establishes his own magnificent garden (in reality a slimy swamp) on the site of Ännchen's cultivated plot. In all of these cases, the supernatural forces merely activate and encourage psychic tendencies that are latent from the beginning. Huldbrand's vulnerability to the water-sprites reflects a hidden susceptibility to the voice of his own neglected conscience. Florio's initial fascination with Bianca escalates immediately to a general state of erotic excitement that opens him to the pernicious influence of Venus. Ännchen's horticultural interests suggest a preoccupation with earthly things that is further manifested in her vanity and pride, and which temporarily blinds her to Carota's true nature. The horizontal spatial opposition between the community and the supernatural realm is augmented, then, through an implied *vertical* tension operating within the protagonist, a tension that pits the conscious self, with its various accommodations to family and society, against such powerful subliminal forces as narcissism, atavistic or misanthropic impulses, sexual lust, or an innate and absolute sense of conscience.

The successive interactions of the two spatial zones, together with corresponding maneuvers on the vertical axis, define the temporal scheme of the psychological tale. Here there can be no talk of mutual attraction of opposites or movement toward synthesis. The goal of the numinous realm is to arouse the slumbering subliminal impulses in the protagonist and to draw him away from the community, into the haunted zone and a state of obsession as complete as it is irrevocable. For this reason, many of these tales are termed *Wahnsinnmärchen*, but that designation fails to cover the occasional instances in which the supernatural exerts a benign or at least an ambiguous influence, as in *Undine*, Tieck's "Die Elfen," or "Der Runenberg." Even at best, however, confinement in the numinous realm represents a condition of arrested development and loss of temporal continuity. At worst it means a terminal state of existential paralysis. The pervasive fear of live burial in the late nineteenth century may be traced in part to the Romantic preoccupation with terrifying possibilities of incarceration in unending spiritual darkness.

Typically, the psychological tale opens with a description of the unstable situation of the hero, followed by his initial encounter with the supernatural realm. The psychic effect of this first collision resembles a subterranean detonation that sends shock waves to the surface but otherwise gives little visible evidence of the inner upheaval. Subsequent encounters recur at an accelerating pace, as the liberated subliminal drives within the hero form an increasingly tighter alliance with the supernatural forces. The protagonist becomes visibly erratic and spatially mobile. He finds himself pulled away from the matrix of the community, drawn by the allure of a region that defies all societal restraints in its satisfaction of subconscious needs. In the end, the hero is either totally engulfed by the supernatural realm or snatched away at the last moment by a redeeming figure who represents higher spiritual agencies within the human community.[25] In neither instance does the hero demonstrate anything like sovereign control over his own fate. As we have seen with "Der blonde Eckbert," the psychological tale contains a certain unresolved tension. Although it makes an ethical statement by vigorously condemning certain aspects of human behavior, it frequently denies the freedom of choice on which moral action is predicated. In this respect, the psychological tale anticipates one of the central predicaments of the nineteenth century:

the dilemma of reconciling traditional Western ethics with an increasingly deterministic view of human nature.

In the context of a movement that made a veritable cult of emotional intensity, it is scarcely remarkable that the Romantic psychological *Märchen* addressed itself above all to the unpredictable and mercurial passion of love.[26] A large number of psychological tales take up the archetypal phenomenon of the demon lover, the awesome, uncanny figure who promises erotic satisfaction beyond all human surmise. Under the influence of such a figure, the subconscious sexual fantasies of the hero develop into a relentless fixation, and he becomes drained of human warmth, incapable of the voluntary accommodations and compromises demanded by a reciprocal love relationship.[27] In "Der blonde Eckbert," Tieck explores a different sort of threat to mature love: an innate and anxious narcissism that refuses to entertain any emotions save those that fortify the self in its isolation. Like the tales of the demon lover, "Eckbert" exposes the frightful emptiness of a love that has degenerated into self-infatuation.

The bleakest commentary on love, however, is provided in Tieck's "Liebeszauber," a tale of such unremitting gloom that secondary literature has generally avoided dealing with the story at all. Here the enemy of love is a cold, inflexible idealism coupled with the conviction that human nature is intrinsically depraved and insane, a combination reminiscent of the student Raskolnikov in *Crime and Punishment*. Emil, the protagonist of Tieck's *Märchen*, likewise attempts to avoid the ambiguities of existence through a strategy of withdrawal. He seals himself off in a barren, lonely room with a single window opening out onto a courtyard. Directly across from him lives a woman whose solitary habits match his own. Through surreptitious observation of each other, the two fall in love; neither is aware of the other's affection. In this juxtaposition of two isolated and introspective lives, Tieck presents the most morbid variant of Romantic window imagery. As experienced by Emil and the unnamed woman,[28] love is degraded to a perverse double-sided voyeurism. Both Emil and the woman are too proud, and too uncertain of themselves, to establish contact through conventional formulas of courtship. In desperation, the woman enlists the aid of an evil hag who promises to seal the love-bond through the sacrificial murder of a child. The woman's fatal mistake lies in her failure to realize that Emil is as much of a voyeur as she is; peeping through his window, Emil witnesses the murder and falls into a lifeless faint, overcome with horror. When he regains consciousness, his memory of all but his earliest years has been obliterated. In a susceptible, childlike state Emil encounters the woman again. While he has no conscious memory of her, he promptly and impulsively confesses his love for her.[29] On the day of their wedding, however, accidental circumstances restore details of the murder scene to Emil's mind, and he stabs his bride to death in a paroxysm of loathing and despair.

The nightmarish world of "Liebeszauber" is a study in extremes. The rigid, artificial timelessness of Emil's life-negating idealism contrasts with the extemporaneous existence of his alter-ego Roderich, who acts and reacts solely on the basis of momentary whims. Both Emil and Roderich live outside of time. Emil categorically rejects the fluidity of human life, while Roderich refuses to acknowledge its continuity and purposiveness. Similarly, the well-defined spatial image of the two opposing windows is contrasted with the obscure image of the labyrinth, represented in the maze of narrow city streets, the chaotic movements of the masked ball, and the theaterlike architecture of interconnecting doors, passageways, and balconies in the country house that Emil purchases for his bride. If the facing windows reflect lonely self-containment and all but autistic withdrawal, the labyrinth provides a setting for the sort of cynical self-abandonment that Roderich practices in his love of intrigue, masks, and mystification. Both spatial configurations represent psychic extremes bordering on insanity. When forcibly dislodged from his idealistic cocoon and confronted with the frightful ambiguity of existence, Emil has neither compassion nor common sense to fall back on. Instead, he becomes precisely what he dreads in other people: an insane, murderous beast who destroys everything in his path, including, in the end, himself.

I have discussed "Liebeszauber" in some detail because it represents a radical form of the psychological *Märchen*, a study in emotional pathology that grimly outlines opposing possibilities of insanity. There is no redeeming agency here, not even a shimmer of hope that the extremes embodied in Emil and Roderich can be integrated to form a fruitful and balanced existence.[30] At the other end of the spectrum of psychological tales lies Fouqué's *Undine*, which ends tragically but nevertheless confirms the existence of no less than two beneficent supernatural agencies. Huldbrand, the knight who marries the water-nymph Undine, finds himself admonished to kindness and love not only by God-fearing folk such as the elderly priest and the fisherman, but also by the water-sprite Kühleborn, who exhibits a primitive but seemingly unerring sense of justice. In this remarkable mixture of Christian theology and *Naturdämonie*, *Undine* comes dangerously close to a fuzzy sort of sentimentality. The heroine's acquisition of an eternal soul may estrange her from the innocent, ephemeral existence of the elementary spirits, but her former life seems nevertheless to provide her with the best possible preparation for timeless participation in God. Undine's newly acquired soul turns out to be superior in every respect to the souls of the weak, callous human beings around her. In order to provide internal conflict for this perfect creature, Fouqué introduces the condition that Undine must return, soul and all, to her watery home if her selfless love is not faithfully returned by her husband. Under the terms of this stipulation, Undine is subjected to ceaseless torment at the hands of Huldbrand. Indeed, her tearful but unflaggingly gallant suffering would soon become almost unbearable to the modern reader, if it were not counterbalanced by the sharply perceived characterizations of Huldbrand and Undine's rival Bertalda. It is in the portrayal of these complicated human beings that *Undine* emphatically rises above its melodramatic premises. Accosted on all sides by voices of supertemporal moral authority, Huldbrand and Bertalda nevertheless insist on short-term solutions to their problems. They live impulsively and provisionally, improvising their way from one situation to the next, hoping against all reasonable expectation to devise a workable ménage à trois with Undine. The spatial development of the tale records their successive foredoomed attempts to locate a setting in which the love triangle can flourish. As in "Der blonde Eckbert" and "Der Runenberg," erratic movements in space are a symptom of temporal discontinuity. In their pride, their self-delusion, and their superstitious fear, Huldbrand and Bertalda refuse to learn from past experience, preferring instead to make one similar false start after another. Like so many characters in the psychological tale, they are motivated by half-conscious drives that prevent them from establishing moral priorities and making consistent sense of their lives. The implication of Undine's enforced return to the sea is that the soul can develop to its fullest potential only in the context of mutual love. Huldbrand and Bertalda not only prevent Undine's soul from achieving such fulfillment, their own souls likewise become atrophied from neglect and mistreatment. No less than Undine, who with her new-found immortality must live forever in the evanescent world of elementary spirits, Huldbrand and Bertalda remain suspended in a spiritual limbo. It is only at the conclusion of the tale, and not altogether voluntarily, that Huldbrand finally acknowledges his disregarded conscience, as he is confronted with the avenging figure of Undine and the imminence of his own death. Like other psychological *Märchen*, *Undine* relies on the intervention of higher agencies to resolve the inner conflicts of the protagonist and bring the narrative to a satisfactory close. There is little indication in the tale that Huldbrand, without the intervention of Undine, would ever have the moral strength to pull his life into focus and to accept the consequences of self-knowledge.

In one sense, *Undine* enlarges the scheme of the psychological *Märchen* by making a representative of the supernatural realm a principal character with a well-defined internal viewpoint and psychological adjustments of her own. Much of the poignancy of *Undine* derives from the efforts of the title figure to accommodate herself to the bewildering and contradictory world of human motivation. The use of the supernatural perspective to illuminate human nature was scarcely new with Fouqué, however. Within German Romanticism itself the most radical and innovative application of this technique is to be found in Wackenroder's "Ein wunderbares morgenländisches Märchen von einem nackten Heiligen," our final example of the psychological tale. Wackenroder's brief and exquisitely compact story concerns the plight of a sidereal being, identified at the conclusion as the spirit of music and love, who has wandered out of the firmament and become entrapped in the body of a man. His transcendent origins cause him to experience the human condition with the stark immediacy of abstraction, unsoftened by habit or trivial preoccupations. What other men sense only dimly, the naked saint apprehends with horrifying intensity and clarity: the essence of human existence is the experience of time. His acutely receptive mind perceives the passage of time as a deafening roar produced by the massive fury of a colossal rotating wheel. In the midst of the perpetual crashing and thundering of the wheel, the saint is overcome by confusion that approaches hysteria. The pandemonium of time fills his soul to the exclusion of all other concerns. He equates his very existence with the experience of time. With the single-mindedness of desperation, he keeps himself in frantic motion day and night, driven by the need to maintain the ceaseless momentum of the wheel and consumed by the nameless anxiety that he himself will cease to be if the wheel stops. In the ferocity of his obsession he becomes like a tormented beast, fully capable of springing out of his solitary cave and striking dead any human being who is tactless enough to engage in some self-contained, practical activity in his presence. Wackenroder's portrait of the agonized saint serves as a radical commentary on the psychology of human existence in time. The distraction, the anxiety, and the mindless brutality of the saint reflect, in nightmarish magnification, the situation of all human beings who know of no other way to verify their own existence than to fill every instant of time with hectic busywork. In their confusion and endless frenzy they become, like the naked saint, solitary and unapproachable, incapable of happiness but altogether too capable of irrational hatred toward those who appear to lead calm, purposeful lives.

The naked saint is finally released from his agony on a moonlit night, as he catches sight of two lovers sailing upstream near his cave. Wondrous, ethereal music rises spontaneously from their small boat, and at the first tone of the music, the roaring wheel of time suddenly vanishes. The disappearance of the wheel does not, however, signify the abolition of time, but rather its transformation. If the rotating movement of the wheel represented an experience of time as monotonous, senseless repetition and dizzying confusion, the horizontal movement of the boat evokes the serene, purposive temporal development of two lives synchronized in mutual love. The thundering cacophony of the wheel had been produced by a chaotic jumble of thousands of single tones. Under the unifying influence of love, the tones realign themselves in the sonorous configurations of harmony, and the mechanical, rhythmic pounding of the wheel is transformed into the living pulse of music. Indeed, the conclusion of the tale prompts an enlarged interpretation of the wheel itself as a ghastly perversion of the music of existence, as the disintegration of existential harmony into unbearable noise when life is no longer informed and animated by love.[31] Confronted at last by the earthly affirmation of his own essence, the spirit of music and love rises in ecstasy from his bondage. His once frantic movements are transformed into dancing steps to the beat of the music, and he ascends, pivoting and turning, homeward into the firmament.

It should be evident from the foregoing discussion that the designations "allegorical *Märchen*" and "psychological *Märchen*" represent nothing more than characteristic labels that help to distinguish the tales derived from the *Volksmärchen* from those based on the format of the *Volkssage*. Precisely because of the major structural differences in these two antecedent forms, Romantic fairy tales tend strongly toward one group or the other. Despite considerable variations within each group, there is no clear evidence of a continuum along which, for instance, the allegorical tale gradually merges with the psychological tale. Given the extraordinary deftness with which Romantic writers invented narrative structures to suit their needs, however, it seems clear that intermediary forms of the fairy tale could have been produced, if the psychological and allegorical tales had not, in themselves, corresponded fairly exactly to two prominent and opposing tendencies within Romanticism.

To use a suggestive play on words, allegorical and psychological *Märchen* may be redesignated as "prescriptive" and "proscriptive" tales. The former prescribe an ideal course of action; they spell out a methodology of intellectual and emotional advancement with the aim of integrating the mind and consolidating it with external nature. The latter group of tales is no less concerned with the enrichment of human existence, but it focuses on the various temptations and preoccupations that benumb the mind and lead to an enduring state of arrested development. The proscriptive tale admonishes the reader to avoid certain universal pitfalls of human nature, and it underscores the urgency of its message by indicating that supernatural forces are involved.

The prescriptive tale is an outgrowth of the progressive tendency in Romanticism, with its faith in the redemptive powers of myth, its confidence in the essential rightness and latent perfectability of human nature. Through the devices of allegory, the prescriptive tale isolates the components of the mind in order to rearrange them and to demonstrate their marvelous capacity for recombination. The experience of time and space is exposed as a pernicious illusion, an anxious dream[32] produced by piecemeal comprehension of the world and a disjointed vision that perceives only boundaries, deadlines, and limitations. As preliminary cognitive tools, time and space make order and meaning out of random sensory data, but they also eventually lock the mind into the false security of familiar and habitual thought patterns. The prescriptive tale outlines the liberation of the mind from its own basic operations and describes its triumphant reintegration in the context of a boundless present—a state in which time and space function no longer as existential constraints, but as options of aesthetic diversion.

The proscriptive tale, on the other hand, voices the concerns of the ethical tendency in Romanticism, a sadder, more cautious, and generally later aspect of the movement. Writers of the proscriptive tales had witnessed, in themselves and in their Romantic associates, the consequences of uncompromising spiritual or emotional exaltation. Their works deal not only with universal problems of human frailty, but, more specifically, with the darker sides of Romanticism itself: its solipsistic cultivation of emotions, its morbid idealism, its aloof and elitist spirituality. This self-critique of Romanticism questions, among other things, the central assumptions of the prescriptive tale. It detects malignant forces in the mind and in nature, forces that make a mockery of the ideal of sovereign self-control and the exuberant attempt to model one's life according to mythic patterns. The protagonists of the proscriptive tale face time and space on psychological rather than epistemological terms. They are familiar with the anxiety of spatial separation, and they experience time with the routine and desperate frustration of those who have lost touch with the sense or purpose of their lives. Rather than undertaking the complicated task of self-integration in time and space, they seize on tactics of evasion. They abandon themselves mindlessly and completely to the treadmill of time, like Wackenroder's naked saint or Roderich in Tieck's "Liebeszauber," or they seek out sanctuaries of artificial timelessness and spacelessness, like Eckbert or Florio in *Das Marmorbild*. The proscriptive tale views such tactics as reprehensible and foredoomed, and it appeals to the reader's ethical sense to confirm the rightness of this assessment.

In general, the proscriptive tale is prepared to abandon the noble ambitions of the prescriptive tale in favor of a commitment to moderation, balance, and self-control. These values may invoke unexpected memories of Weimar Classicism. Nevertheless, the proscriptive tale is distinctly Romantic in tone as well as content. The urgency—often, indeed, the fury—with which the proscriptive tale exposes human deficiency is altogether foreign to the temperament of Goethe or Schiller. Moreover, the notion that the unconscious mind is at the mercy of supernatural forces could perhaps only have developed in the framework of a movement that from the very beginning made spectacular claims for the metaphysical range and inclusiveness of mental operations.

With the distinction between prescriptive and proscriptive, or allegorical and psychological, *Märchen*, I do not mean to imply anything so dramatic as a dichotomy within Romanticism. On the other hand, even if the wide variations within each category are taken into account, it is clear that the two types of fairy tales represent two quite divergent views of the nature of man's existential responsibilities and the permissible limits of human aspirations. The prescriptive tale is by no means blind to the presence of evil in the world, but it perceives evil largely as passivity, as a failure to fulfill the human potential for continual self-advancement. In this sense, evil acts represent crimes of omission in the context of an essentially harmonious universe. The proscriptive tale, retaining the features of Christian dualism, views evil as an altogether active force in perpetual competition with the agencies of goodness for the domination of man's soul. Against the backdrop of a divided universe, the individual cannot presume to gather all elements of existence into a sublime synthesis. He can cultivate his best instincts and protect them from corruption, but he can never strive for an oceanic sense of oneness with all creation without opening himself to the risk of spiritual derangement or self-delusion.

Within the broad and variegated framework of Romanticism, the prescriptive tale celebrates the unity of being beyond space and time; the proscriptive tale laments the disunity of being, but admits the possibility of a personal and limited transcendence of time and space through acts of selfless love and human accommodation.

Notes

Introduction

1. Friedrich Schlegel, *Kritische Friedrich-Schlegel-Ausgabe*, ed. Ernst Behler, Jean-Jacques Anstett, and Hans Eichner (München: Ferdinand Schöningh, 1967), II, 154.
2. Novalis's tales are untitled in the original texts; I have supplied titles merely for the sake of convenience. The Klingsohr tale (Chapter 9 of *Heinrich von Ofterdingen*) will also be referred to as "Eros und Fabel."
3. For a comprehensive theoretical discussion of this aspect of literary structure, see Roman Ingarden, *Das literarische Kunstwerk*, 3rd. ed. (Tübingen: Max Niemeyer, 1965), esp. pp. 235–56, which deal specifically with spatial and temporal structure. Also pertinent in this context is Günther Müller's distinction between *Erzählzeit* ("narrative time") and *erzählte Zeit* ("narrated time"), in *Festschrift für Paul Kluckhohn und Hermann Schneider*, edited by "their students at Tübingen" (Tübingen: Mohr, 1948), pp. 195–212. "Narrative time" refers to the time it takes the author to relate a given passage; as such it may be measured roughly according to lines or pages of print. "Narrated time," on the other hand, refers to the length of a time span related in a work or in a phase of a work.
4. By "phases" I mean not only such large, obvious units as chapters or volumes, but any section of the text that is structurally set off; e.g., by concentration and specificity of spatial or temporal detail, by repetition of action, by restriction to a fixed spatial area, or by a fixed point of view. For a perceptive discussion of the ways in which phases operate within narrative fiction, see Eberhard Lämmert, *Bauformen des Erzählens* (Stuttgart: J. B. Metzler, 1955), esp. pp. 73–82.
5. For a lucid analysis of the distinction between *Lokal* and symbolic space, see Herman Meyer, "Raumgestaltung und Raumsymbolik in der Erzählkunst," in his *Zarte Empirie: Studien zur Literaturgeschichte* (Stuttgart: J. B. Metzler, 1963), pp. 33–56.

Chapter I

1. Novalis, *Schriften: Die Werke Friedrich von Hardenbergs*, ed. Paul Kluckhohn and Richard Samuel, 2d ed. (Stuttgart: Kohlhammer, 1968), III, 403. Unless otherwise noted, all of the following quotations from Novalis are cited from this edition; volume and page number will be indicated in parentheses after each quotation.
2. Paul Kluckhohn makes a convincing case for this early date in his excellent introduction to Volume I of the critical edition (I, 43). See also Friedrich Hiebel, *Novalis: Der Dichter der blauen Blume* (Bern: Francke, 1951), p. 136. Hiebel's work is available in English translation, as *Novalis: German Poet, European Thinker, Christian Mystic* (Chapel Hill: The University of North Carolina Press, 1954).
3. *Ausführliches Lexikon der griechischen und römischen Mythologie*, ed. W. H. Roscher (Leipzig: B. G. Teubner, 1884), I, 2598. The Latin poets (e.g., Vergil, Ovid, and Plinius) generally located the Hesperides in the Atlas Mountains on the northwestern edge of Africa, due west of Sais.
4. Novalis probably found the idea of standing at an open window rather too passive a posture; in his narrative fiction as well as his fragments he was far more concerned with the active process leading toward perfection (see below, Chapter 3).

5. See August Langen, *Anschauungsformen in der deutschen Dichtung des 18. Jahrhunderts (Rahmenschau und Rationalismus)* (Jena: Eugen Diederich, 1934), p. 21: "Das Charakteristische des künstlerischen Bildes zumal dieser Zeit ist Auswahl und Eingrenzung, Gruppierung, Aufbau und Komposition, Zusammendrängung des Wesentlichen auf ein kleines umrahmtes Apperzeptionsfeld."
6. Ibid., p. 14.
7. Romantic irony, of course, has its roots in Fichtean philosophy. Helmut Rehder, in his discussion of Fichte's contribution to Romantic natural philosophy, notes the crucial importance of the frame, or boundary, in orienting the mind toward infinity: "Das Bewußtsein der Grenze verleiht dem Geist einen Ausblick auf unendliche Möglichkeiten." H. Rehder, *Die Philosophie der unendlichen Landshaft: Ein Beitrag zur Geschichte der romantischen Weltanschauung* (Halle/Saale: Max Niemeyer, 1932). p. 60.
8. Friedrich Schlegel, *Kritische Friedrich-Schlegel-Ausgabe*, ed. Ernst Behler and Hans Eichner (München: Ferdinand Schöningh, 1962), V, 8.
9. For a lively discussion of Eichendorff's window imagery, see Richard Alewyn's *Nachwort* to Joseph von Eichendorff, *Werke in einem Band*, ed. Ingeborg Hillmann (Hamburg: Hoffmann und Campe, 1966), pp. 579–81. Alewyn seeks to exonerate Eichendorff from the charge of shallowness by demonstrating, as a case in point, that Eichendorff's insistent use of windows reflects an experience that is universally and archetypically human: the experience of interior space as restrictive and stultifying, and the longing for release in unbounded exterior space. Alewyn's point is well argued, but he overlooks Eichendorff's great indebtedness to Romantic tradition in this and other regards.
10. Heinrich Heine, *Sämtliche Schriften*, ed. Klaus Briegleb (München: Carl Hanser, 1971), III, 442–45.
11. It seems to me not too farfetched to see in the old man and the old woman a reiteration of this use of masculinity and femininity to symbolize mind and nature respectively. The old man and his book represent the lure of absolute knowledge and the celebration of the intellect; and it is at the old woman's behest that Hyazinth sets out to traverse the natural world.
12. In Chapter 3, we shall see that this spatial reversal has important implications for Hyazinth's temporal experience.
13. The preliminary synthesis expressed in this scene is also apparent in the narrative tone with which it is related. It can be shown, for instance, that the narrative voice moves from the naive viewpoint of nature in the opening passages to an exalted lyrical style that reflects Hyazinth's internal ascent to perfection. Here elements of *both* viewpoints are present: the poetic diction of "kristallner Quell" and "schwarze himmelhohe Säulen" is combined with the ingenuous colloquialism "eine Menge Blumen" and the syntax of the folk fairy tale ("Er begegnete . . . einer Menge Blumen, die kamen in ein Tal herunter zwischen schwarzen himmelhohen Säulen").
14. Ulrich Gaier, *Krumme Regel: Novalis' 'Konstruktionslehre des schaffenden Geistes' und ihre Tradition* (Tübingen: Max Niemeyer, 1970), p. 221.
15. Thus in his earliest conception of the tale Novalis envisioned this scene as follows: "Einem gelang es—er hob den Schleyer der Göttin zu Sais— / Aber was sah er? Er sah—Wunder des Wunders—Sich Selbst" (II, 584).
16. That Hyazinth's return could so transform the entire community is clearly anticipated in the *Lehrlinge*. The Teacher has sent out into the world a beautiful child with dark-blue eyes who closely resembles Hyazinth; of his return, the Teacher prophesies: "Einst wird es wiederkommen . . . und unter uns wohnen, dann hören die Lehrstunden auf" (I, 80–81).
17. In the *Blütenstaub* collection, Novalis describes this final state "after abstraction" as follows: "Vor der Abstrakzion ist alles eins, aber eins wie Chaos; nach der Abstrakzion ist wieder alles vereinigt, aber diese Vereinigung ist eine freye Verbindung selb-

ständiger, selbstbestimmter Wesen. Aus einem Haufen ist eine Gesellschaft geworden, das Chaos ist in eine mannichfaltige Welt verwandelt" (II, 455–57).

18. The German word *Gegenwart* is doubly appropriate here, for its signifies both "presence" (in a spatial sense) and "present" (in a temporal sense); as we shall see in Chapter 3, the final state also represents a synthesis of time and timelessness.

19. Bruce Haywood contends—justifiably, I think—that this conflict is one of the principal themes of *Heinrich von Ofterdingen*. B. Haywood, *Novalis: The Veil of Imagery. A Study of the Poetic Works of Friedrich von Hardenberg (1772–1801)* (Cambridge, Mass.: Harvard University Press, 1959), p. 97.

20. While Novalis himself does not mention the poet's name, the tale is clearly adapted from Herodotus's account of Arion's voyage in the *History*, I, 23–24.

21. Max Lüthi, *Es war einmal . . . : Vom Wesen des Volksmärchens*, 3rd ed. (Göttingen: Vandenhoeck & Ruprecht, 1968), p. 34.

22. Ibid., p. 34.

23. Lawrence Frye, "Spatial Imagery in Novalis' 'Hymnen an die Nacht,'" *Deutsche Vierteljahrsschrift*, 41 (1967), 568–91.

24. Hayward, *Novalis: The Veil of Imagery*, p. 101.

25. The cave is, of course, an exception to the other enclosed spaces. We have seen that it, too, represents a preliminary synthesis of inside and outside—a room in a forest, so to speak. Details inside the cave such as the lute and the almond branch—representing poetry and nature—reinforce this interpretation.

26. It is characteristic of Novalis's reluctance to describe the final state of perfection that the dissolving of Atlantis is not part of the narrative proper, but is mentioned as a kind of afterthought by the merchants: the land "is *said* to have" sunk beneath the waves. While on the one hand the indirectness of this statement relieves the narrators of a certain authorial responsibility, on the other hand the appeal to legend substantiates the truth of their assertion on a higher level of authority.

27. Ricarda Huch, *Die Romantik: Ausbreitung, Blütezeit und Verfall* (Tübingen: Rainer Wunderlich, 1951), p. 297.

28. H. A. Korff, *Geist der Goethezeit: Versuch einer ideellen Entwicklung der klassisch-romantischen Literaturgeschichte*, 3rd rev. ed. (Leipzig: Koehler & Amelang, 1959), III, 585.

29. As an indication of the heightened complexity of this tale, we may note that not one couple, but *two* are now separated by spatial polarity (Eros and Freya, Arcturus and Sophie).

30. Peter Küpper, *Die Zeit als Erlebnis des Novalis* (Köln: Böhlau, 1959), pp. 83–84, notes this correspondence between the stars and the main figures of the tale. Strangely enough, he overlooks the temporal implications of these movements. We have discovered, of course, a similar structural correlation between mind and nature in "Hyazinth und Rosenblüte."

31. The various groupings are by no means arbitrary. After apparently engaging in sexual intercourse with the Father (Sense), Ginnistan (Fantasy) busies herself opening the windows, letting in fresh air, making a delicious meal—all activities relating to the senses (sight, smell, taste). A more obvious example of the same kind of thing is Eros's transformation into Cupid after intercourse with Ginnistan.

32. J. Christopher Middleton, in his discussion of the mythical antecedents of Arcturus's mountain, writes, "I do not know how much significance should be attached to the detail about the events in the city being reflected in the frozen sea. But this detail does introduce the cosmorama of central mountain, encircling sea, and distant ring of mountains, almost as if it were by afterthought, even with some carelessness in the visual presentation." "Two Mountain Scenes in Novalis and the Question of Symbolic Style," in *Literary Symbolism: A Symposium*, ed. Helmut Rehder (Austin, Texas: University of Texas Press, 1965), pp. 87–88. Middleton suggests that the mountain functions

merely as a mythic image rather than as "one detail in a symbolism that is contained in its context and analytic in its function" (p. 88), with which I would tentatively agree; but the image is clearly not as isolated as he indicates.

33. Spatial images suggesting analytical and synthetic thought may also be found in Heinrich's first dream (I, 196–97), in which the two psychic directions are expressed through an alternate succession of entry and emergence, movement to closed and movement to open space. As the final sequence of the dream begins, Heinrich is walking through a dark forest that gradually *opens* out onto a meadow; he then *enters* a cave which in turn *opens* into a cavern; here he climbs *into* a large basin full of a wondrous bluish liquid (first symbol of unity in diversity) whose current he ultimately follows *out* of the basin and *into* the rocks, where he falls asleep; later he regains consciousness on an *open* meadow, where he discovers the blue flower. Not the least of the symbolic properties of the flower, incidentally, is its combination of open and enclosed space in the configuration of its petals.

34. Their punishments differ slightly in accordance with their allegorical functions: the Mother is chained in iron bands to deprive her of spatial mobility and the chance to extend herself to other characters, while the Father (Sense) is condemned to bread and water, i.e., the most meager sensory experiences.

35. Her "other half," the flame, also operates as a source of unity and communion, by dissolving the frozen sea. The Mother thus helps to redeem the realms of both Mind and Nature simultaneously.

36. From the initial description of Arcturus's realm (I, 291), one might be tempted to view his domain as encompassing only *inorganic* nature: stars, minerals, metals, and the like. Yet at the conclusion of the tale, the "Gestirne" and the "Geister der Natur" (unqualified!) descend from the cupola of Arcturus's palace (I, 313). If the spirits of Nature per se reside in Arcturus's cupola, one must seek a broader explanation for the apparent exclusion of organic life from this realm. As I see it, the metallic flowers and plants described in the opening episode are best interpreted as timeless *Urformen* of their earthly counterparts, *natura naturans* as opposed to *natura naturata*. The frozen condition of all forms of nature in Arcturus's realm is a further complication, to be taken up in Chapter 3.

37. H. J. Schueler discusses some of the Gnostic allusions in the Klingsohr tale, in "Cosmology and Quest in Novalis' 'Klingsohrs Märchen,'" *Germanic Review*, 49 (1974), 259–66. The principal spatial model that Schueler sees in the tale, however, is the Ptolemaic geocentric cosmos with its hierarchy of existence. The highest level, that of God and divine grace, is represented by the "soft music" in Arcturus's throne room; the "lower heaven or sky" appears as Arcturus's island kingdom and the realm of the Moon; the House and the domain of the Fates represent, respectively, the level of ordinary human existence and the level of chaotic, demonic forces. Schueler's analysis is ingenious and illuminating, though he fails to take into account Novalis's deliberate deviations from Ptolemaic cosmology (Arcturus's kingdom encompasses, for instance, subterranean as well as celestial nature, and the Moon is associated with this kingdom only in a very limited sense), and he does not acknowledge the various other spatial configurations that operate alongside the Ptolemaic system.

38. Middleton, "Two Mountain Scenes," pp. 88–90, traces the history of the concentric cosmorama back to Plato's description of Atlantis in the *Timaeus*, and further to Chinese, Indian, and Sumerian mythology.

39. Fabel descends from Sophie's altar to the land of the Fates, but ascends straight up to Arcturus's throne room. The domain of Death extends to Nature as well as Mind.

40. Max Diez points out this exchange of gender, in "Metapher und Märchengestalt III, Novalis und das allegorische Märchen," *PMLA*, 48 (1933), 495.

41. Werner Kohlschmidt, "Der Wortschatz der Innerlichkeit bei Novalis," in his *Form und Innerlichkeit: Beiträge zur Geschichte und Wirkung der deutschen Klassik und Romantik* (Bern: Francke, 1955), pp. 120–56.

Chapter II

1. André Gottrau's dissertation on Tieck is typical of this line of criticism: "Es findet sich keine Möglichkeit, den Gang der Handlung von irgend einem Punkte aus als Ganzes zu verstehen. . . . Das ist die traumhafte Welt des jungen Tieck in ihrer ganzen Zauberhaftigkeit und Nichtigkeit." A. Gottrau, "Die Zeit im Werk des jungen Tieck," Diss. Zürich 1947, pp. 86–87.
2. Ludwig Tieck, *Werke*, ed. Marianne Thalmann (Darmstadt: Wissenschaftliche Buchgesellschaft, 1968), II, 9. Further page references to this edition (and this volume) will be indicated in parentheses following the individual quotations.
3. The old woman's coughing and the uncanny shifting of her facial features introduce a disturbing note into the general harmony. These ominous undertones anticipate the old woman's ambiguity in the tale as a whole. I will deal with her problematic role in detail in Chapter 4.
4. Victoria L. Rippere notes the importance of self-limitation and "assent . . . to the restrictions of 'prosaic reality' " in the idyll of "Waldeinsamkeit," in " 'Der blonde Eckbert': A Psychological Reading," *PMLA*, 85 (1970), 482.
5. Representatives of the "ethical" interpretation include Janis Gellinek, "*Der blonde Eckbert*: A Tieckian Fall from Paradise," in *Lebendige Form: Interpretationen zur deutschen Literatur: Festschrift für Heinrich E. K. Henel*, ed. Jeffrey L. Sammons and Ernst Schürer (München: Wilhelm Fink, 1970), pp. 147–66; Rippere, " 'Der blonde Eckbert': A Psychological Reading"; Otto K. Liedke, "Tieck's *Der blonde Eckbert*: Das Märchen von Verarmung und Untergang," *German Quarterly*, 44 (1971), 311–16; and Ralph W. Ewton, Jr., "Childhood without End: Tieck's *Der blonde Eckbert*," *German Quarterly*, 46 (1973), 410–27. The "demonic-force" interpretation is advanced by, among others, Ingrid Merkel, "Wirklichkeit im romantischen Märchen," *Colloquia Germanica*, 3 (1969), 162–83; Valentine C. Hubbs, "Tieck, Eckbert und das kollektive Unbewußte," *PMLA*, 71 (1956), 686–93; Richard W. Kimpel, "Nature, Quest, and Reality in Tieck's *Der blonde Eckbert* and *Der Runenberg*," *Studies in Romanticism*, 9 (1970), 176–92; Richard Benz, *Märchen-Dichtung der Romantiker* (Gotha: Perthes, 1908), pp. 109–10; and Raymond Immerwahr, "The Outer World in *Der blonde Eckbert*," in *Studies in Nineteenth Century and Early Twentieth Century German Literature: Studies in Honor of Paul K. Whitaker*, ed. Norman H. Binger and A. Wayne Wonderley (Lexington, Kentucky: APRA Press, 1974), pp. 52–70. After acknowledging the limited relevance of an ethical interpretation, William J. Lillyman also finally opts for this position, in "The Enigma of *Der blonde Eckbert*: The Significance of the End," *Seminar*, 7 (1971), 144–55.
6. Hubbs, "Tieck, Eckbert und das kollektive Unbewußte," p. 688.
7. For an excellent discussion of the role of narcissism in "Der blonde Eckbert," see Rippere, " 'Der blonde Eckbert': A Psychological Reading."
8. I must disagree emphatically with Marianne Thalmann, *Das Märchen und die Moderne: Zum Begriff der Surrealität im Märchen der Romantik* (Stuttgart: Kohlhammer, 1961), pp. 55–56, who interprets the incest motif as a gratuitous concession to Nicolai and the Enlightenment reading public, a prosaic explanation for Eckbert's secret. Drawing a false analogy to "Der Runenberg" and particularly to "Die Elfen," Thalmann overlooks the crucial significance of confession in "Eckbert" and interprets Bertha's story as a *betrayal* of her wonderful secret, a source of guilt rather than redemption. Even more disturbing, however, is Walther L. Hahn's contention, "Tiecks Blonder Eckbert als Gestaltung romantischer Theorie," *Proceedings, Northwest Conference on Foreign Languages*, 18 (1967), 78, that the incest motif reflects the Romantic wish for perfect unity and the attempt to overcome conventional mores. Misinterpretations of this sort abound in Hahn's article. Like Thalmann, he is too much concerned with extraneous analogies. While the attempt to find parallels to Romantic theory, or to other tales of Tieck, in "Der blonde Eckbert" is sound enough in principle, this procedure surely presupposes a careful interpretation of the work and a willingness to acknowledge elements that do not conform to one's general scheme.

9. Immerwahr, "The Outer World in *Der blonde Eckbert*," p. 61, also points out the ominous implications of the words "bis jetzt."

10. The parallel here to Freud's concepts of the superego and the id is fairly obvious and needs, I think, no further elaboration.

11. Lillyman's "The Enigma of *Der blonde Eckbert*," which deals quite sensibly with the problem of original sin and is generally one of the better pieces on "Eckbert," neglects to consider these internal impulses as a central aspect of original sin. Instead, Lillyman contends that *all* of Eckbert's and Bertha's transgressions derive directly or indirectly from their father's adultery.

12. Immerwahr, "The Outer World in *Der blonde Eckbert*," p. 54, makes the valid and long overdue point that the old woman's domain encompasses not merely "nature," but "all forces surrounding human life—spatially and temporally, metaphysically and ethically, externally and psychologically—which control man's destiny." It seems to me, however, that Immerwahr takes his argument one step too far. In viewing the old woman's influence as all-inclusive, he deftly avoids the problem of establishing the degree to which Eckbert and Bertha are motivated by impulses beyond the old woman's knowledge or control. We have seen, for instance, that both Eckbert and Bertha are split between the drive toward existential openness and the drive toward self-defensive isolation. Following Immerwahr's interpretation, one would have to assume that the old woman, inscrutable as she is, somehow supports and even dictates *both* of these contradictory psychological impulses. Throughout the story, however, she encourages the first impulse and displays an altogether inadequate understanding of the second.

13. His meeting with the peasant on the way represents an abbreviated version of his dealings with Walther and Hugo: friendly interaction, suspicion on Eckbert's part, immediate confirmation of his suspicion.

14. The final pages of the tale present a special problem of narrative perspective. It is possible, for instance, to interpret Hugo, the peasant, and the old woman herself as phantoms of Eckbert's deranged mind. From a psychological standpoint, it makes good sense that Eckbert should impute objective reality to these hallucinations, which represent externalizations of his guilt feelings. Such a reading, however, robs the natural world of the autonomous power it formerly demonstrated through Walther's uncanny knowledge of the dog's name—the one imponderable act in the tale which both Eckbert and Bertha witness, and which must be considered an objective event. It seems to me that Tieck purposefully creates an atmosphere of ambiguity around the supernatural incidents at the end of the tale in order to draw the reader into Eckbert's confusion and horror. Thus some of the occurrences are viewed only through Eckbert's senses: "Indem er noch immer hinstarrte, sah er plötzlich Walthers Gesicht" (24); "Es war, als wenn er ein nahes munteres Bellen vernahm . . . er hörte mit wunderlichen Tönen ein Lied singen" (25). Others are presented through the neutral eyes of a presumably objective narrator: "Es war niemand anders als Walther" (25); "Eine krummgebückte Alte schlich hustend mit einer Krücke den Hügel heran" (25–26).

15. In a similar vein, Bertha is "pleasantly surprised" at the appearance of the old woman; later the two walk together over a "pleasant meadow." The repetition of the word "angenehm" prepares the reader for the kind of existence that Bertha is about to enter into: a low-keyed, muted happiness, an enjoyable state of mind that places no severe demands either on the intellect or the emotions. The paradise of "Waldeinsamkeit" is not to be confused with Novalis's second Golden Age, as we shall see below.

16 They also transgress against the second part of the categorical imperative: to act as if the maxim of one's action were to become, by one's own will, a universal law of nature. Appropriately, the old woman's strategy in punishing Eckbert is to make the "as if " come true—against Eckbert's will. The betrayal and mistrust that he has made the maxim of his actions become the maxim of the world around him; each misdeed of Eckbert's is immediately repaid in like kind, with the merciless consistency of natural

law. The parallel to Kantian thought is more or less coincidental. Tieck never studied philosophy in any kind of systematic way and probably knew the *Critique of Practical Reason* only from hearsay. At any rate, Kant's moral precepts represent to a large extent a reformulation of the Christian ethics which Tieck's mother, a devout Lutheran, must have attempted to instill in her son from his earliest childhood.

17. This qualified sense of satisfaction is to be contrasted with the smug, self-congratulatory attitude presented by Ewton, "Childhood without End," p. 425, who observes in his closing remarks, "When we finally detach ourselves from these characters at the end and conclude that their fate was inevitable we have an emerging sense of having successfully withstood the trial in which they failed. From this unconscious interpretation of the story the reader derives a large measure of his pleasure in reading." I find this attitude insensitive, particularly in the context of a study that otherwise displays some degree of psychological finesse.

18. Cf. Emil Staiger, "Ludwig Tieck und der Ursprung der deutschen Romantik," in his *Stilwandel: Studien zur Vorgeschichte der Goethezeit* (Zürich: Atlantis, 1963), pp. 175–204. Staiger seeks to identify a more fundamental affinity between Tieck and the members of the Jena group: Tieck emerges as the prototypical Romantic, whose early works stand as "Zeugnis eines gewichtlosen Daseins, das, eben um seiner Leere willen, unendlich bestimmbar und reizbar ist" (p. 194). Moreover, Tieck anticipates and exemplifies a deep-seated indifference [Gleichgültigkeit], in terms of which all values appear interchangeable and devoid of substance, the world becomes an aesthetic toy, literature predominates over life, and the dalliance with moods and sensations supplants any commitment to moral issues.

19. Edwin H. Zeydel, *Ludwig Tieck, the German Romanticist: A Critical Study* (Princeton, N.J.: Princeton University Press, 1935), p. 81.

20. As Erika Voerster maintains (echoing Marianne Thalmann), in *Märchen und Novellen im klassisch-romantischen Roman*, 2d ed. (Bonn: H. Bouvier, 1966), p. 86.

21. Gellinek, "*Der blonde Eckbert*: A Tieckian Fall from Paradise," pp. 150–57.

22. Zeydel, *Ludwig Tieck, the German Romanticist*, p. 34, points out that the ideal of altruism as a counterforce to unstable subjectivism is one of the most conspicuous themes in Tieck's early works. Curiously, he overlooks this theme in "Eckbert" and adds his voice to the chorus of those who see little more in the tale than a dreamlike atmosphere of enchantment and horror. "A veil of poetry is cast about the whole story, and not even an echo of the real world penetrates it.... What counts here is not so much Bertha's guilt as the fastening of the mood of guilt upon helpless human beings.... *Der blonde Eckbert* is a product of dreams and fancies, which spin a web of varicolored moods and atmospheres." Zeydel, p. 84.

23. The fact that the new village appears quite different to Christian may be attributed to his internal reversal of values: what previously seemed "hateful" is now "charming and enticing."

24. As will be pointed out in Chapter 4, the piety of the village contains elements that deviate from Christian orthodoxy in the direction of primitive vegetative rites. In this chapter, however, I stress only the conventional aspects of the village religion, since the unorthodox aspects become apparent only in a discussion of the kind of temporal experience the village has to offer.

25. Immerwahr, "Reality as an Object of Romantic Experience in Early German Romanticism," *Colloquia Germanica*, 3 (1969), 140.

26. Max Diez points out the metaphorical identity of the woman and the mountains in "Metapher und Märchengestalt IV: Tiecks Frau vom Runenberg," *PMLA*, 48 (1933), 879–80.

27. Lillyman points out this analogy to Christian communion in his very perceptive article, "Ludwig Tieck's 'Der Runenberg': The Dimensions of Reality," *Monatshefte*, 42 (1970), 236.

28. Cf. Elisabeth's words to Christian's father: "Immer spricht er von dem Fremden,

und behauptet, daß er ihn schon lange gekannt habe, denn dieser fremde Mann sei eigentlich ein wunderschönes Weib" (75). Unless one assumes that Christian is losing his mind—the usual interpretation of this scene and later ones—one must take his assertion of the stranger's true identity at face value.

29. At least three studies have attempted to identify the precise nature of the forces Christian encounters on the mountain: Wolfdietrich Rasch, "Blume und Stein: Zur Deutung von Ludwig Tiecks Erzählung *Der Runenberg*," in *The Discontinuous Tradition: Studies in German Literature in Honour of Ernest Ludwig Stahl*, ed. P. F. Ganz (London: Oxford University Press, 1971), pp. 113–28; Ewton, "Life and Death of the Body in Tieck's *Der Runenberg*," *Germanic Review*, 50 (1975), 19–33; and Harry Vredeveld, "Ludwig Tieck's *Der Runenberg*: An Archetypal Interpretation," *Germanic Review*, 49 (1974), 200–214. While one may commend the resourcefulness of these works, all three are open to the charge of special pleading for psychological theses external to the text of "Der Runenberg." Rasch maintains that Christian's experiences on the mountain represent a symbolic confrontation with, and submission to, nothing other than his own morbid "death instinct" as defined by Freud in *Jenseits des Lustprinzips*. Apart from some serious oversimplifications in dealing with the plant world, Rasch's interpretation ultimately stands or falls according to one's willingness to accept the validity of the idea of the death instinct, a concept that has become generally discredited among psychologists. (Cf. Erich Fromm, *The Anatomy of Human Destructiveness* (New York: Holt, Rinehart and Winston, 1973), pp. 15–16.) For Ewton, too, the woman and her tablet symbolize self-encounter: Christian experiences an ecstatic "rebirth of the body" (p. 25), in which the self is recognized as fundamentally physical in nature. Ewton is clearly inspired here by the works of Norman O. Brown (notably *Love's Body* and *Life Against Death*), but his application of Brown's ideas to "Der Runenberg" is forced and unconvincing. To justify his assertion that the mineral world symbolizes an exaltation of the physical body, Ewton alludes to Jacob Böhme's mystique of the pure body and identifies elements of Böhmian mineral imagery in the woman's song. The connection is interesting but not compelling. More disturbingly, Ewton finds it necessary to support this interpretation of the mountain world by claiming that the plant world is life-negating, oppressively spiritualized, and self-deluded about the reality of physical death. This assessment of Christian culture, explicitly derived from Brown and from Freud's *Das Unbehagen in der Kultur*, cannot be applied to the Christianity of Tieck's tale, which places an almost pagan emphasis on the organic life cycle of growth, maturation, and decay. Vredeveld's Jungian analysis promptly and unequivocally identifies the woman in the castle as the "Great Mother Goddess" (p. 203). The principal weakness of this interpretation is that it reduces the tale to a rather specialized case study in developmental pathology. Christian displays a distorted and unstable relationship to the Great Mother because his own physical mother has been overshadowed by a dominant father figure who relentlessly champions consciousness and rationality. The employment of Jungian archetypes is capricious here, too. If the father functions as an advocate of consciousness, it is curious that Tieck should have made him a gardener—an occupation closely associated with the earth and the dark, irrational realm of the Great Mother. Moreover, although Vredeveld views the woman in the castle as an ambivalent figure (the Good Mother of the beginning is transformed into the Terrible Mother of the conclusion of the tale), he is unable to account satisfactorily for this shifting function. Surely the Terrible Mother would be more likely to engulf Christian at the beginning, when his consciousness is ostensibly more vulnerable and superficial.

30. A similar ambivalence is generated within him when he later reenters this intermediate zone on his journey back to his home village. Cf. p. 72 of the text.

31. E. T. A. Hoffmann, *Poetische Werke* (Berlin: Walter de Gruyter, 1961), X, 241.

32. August Langen, *Anschauungsformen in der deutschen Dichtung des 18. Jahrhunderts (Rahmenschau und Rationalismus)* (Jena: Eugen Diederich, 1934), pp. 68–69.

33. If Novalis had written "Der Runenberg," for instance, Christian would have

found the woman on Rune Mountain to be none other than *Elisabeth*—but an Elisabeth who was elevated along with him to a higher mode of being.

34. Lillyman, "Ludwig Tieck's 'Der Runenberg,'" pp. 231–32, presents very convincing arguments for the existence of this paradoxical double validity. The most striking proof that Christian's experience on the mountain cannot be dismissed as mere madness is, of course, the reappearance of the tablet near the village. Since Christian's father sees the tablet, and takes its mystical import quite seriously, one must assume that it does indeed exist objectively.

Chapter III

1. H. A. Korff, "Das Wesen der Romantik," in *Begriffsbestimmung der Romantik*, ed. Helmut Prang (Darmstadt: Wissenschaftliche Buchgesellschaft, 1968), pp. 204–6.

2. For a comprehensive discussion of the triadic development of time in Early Romanticism, see Hans Joachim Mähl, *Die Idee des goldenen Zeitalters im Werk des Novalis: Studien zur Wesensbestimmung der frühromantischen Utopie und zu ihren ideengeschichtlichen Voraussetzungen* (Heidelberg: C. Winter, 1965).

3. For a clarification of the terms "narrative time" and "narrated time," see the Introduction, note 3.

4. Kafka, unlike Novalis, makes the deceleration of time tangible to the reader by progressively extending the narrative time employed in describing each day of narrated time. He expends, for instance, only 57 pages on K.'s first three days in the village and 365 pages on his last three or four days. Cf. Heinz Politzer, *Franz Kafka: Parable and Paradox*, 2d ed. (Ithaca, N.Y.: Cornell University Press, 1966), pp. 248–52.

5. Cf. Helmut Schanze, *Romantik und Aufklärung: Untersuchungen zu Friedrich Schlegel und Novalis* (Nürnberg: Hans Carl, 1966), p. 31: "Diese Doppelbewegung des Begreifens, der mit Bewußtsein gefundene Zusammenhang von Denken und Fühlen, die 'Hin und *her* Direktion' des anschauenden Begreifens, [ist] nach Novalis die 'Basis alles Philosophierens'." In this connection, Schanze also emphasizes the high importance that Novalis ascribed to *Besonnenheit* as opposed to fretful, impatient philosophizing.

6. It may be noted—again in analogy to the spatial development of the tale—that articulated time begins to reappear in the final phases of Hyazinth's journey, primarily in the image of the endless chambers through which he travels. Here too, as with space, the fusion of definite and indefinite time anticipates the concluding synthesis of time and timelessness.

7. Mircea Eliade discusses the significance of ritual events as reenactments of a mythic process in *The Myth of the Eternal Return* (New York: Pantheon Books, 1954). For an examination of ritual forms and themes in the history of narrative literature, see Robert Scholes and Robert Kellogg, *The Nature of Narrative* (New York: Oxford University Press, 1966), pp. 220–26.

8. This passage also indicates that the House is slowly returning to nature—precisely as its inhabitants are doing on the allegorical level of the tale. A particularly nice touch here is the moss which upholsters the steps: it is as if Nature were at work redecorating the house.

9. This attack on the notion of objective time corresponds to the related attack on objective space that we noted in Chapter 1.

10. Hence the anguished beginning of the second "Hymne an die Nacht": "Muß immer der Morgen wiederkommen?" (II, 133).

11. According to Father Moon, the drama is to last "until the sign is given for departure," i.e., until the moon rises again several hours later.

12. The Lily is probably the constellation Virgo, which appears to the right of Libra (the Scales) on the ecliptic (or, from Arcturus's point of view, to the left). The position of the other constellations alluded to here—Corona Borealis, Aquila, and Leo—also corresponds exactly to their location in the sky.

13. Cf. Peter Küpper, *Die Zeit als Erlebnis des Novalis* (Köln: Böhlau, 1959), p. 48.

14. In Chapter 1, Arcturus's mountain island was designated as the realm of ideal nature, in which the timeless *Urformen* of organic and inorganic nature reside. Nevertheless, even this ideal kingdom remains in some respects susceptible to change. With Sophie's descent to the lower level of prosaic reality and immature mind, the timeless forms are bereft of their animating force. They become frozen into indifferent templates that mechanically generate imperfect reproductions in the temporal world. In the concluding apotheosis of Eternal Spring, the gap between ideal and temporal nature closes. The living flowers and trees are released from time and become spiritually animated (they speak and sing), while their metallic counterparts in Arcturus's realm begin to move and likewise to sing, as they reverberate with melodious sound: "Die Blumen und Bäume [in der Welt] wuchsen und grünten mit Macht. Alles schien beseelt. Alles sprach und sang. . . . Im Hofe sprang der lebendiggewordne Quell, der Hain bewegte sich mit den süßesten Tönen, und ein wunderbares Leben schien in seinen heißen Stämmen und Blättern, in seinen funkelnden Blumen und Früchten zu quellen und zu treiben" (I, 312–13).

15. "Er war in dieser Nacht um mehrere Jahre älter, aus einem Jünglinge zum Manne geworden" (I, 222).

16. Ricarda Huch, for instance, speaks caustically of the "unverständlicher allegorischer Kleinkram" in "Eros und Fabel" and Goethe's "Märchen." R. Huch, *Die Romantik: Ausbreitung, Blütezeit und Verfall* (Tübingen: Rainer Wunderlich, 1951), p. 296. Rudolf Haym attacks the Klingsohr tale for its harsh allegorical meaning and the "zufällige Bewegungen . . . der sich hier durcheinander tummelnden Redoutenfiguren." R. Haym, *Die romantische Schule* (Berlin: R. Gaertner, 1870), pp. 383–84.

17. Schanze, *Romantik und Aufklärung*, p. 54.

18. It is of particular significance that the name "Fabel" suggests not only poesy or literature but, more specifically, narrative with a *plot*. Fabel thus represents the temporal force of development, change, and direction, as well as the spatial force of cohesiveness and unity. (In the eighteenth century the word "Fabel" had a variety of meanings, including "epic poetry," "fairy tale," and "fable" in the English sense.)

19. That Fabel is related to the Fates as an agent of death in her own right is suggested by her reference to them as her aunts (I, 303). It is also worth noting here that Fabel's activity most frequently takes the form of *awakening* (as with the Father, Atlas, and Freya). The experience of waking up signifies, of course, a continuation of the same existence on a higher level of vitality and consciousness.

20. Schanze, *Romantik und Aufklärung*, pp. 51–52.

21. Theodor Haering, *Novalis als Philosoph* (Stuttgart: Kohlhammer, 1954), pp. 536–37.

Chapter IV

1. Henry D. Thoreau, *Walden; or Life in the Woods*, ed. Edwin Way Teale (New York: Dodd, Mead & Co., 1946), p. 7.

2. As Victoria L. Rippere points out, in "Ludwig Tieck's 'Der blonde Eckbert': A Psychological Reading," *PMLA*, 85 (1970), 483. From a strictly psychological viewpoint, it is, incidentally, altogether fitting that the old woman and her pets, as images of guilt generated by Eckbert's subconscious mind, should be supertemporal. Cf. Freud: "The events of the unconscious system are timeless, that is they are not ordered in time, are not changed by the passage of time, have no relation whatsoever to time. Temporal relations, too, are connected with the working of the conscious mind." From "Das Unbewußte," quoted in Hans Meyerhoff, *Time in Literature* (Berkeley, Calif.: University of California Press, 1955), p. 58. Once again, however, it must be emphasized that the old woman and the animals, far from being mere images of Eckbert's guilt, must be considered as existing in their own right, as autonomous, objective figures. It is precisely this horrible and unaccountable congruence of guilty subconscious and external reality that ultimately pitches Eckbert into madness.

3. Gerhard Haeuptner, "Ludwig Tiecks Märchen 'Der blonde Eckbert,'" in *Verstehen und Vertrauen: Otto Friedrich Bollnow zum 65. Geburtstag*, ed. Johannes Schwartländer (Stuttgart: Kohlhammer, 1968), p. 24.

4. André Jolles, *Einfache Formen: Legende, Sage, Mythe, Rätsel, Spruch, Kasus, Memorabile, Märchen, Witz*, 2d ed. (Halle/Saale: Max Niemeyer, 1956), pp. 200–201.

5. By way of contrast, the interdictions in folk fairy tales are quite specific: "do not pick the apples," "do not speak to the wolf if he comes to the door," "do not leave the tower," etc. Raymond Immerwahr, "The Outer World in *Der blonde Eckbert*," p. 59, takes the view that the old woman is *intentionally* vague in her warning: "The Old Woman's rasping admonition can have no effect or *purpose* other than to tempt Bertha into sin" (emphasis added). This reading attributes altogether too much malevolence to the old woman. Despite her various ominous characteristics, she has up to this point played a wholly positive and beneficent role in Bertha's life.

6. Karl S. Guthke, *Die Mythologie der entgötterten Welt: Ein literarisches Thema von der Aufklärung bis zur Gegenwart* (Göttingen: Vandenhoeck & Ruprecht, 1971), p. 107.

7. To defend the old woman's lack of knowledge as congruent with her role as the representative of unconscious nature does not seem to me to be a convincing argument. She is certainly knowledgeable enough in other respects, as the ending of the tale makes clear.

8. Rippere, "Ludwig Tieck's 'Der blonde Eckbert,'" p. 478.

9. Haeuptner, "Ludwig Tiecks Märchen 'Der blond Eckbert'," p. 23.

10. Immerwahr, "'Der blonde Eckbert' as a Poetic Confession," *German Quarterly*, 34 (1961), 103–17, sees "Waldeinsamkeit" as a refuge for the "imaginative self," in which "a poetically gifted imagination" may develop without the distraction of social commitments or expectations. William J. Lillyman, "The Enigma of *Der blonde Eckbert*," p. 146, is unimpressed with this argument: "Immerwahr's central point, that Bertha represents *poetic* imagination, is untenable since her imaginings are trite, composed of nothing but clichés: desire for wealth, for the love of a knight, etc." The implied value judgment in Lillyman's statement is invalid: the sole proof of poetic imagination, and especially childish poetic imagination, does not necessarily lie in originality. Here again, however, "Waldeinsamkeit" makes no concession to future development. Bertha's dreamy meditations in the valley of birches in no way prepare her for the technical and imaginative difficulties of mature artistic production.

11. Edwin H. Zeydel, *Ludwig Tieck, the German Romanticist*, (Princeton, N.J.: Princeton University Press, 1935), p. 8.

12. Ralph W. Ewton, Jr., "Childhood without End: Tieck's *Der blonde Eckbert*," pp. 415–20, discusses the self-enclosed nature of "Waldeinsamkeit" as well as Eckbert's and Bertha's inability to assume adult roles. What I find troublesome in Ewton's interpretation is the assertion that "Waldeinsamkeit" exists solely as a wish-fulfillment for Bertha's escapist self. He says, for example: "Even as vague a character as the old woman clutters the desired simplicity of Bertha's wish world, *so* the mother figure simply disappears for longer and longer periods of time" (p. 417; emphasis added). In this way the old woman and her valley are divested of any autonomous existence. Indeed, almost everything in the tale—"Waldeinsamkeit," the old woman, the confessions, even Bertha's death—emerges in Ewton's interpretation as a childish maneuver devised by Eckbert or Bertha to avoid adult responsibility. Whenever Ewton approaches the problem of admitting the old woman's role as a force independent of Eckbert and Bertha, he takes refuge in the passive voice, suppressing the agent: "For some six years Bertha is granted her desires" (p. 418); "The whole complex of hidden transgressions . . . is forced into awareness" (p. 425). Similarly, he is unable to explain why the "magic" in the tale recoils on Eckbert and Bertha, as the old woman abruptly changes from a benevolent and obedient wish-fulfillment to a punitive figure.

13. In the notes to her edition of "Der blonde Eckbert," Marianne Thalmann points out that the old woman herself displays typical features of the eighteenth-century em-

issary figure: notably her raspy voice, her grimace, and her dissonant laughter (pp. 892–93 of the edition and volume cited).

14. Max Lüthi examines this structural device at some length in his discussion of the tale of the dragon-killer, in *Es war einmal . . . : Vom Wesen des Volksmärchens*, 3rd ed. (Göttingen: Vandenhoeck & Ruprecht, 1968), pp. 37–38. See also M. Lüthi, *Das europäische Volksmärchen: Form und Wesen*, 2d revised ed. (Bern: Francke, 1960), pp. 33, 38.

15. The last remnant of authorial commentary occurs in the Hugo episode: "Es schien aber seine Verdammnis zu sein, gerade in der Stunde des Vertrauens Argwohn zu schöpfen" (24).

16. Thalmann, *Das Märchen und die Moderne*, pp. 55–56; Gottrau, "Die Zeit im Werk des jungen Tieck," p. 86; Zeydel, *Ludwig Tieck, the German Romanticist*, p. 84.

17. In the context of "Der blond Eckbert," I mean by "original sin" an innate and uncontrollable disposition to greed and self-protective insularity. Lillyman, "The Enigma of *Der blonde Eckbert*," p. 151, uses the term to refer to the irrational law that hangs over Eckbert and Bertha as a consequence of their father's sin of adultery. Although I concur with Lillyman's assertion that this initial sin sets up the chain of transgressions committed by Eckbert and Bertha, I am not convinced that their disposition to evil should be attributed solely to the warped situation created by their father. Lillyman views Eckbert, for instance, as infected by his wife's greed and mistrust (pp. 151–52), but he does not examine Eckbert's *original* attraction to Bertha. The fatal allure of her solitary upbringing and her wealth cannot convincingly be ascribed to the father's influence.

18. Ralph Tymms, *German Romantic Literature* (London: Methuen & Co. Ltd., 1955), p. 83.

19. Ewton, "Life and Death of the Body in Tieck's *Der Runenberg*," p. 31, cites the concluding stanza of the song as evidence of the spirituality of the plains culture: the fragrance emitted by the dying flowers suggests "the release of the soul in death." I would argue, however, that these spirits (*Düfte*) do not function as "allusions to an afterlife," either for Christian or his father; they are wholly immanent, both in their origin and in their brief, intoxicating effect. The life-spirit poured out by the exhausted and dying flowers in no way indicates an ascent to otherworldly existence.

20. An old *tree*, on the other hand, might command a certain reverence; but trees, significantly enough, appear primarily in the mountain realm. Cf. Christian's description of his homeland: "wenige Bäume schmückten den grünen Plan" (63). As organic forms whose life spans are indefinitely extended, trees logically occupy the middle range between the plant world and the stone world. They do not appear, of course, in the high mountains, where every trace of green disappears (66).

21. The point is worth emphasizing, since critics have generally been pleased to view the religion of the village as perfectly orthodox Christianity, in contrast to the diabolical or demonic forces residing in the mountains. See for example Richard W. Kimpel, "Nature, Quest, and Reality in Tieck's *Der blonde Eckbert* and *Der Runenberg*," pp. 182–83, 186.

22. Theoretically, the participation in Holy Communion should also serve to promote entrance into the timelessness of Christian salvation. This aspect is, however, not stressed in the context of the story. The father's song, which represents the most important ideological statement of the plant world, makes no mention whatsoever of Christian transcendence of time.

23. Gotthilf Heinrich von Schubert, *Ahndungen einer allgemeinen Geschichte des Lebens* (Leipzig: Reclam, 1806), I, 230–31. I am not suggesting, of course, that Schubert's *Ahndungen* was influenced in any way by "Der Runenberg," but rather that both documents reflect a common thesis of Romanticism and that the possibility of transcendence of self through union with the life-force, which is none too clearly stated in the father's song (and which seems to have eluded most modern readers), would have been much more obvious to Tieck's contemporaries.

24. "Sein Gespräch machte ihn selbst wie trunken, und er fühlte im Reden erst recht, wie nichts mehr zu seiner Zufriedenheit ermangle" (73). Language, the medium of the collective, serves to suppress the internal and incommunicable reality of the mountain world. This passage also offers further evidence that Christian's experience of the plant realm is by no means rational (in contrast, say, to his irrational response to the mountains): the conversation with his father intoxicates him into an affirmation of his life on the plains.

25. Zeydel, *Ludwig Tieck, the German Romanticist*, pp. 159–60.

26. Edmund Burke, *A Philosophical Enquiry into the Origin of our Ideas of the Sublime and the Beautiful; with an Introductory Discourse Concerning Taste*, 2d rev. ed. (London: Vernor and Hood, 1798), pp. 99–159.

27. Ibid., pp. 96–97.

28. Ibid., pp. 210–39.

29. Ibid., pp. 59–60 and 69—70 respectively.

30. For the sake of precision, it should be noted that the gold in "Der Runenberg" does represent a certain advancement in Christian's progress. As Lillyman has pointed out, the gold and the tablet may be interpreted as elements (blood and communion tablet, respectively) of Christian's communion with the mountain realm. "Ludwig Tieck's 'Der Runenberg': The Dimensions of Reality," pp. 236, 240.

31. As early as the *Fichte-Studien*, he wrote, "Sollte der Fehler, warum ich nicht weiter komme, etwa darinn liegen—daß ich nicht ein Gantzes fassen und festhalten kann?" (II, 282).

32. Five years pass between Christian's first reencounter with the mountains (during his journey back to his homeland) and the arrival of the stranger. A year and some months later, Christian invests the gold in land holdings, and "soon" thereafter Elisabeth alerts the father to Christian's alarming and incomprehensible behavior. One may assume, though no temporal datum is supplied, that the ensuing discussion is followed directly by the harvest festival and the rediscovery of the tablet, after which no more than a few hours pass before Christian disappears into the mountains for good.

33. Richard Benz, *Märchen-Dichtung der Romantiker*, p. 115.

Chapter V

1. In Brentano's "Das Myrtenfräulein," for instance, the title figure is dismembered by envious rivals, and her spatial dispersal leads to a state of impoverishment that can be rectified only by love and patient devotion. However, time and space are not *consistently* meaningful throughout the tale, and the significance of the dismemberment is in any event so immediately evident that conceptual clarification is both unnecessary and inappropriate. Clemens Brentano, *Werke*, ed. Max Preitz (Leipzig: Bibliographisches Institut, 1914), III, 30–42.

2. For a superb account of the way in which Neoplatonic concepts were incorporated into Romantic thought, see M. H. Abrams, *Natural Supernaturalism: Tradition and Revolution in Romantic Literature* (New York: Norton 1971), pp. 143–95.

3. "Bedeutender Zug in vielen Mährchen, daß wenn Ein Unmögliches möglich wird—zugl[eich] ein andres Unmögliches unerwartet möglich wird . . . Die *Zauberbedingungen* z.B. die Verwandl[ung] des Bären in einen Prinzen, in dem Augenblicke, als der Bär geliebt wurde etc. Auch bey den Mährchen der beyden Genien" (III, 389).

4. The fact that substitutions such as this are possible accounts for the numerous variants of what is considered to be the same tale. If "Hänsel und Gretel" were a literary fairy tale, on the other hand, one would be well within one's rights to question why the author selected a white bird instead of, say, a brown mouse, and what symbolic or evocative meanings, if any, may be associated with the figure of the bird.

5. Max Lüthi, *Volksmärchen und Volkssage: Zwei Grundformen erzählender Dichtung*, 2d ed. (Bern: Francke, 1966), pp. 35–39.

6. Ibid., p. 28.

7. Ibid., p. 30.

8. Ibid., p. 41. The following discussion of the *Sage* is also indebted in many particulars to Lüthi's analysis.

9. Wilhelm Hauff opts, in fact, for *both* terms. The tales from *Das Wirtshaus im Spessart* were composed as "Märchen für Söhne und Töchter gebildeter Stände," but in the frame story of *Das Wirtshaus* they are referred to as *Sagen*. Wilhelm Hauff, *Sämtliche Werke in sechs Bänden* (Leipzig: Max Hesses, 1899), V, 164–288. In view of the late date of these tales (1830/31), it seems probable that Hauff was influenced by the terminology of the Grimm collections.

10. For a detailed account of the theory and practice of embedding, see Erika Voerster, *Märchen und Novellen im klassisch-romantischen Roman*, 2d ed. (Bonn: H. Bouvier, 1966). The principal shortcoming of this perceptive and well-documented book lies in its restriction to interpolated fairy tales and novellas. The author neglects other important imbedded forms such as the lyrical *Einlage* and the dream.

11. In the case of Goethe's "Märchen," one may justifiably relax the conventional distinction between Classicism and Romanticism, since this astonishing tale directly influenced many of the Romantic *Märchen* that followed it.

12. See, for example, Emil Staiger, "Ludwig Tieck und der Ursprung der deutschen Romantik," in his *Stilwandel: Studien zur Vorgeschichte der Goethezeit* (Zürich: Atlantis, 1963), pp. 202–3.

13. Quoted in Walter Wetzels, "Aspects of Natural Science in German Romanticism," *Studies in Romanticism*, 10 (1971), p. 43.

14. Both the will-o'-the-wisps and the youth, for instance, cross the river in search of the kingdom of the lily, only to discover that her realm is on the shore they just left behind.

15. For example, the body of the giant is helpless, although his shadow is all-powerful; the snake forms herself into a bridge over the river, but only at noon; those who cross the river via the ferry must discharge their debt to the river within twenty-four hours or suffer irreversible decay; the old man's lamp transmutes stones into gold but destroys metallic substances.

16. The old man is able to cross the river on his own power; the snake forms a bridge at midnight rather than at noon, her otherwise appointed hour; the subterranean temple rises and crosses under the river to emerge above ground in the land of the lily; the snake sacrifices herself to become an eternal bridge over the river.

17. In the first mythic cycle, the turbulent waters are swallowed by the black jaws of the abysses. In the second cycle, the valley of flowers is enshrouded by dark, toxic clouds issuing from the black hill. In the third, the winged fire-lily is captured and encircled by the black dragon. In the fourth, the green snake takes to flight and descends to the confinement of earthly existence along with her impetuous lover, the Salamander-Prince (Lindhorst). In the fifth, Anselmus himself is incarcerated in a glass bottle after defacing Lindhorst's parchment in a moment of recklessness and distraction.

18. See Kenneth Negus, *E. T. A. Hoffmann's Other World: The Romantic Author and his "New Mythology"* (Philadelphia: University of Pennsylvania Press, 1965), pp. 55–59, for a detailed interpretation of the mythic cycles and their relationship to the main text of *Der goldne Topf*.

19. Hoffmann provides no less than three distinct commentaries on the meaning of the "Urdarquelle" episode: Ophioch explains the transformation to Liris; Hermod reformulates the entire tale in abstract terms; and the painter Franz Reinhold, on the realistic level of events in Rome, relates the effect of the "Urdarquelle" to German humor.

20. Similarly, Anselmus's ultimate fate in *Der goldne Topf* is not directly depicted. Instead, the narrator invites the reader to join him in a poetic trance that evokes dream images of Anselmus's utopian existence in Atlantis.

21. Similarly, at the conclusion of the first chapter of *Heinrich von Ofterdingen*, as

Heinrich dreams of approaching the blue flower, he is awakened by his mother, the first of a series of feminine guides whose various functions are collectively symbolized in the flower (I, 197).

22. For an excellent account of the ways in which love and revolution are synchronized in Eichendorff's novella, see Helmut Koopman, "Eichendorff, *Das Schloß Dürande* und die Revolution," *Zeitschrift für deutsche Philologie*, 89 (1970), 180–207.

23. The allegorical *Märchen* also admits a psychological reading, but it is not concerned immediately and primarily with extreme or obsessive states. Moreover, the psychological *Märchen* is structured in such a way that an examination of the protagonist's mental disposition becomes one of the central tasks of interpretation. With the term "psychological *Märchen*" I am not suggesting, however, that such tales demand a rigorous psychoanalytical reading. Nevertheless, they do require some astuteness in recognizing and interpreting complex mental behavior.

24. Undine's uncle Kühleborn is a splendid, if exaggerated, example of the omnipresence of supernatural figures in the psychological tale. His relentless appearance in every lake, fountain, cistern, and brook becomes so predictable that it finally has an almost humorous effect.

25. Hoffmann's *Die Königsbraut* offers a witty and satirical variation on this theme: the force that conquers Carota and sends him fleeing back into the earth is not wisdom or an ennobling spirit of humanity, but the unbelievably trite poetry of Ännchen's suitor, the university student Amandus von Nebelstern.

26. A limited number of tales, for example Hauff's "Der Hirschgulden" and "Das kalte Herz," deal with more specific problems such as pride or greed. Here again, however, the problems generally extend to a crisis of love.

27. Examples of this kind of tale include Tieck's "Der getreue Eckart und der Tannenhäuser" and (in a limited sense) "Der Runenberg"; E. T. A. Hoffmann's *Die Königsbraut, Der Elementargeist*, and *Die Bergwerke zu Falun*; Eichendorff's "Die Zauberei im Herbst," *Das Marmorbild*, the tale of the strange ring from *Ahnung und Gegenwart*, and the fragmentary "Roßtrappmärchen" from *Viel Lärmen um Nichts*.

28. It is symptomatic of Emil's arrogant and misanthropic idealism that he glorifies individuality in himself but denies it to others. The woman remains nameless throughout the story, even after her betrothal and marriage to Emil.

29. Tieck characteristically leaves the question of supernatural influence open. It remains uncertain whether Emil's sudden ability to make an open declaration of his love results from black magic or from his psychic trauma and amnesiac rebirth. What matters here is after all not the objective reality of the supernatural, but the exceptional frame of mind that is revealed in the *interpretation* of the supernatural. Emil collapses because he sees his idealized lover suddenly linked with the venal, diabolical forces that he associates with ordinary humanity.

30. Near the conclusion of the tale, Tieck presents a contrasting image in the wedding of a young stable boy and an older, unattractive servant woman, who exhibit a humble, unselfish love that fears neither time nor social ridicule. In the framework of a story that relentlessly exposes the susceptibility of human beings to their worst instincts, however, this sugary counter-image has little persuasive force.

31. In this light, it is worth noting that the tale appears in the fictive framework of "Musikalische Aufsätze von [dem Komponisten] Joseph Berglinger."

32. Novalis, I, 338.

Bibliography of Works Cited

Abrams, M. H. *Natural Supernaturalism: Tradition and Revolution in Romantic Literature.* New York: Norton, 1971.
Albrecht, Luitgard. *Der magische Idealismus in Novalis' Märchentheorie und Märchendichtung.* Hamburg: Hansischer Gildenverlag, 1948.
Benz, Richard. *Märchen-Dichtung der Romantiker.* Gotha: Perthes, 1908.
Brentano, Clemens. *Werke.* Ed. Max Preitz. Leipzig: Bibliographisches Institut, 1914. Vol. III.
Burke, Edmund. *A Philosophical Enquiry into the Origin of our Ideas of the Sublime and the Beautiful; with an Introductory Discourse Concerning Taste.* 2d rev. ed. London: Vernor and Hood, 1798.
Diez, Max. "Metapher und Märchengestalt III, Novalis und das allegorische Märchen." *PMLA,* 48 (1933), 488–507.
———. "Metapher und Märchengestalt IV, Tiecks Frau vom Runenberg." *PMLA* 48 (1933), 877–87.
Eichendorff, Joseph Freiherr von. *Werke und Schriften.* Ed. Gerhard Baumann. Stuttgart: Cotta, 1957. Vol. II.
Eliade, Mircea. *The Myth of the Eternal Return.* New York: Pantheon Books, 1954.
Ewton, Ralph W., Jr. "Childhood without End: Tieck's *Der blonde Eckbert.*" *German Quarterly,* 46 (1973), 410–27.
———. "Life and Death of the Body in Tieck's *Der Runenberg.*" *Germanic Review,* 50 (1975), 19–33.
Fromm, Erich. *The Anatomy of Human Destructiveness.* New York: Holt, Rinehart and Winston, 1973.
Frye, Lawrence. "Spatial Imagery in Novalis' 'Hymnen an die Nacht.'" *Deutsche Vierteljahrsschrift,* 41 (1967), 568–91.
Gaier, Ulrich. *Krumme Regel: Novalis' 'Konstruktionslehre des schaffenden Geistes' und ihre Tradition.* Tübingen: Max Niemeyer, 1970.
Gellinek, Janis Little. "*Der blonde Eckbert*: A Tieckian Fall from Paradise." In *Lebendige Form: Interpretationen zur deutschen Literatur: Festschrift für Heinrich E. K. Henel.* Ed. Jeffrey L. Sammons and Ernst Schürer. München: Wilhelm Fink, 1970, pp. 147–66.
Goethe, Johann Wolfgang von. *Werke.* Ed. Benno von Wiese and Erich Trunz. Hamburg: Christian Wegner, 1951. Vol. VI.
Gottrau, André. "Die Zeit im Werk des jungen Tieck." Diss. Zürich 1947.
Guthke, Karl S. *Die Mythologie der entgötterten Welt: Ein literarisches Thema von der Aufklärung bis zur Gegenwart.* Göttingen: Vandenhoeck & Ruprecht, 1971.

Haering, Theodor. *Novalis als Philosoph.* Stuttgart: Kohlhammer, 1954.
Haeuptner, Gerhard. "Ludwig Tiecks Märchen 'Der blonde Eckbert.' " In *Verstehen und Vertrauen: Otto Friedrich Bollnow zum 65. Geburtstag.* Ed. Johannes Schwartländer. Stuttgart: Kohlhammer, 1968, pp. 22–26.
Hahn, Walther. "Tiecks *Blonder Eckbert* als Gestaltung romantischer Theorie." *Proceedings, Northwest Conference on Foreign Languages,* 18 (1967), 69–78.
Hauff, Wilhelm. *Sämtliche Werke in sechs Bänden.* Leipzig: Max Hesses, 1899. Vol. V.
Haym, Rudolf. *Die romantische Schule.* Berlin: R. Gaertner, 1870.
Haywood, Bruce. *Novalis: The Veil of Imagery. A Study of the Poetic Works of Friedrich von Hardenberg (1772–1801).* Cambridge, Mass.: Harvard University Press, 1959.
Heine, Heinrich. *Sämtliche Schriften.* Ed. Klaus Briegleb. München: Carl Hanser, 1971. Vol. III.
Hiebel, Friedrich. *Novalis: Der Dichter der blauen Blume.* Bern: Francke, 1951.
———. *Novalis: German Poet, European Thinker, Christian Mystic.* Chapel Hill: The University of North Carolina Press, 1954.
Hoffmann, E. T. A. *Poetische Werke.* 12 vols. Berlin: Walter de Gruyter, 1957–62.
Hubbs, Valentine C. "Tieck, Eckbert und das kollektive Unbewußte." *PMLA,* 71 (1956), 686–93.
Huch, Ricarda. *Die Romantik: Ausbreitung, Blütezeit und Verfall.* Tübingen: Rainer Wunderlich, 1951.
Immerwahr, Raymond. " 'Der blonde Eckbert' as a Poetic Confession," *German Quarterly,* 34 (1961), 103–17.
———. "Reality as an Object of Romantic Experience in Early German Romanticism." *Colloquia Germanica,* 3 (1969), 133–61.
———. "The Outer World in *Der blonde Eckbert.*" In *Studies in Nineteenth Century and Early Twentieth Century German Literature: Studies in Honor of Paul K. Whitaker.* Ed. Norman H. Binger and A. Wayne Wonderley. Lexington, Kentucky: APRA Press, 1974, pp. 52–70.
Jolles, André. *Einfache Formen: Legende, Sage, Mythe, Rätsel, Spruch, Kasus, Memorabile, Märchen, Witz.* 2d ed. Halle/Saale: Max Niemeyer, 1956.
Kimpel, Richard W. "Nature, Quest, and Reality in Tieck's *Der blonde Eckbert* and *Der Runenberg.*" *Studies in Romanticism,* 9 (1970), 176–92.
Kohlschmidt, Werner. *Form und Innerlichkeit: Beiträge zur Geschichte und Wirkung der deutschen Klassik und Romantik.* Bern: Francke, 1955.
Koopman, Helmut. "Eichendorff, *Das Schloß Dürande* und die Revolution." *Zeitschrift für deutsche Philologie,* 89 (1970), 180–207.
Korff, H. A. *Geist der Goethezeit: Versuch einer ideellen Entwicklung der klassisch-romantischen Literaturgeschichte.* 3rd rev. ed. Leipzig: Koehler & Amelang, 1959.
———. "Das Wesen der Romantik." In *Begriffsbestimmung der Romantik.* Ed. Helmut Prang. Darmstadt: Wissenschaftliche Buchgesellschaft, 1968.
Küpper, Peter. *Die Zeit als Erlebnis des Novalis.* Köln: Böhlau, 1959.
La Motte-Fouqué, Friedrich de. *Fouqués Werke.* Ed. Walther Ziesemer. Berlin: Bong & Co., 1908. Vol. I.

Bibliography

Lämmert, Eberhard. *Bauformen des Erzählens.* Stuttgart: J. B. Metzler, 1955.
Langen, August. *Anschauungsformen in der deutschen Dichtung des 18. Jahrhunderts (Rahmenschau und Rationalismus).* Jena: Eugen Diederich, 1934.
Liedke, Otto K. "Tieck's *Der blonde Eckbert*: Das Märchen von Verarmung und Untergang." *German Quarterly,* 44 (1971), 311–16.
Lillyman, William J. "Ludwig Tieck's 'Der Runenberg': The Dimensions of Reality." *Monatshefte,* 42 (1970), 231–44.
──────. "The Enigma of *Der blonde Eckbert*: The Significance of the End." *Seminar,* 7 (1971), 144–55.
Lüthi, Max. *Es war einmal . . . : Vom Wesen des Volksmärchens.* 3rd ed. Göttingen: Vandenhoeck & Ruprecht, 1968.
──────. *Das europäische Volksmärchen: Form und Wesen.* 2d ed. Bern: Francke, 1960.
──────. *Volksmärchen und Volkssage: Zwei Grundformen erzählender Dichtung.* Bern: Francke, 1961.
Mähl, Hans Joachim. *Die Idee des goldenen Zeitalters im Werk des Novalis: Studien zur Wesensbestimmung der frühromantischen Utopie und zu ihren ideengeschichtlichen Voraussetzungen.* Heidelberg: Carl Winter, 1965.
Merkel, Ingrid. "Wirklichkeit im romantischen Märchen." *Colloquia Germanica,* 3 (1969), 162–83.
Meyer, Herman. "Raumgestaltung und Raumsymbolik in der Erzählkunst." In his *Zarte Empirie: Studien zur Literaturgeschichte.* Stuttgart: J. B. Metzler, 1963.
Meyerhoff, Hans. *Time in Literature.* Berkeley, Calif.: University of California Press, 1955.
Middleton, J. Christopher. "Two Mountain Scenes in Novalis and the Question of Symbolic Style." In *Literary Symbolism: A Symposium.* Ed. Helmut Rehder. Austin: University of Texas Press, 1965.
Müller, Günther. "Erzählzeit und erzählte Zeit." In *Festschrift für Paul Kluckhohn und Hermann Schneider.* Edited by their students at Tübingen. Tübingen: Mohr, 1948, pp. 195–212.
Negus, Kenneth. *E. T. A. Hoffmann's Other World: The Romantic Author and his "New Mythology."* Philadelphia: University of Pennsylvania Press, 1965.
Novalis. *Schriften: Die Werke Friedrich von Hardenbergs.* 2d rev. ed. Ed. Paul Kluckhohn and Richard Samuel. 5 vols. Stuttgart: Kohlhammer, 1960–72.
Politzer, Heinz. *Franz Kafka: Parable and Paradox.* 2d rev. ed. Ithaca, N.Y.: Cornell University Press, 1966.
Rasch, Wolfdietrich. "Blume und Stein: Zur Deutung von Ludwig Tiecks Erzählung *Der Runenberg.*" In *The Discontinuous Tradition: Studies in German Literature in Honour of Ernest Ludwig Stahl.* Ed. P. F. Ganz. London: Oxford University Press, 1971.
Rehder, Helmut. *Die Philosophie der unendlichen Landschaft: Ein Beitrag zur Geschichte der romantischen Weltanschauung.* Halle/Saale: Max Niemeyer, 1932.
Rippere, Victoria L. "'Der blonde Eckbert': A Psychological Reading." *PMLA,* 85 (1970), 473–86.

Roscher, W. H., ed. *Ausführliches Lexikon der griechischen und römischen Mythologie.* Leipzig: B. G. Teubner, 1884. Vol. I.

Schanze, Helmut. *Romantik und Aufklärung: Untersuchungen zu Friedrich Schlegel und Novalis.* Nürnberg: Hans Carl, 1966.

Schlegel, Friedrich. *Kritische Friedrich-Schlegel-Ausgabe.* Ed. Ernst Behler, Jean-Jacques Anstett, and Hans Eichner. Munchen: Ferdinand Schöningh, 1967 and 1962. Vols. II, V.

Scholes, Robert, and Robert Kellogg. *The Nature of Narrative.* New York: Oxford University Press, 1966.

Schubert, Gotthilf Heinrich. *Ahndungen einer allgemeinen Geschichte des Lebens.* 2 vols. Leipzig: Reclam, 1806–21.

Schueler, H. J. "Cosmology and Quest in Novalis' 'Klingsohrs Märchen.'" *Germanic Review*, 49 (1974), 259–66.

Staiger, Emil. "Ludwig Tieck und der Ursprung der deutschen Romantik." In his *Stilwandel: Studien zur Vorgeschichte der Goethezeit.* Zürich: Atlantis, 1963, pp. 175–204.

Thalmann, Marianne. *Das Märchen und die Moderne: Zum Begriff der Surrealität im Märchen der Romantik.* Stuttgart: Kohlhammer, 1961.

Thoreau, Henry D. *Walden; or Life in the Woods.* Ed. Edwin Way Teale. New York: Dodd, Mead & Co., 1946.

Tieck, Ludwig. *Werke.* Ed. Marianne Thalmann. 4 vols. Darmstadt: Wissenschaftliche Buchgesellschaft, 1968.

Tymms, Ralph. *German Romantic Literature.* London: Methuen & Co., 1955.

Voerster, Erika. *Märchen und Novellen im klassisch-romantischen Roman.* 2d ed. Bonn: H. Bouvier, 1966.

Vredeveld, Harry. "Ludwig Tieck's *Der Runenberg*: An Archetypal Interpretation." *Germanic Review*, 49 (1974), 200–214.

Wetzels, Walter D. "Aspects of Natural Science in German Romanticism." *Studies in Romanticism*, 10 (1971), 44–59.

Zeydel, Edwin H. *Ludwig Tieck, the German Romanticist: A Critical Study.* Princeton, N.J.: Princeton University Press, 1935.

www.ingramcontent.com/pod-product-compliance
Lightning Source LLC
Chambersburg PA
CBHW031314150426
43191CB00005B/229